Best Wishes

Bernard F. Coats

15 July 2018

DERBYSHIRE
A Light-Hearted Peek

First published 2014 by DB Publishing, an imprint of JMD Media Ltd, Nottingham, United Kingdom.

ISBN 9781780914312

DERBYSHIRE
A Light-Hearted Peek

Bernard Carter

Contents

In Memory of my Parents.
And the
10:40 Sunday morning Rambler's Train.

A Diverting
Introduction.

The thing about Derbyshire is that its unique topography allows it to present itself as perplexingly multi-faceted. It encompasses vast areas of gritstone giving rise to wild, open moorland with waterlogged peat and smooth-edged rocky escarpments, as well as large areas of limestone that form the dales and deep gorges, carved and sculptured by water over millions of years. It is millstone grit nudging carboniferous limestone with clumps of gritstone, unexpectedly popping up out of the ground like at Cratcliffe Rocks near Birchover, Black Rocks at Cromford and a sandy version at Alport Hill by Wirksworth. Scattered among all this are dollops of basalt, volcanic tuff, clay, shale, coal seams and a wealth of minerals especially lead; which has been hacked out of the earth from way back in the mists of time.

The Saxons certainly had a go at mining lead, as indeed did the Romans who came all that way from Italy to invade us, and when they were not engaged in bashing the locals into submission, bashed out lots of the silver-grey stuff for themselves. Their lust for galena eventually and perhaps rather ironically became greatly contributory to the demise of their empire, from swigging water and wine from too many lead vessels, which did their innards no good at all. It occurs to me that the well-known and slightly smutty innuendo of 'putting lead in your pencil' is particularly apt in the case of the Romans despite its detrimental effect.

On the subject of minerals, Derbyshire can gloatingly lay claim to having the only veins of fluorite (fluorspar) in the entire world called Blue John, which is mined in a place previously referred to as Water Hull mine just outside the village of Castleton. Now far be it from me to become too geological at this point, but I fancy you will be fairly impressed – and this is bound to get you on the edge of your seat with anticipation – when I tell you that sometimes the crystal structure of Blue John can be a combination of octahedron or rhombdodecahedron. (Yeah … whaèver). Mining this rare fluorspar with any degree of seriousness began around 1765 and its value as a decorative stone was soon seized upon by one entrepreneur Mathew Boulton who successfully marketed and created a demand for vases, urns and inlays aimed mainly at the wealthy. This came about after Erasmus Darwin, inappropriately dressed in a wig and a heavy, sweat-inducing topcoat (not quite what you would call top-notch caving gear), had descended the cavern of Treak Cliff and was taken aback at the wonders he saw by the light of a candle. He eventually emerged into daylight utterly thrilled by his subterranean venture (and no doubt in dire need of an under-arm deodorant) and enthused by letter to all his friends – including Boulton – of the mineral wealth he had witnessed.

In truth the Romans had beaten him to it, as a couple of ornaments made from Blue John have been dug out of the lava at Pompeii. However, an advertisement in the late 1830s proclaims that the Centre Museum in Matlock Bath, which at the time was under the, 'Especial Patronage of His Grace the Duke of Devonshire and His Grace the Duke of Rutland', was the place to go and drool over, 'Vases of Amethystine and Topazine Fluor Spars'. Along with, 'Black Marble fashioned into Obelisks, Candelabra, Inlaid Tables, Urns, Altars and Memorials.' There was also available other miscellaneous goods such as 'Stationary, Cutlery, Perfume' and even lumps of Tuffa for the DIY garden grotto and rockery building enthusiast.

Naturally after a few centuries of chipping out lumps of this unique Blue John mineral and heaven knows how many polished vases, urns and bowls down the line the remaining veins are getting a tad thin on the ground, or to be more precise, in the ground and sizeable blocks of the stuff are now as rare as hen's teeth. A 1950s handbill proclaims the Blue John Caverns as being, 'of exceptional Educational and Geological interest, offering the finest example of the action of water that can be seen in this country' and, 'Now Magnificently Transformed by the Installation of Modern Electric Lighting'; and you could still purchase, 'Vases, Chalices, Ash Trays, Pin Trays, Rings, Brooches, Ear-rings, Bracelets, Necklets and Cuff-links', if your wallet would allow.

The multitude of visual aspects the county has on offer are virtually incomparable to anywhere else in the country, with woodlands, hills, vales, cliffs, gorges, tors, escarpments, heathland, rivers and caves. With much of the landscape knitted together by mile after mile of dry stone walls meandering across the countryside, sometimes appearing in the most inaccessible and challenging of places that leave you opened mouthed and asking yourself the question, 'Why would you want to?' The building and topping of a wall without mortar is an ancient skill, which is still alive and kicking today, to the extent that even competition 'walling matches' take place, which could be viewed as a kind of stony version of a sheep dog trial. Not so much *One Man and his Dog*, more *One Man and his Wall*.

Sometimes the hand of man upon the landscape has not always left such an aesthetic impression and blasting out massive chunks of hillsides in the Peak District to provide rail and road ballast and heaven knows what else, has created a bit of a controversial eyesore. Disused quarries mellow with time and nature normally makes a stoic effort to soften the edges and smother the bare rock with whatever growth can get a purchase, but even today there are many active quarries still gobbling up the landscape; and the unmistakable blot on the scene around Edale of the cement factory belching out white smoke that can be seen from miles away has a lot to answer to.

The county is, geographically speaking quite centralised and many see Derbyshire as being the proverbial jewel in the crown. At a place near Coton in the Elms in the south of the county is a post stuck in a piece of scrubland marking the spot that is generally accepted as being some seventy miles from the sea and therefore the furthest place from the coast in the UK. The marker is not a great crowd-puller, just fact. The coast in this instance is to the east at a place called Fosdyke Wash which is not a seaside town and has no particular merits unless you are heavily into estuarial mud and slime. The nearest proper seaside town would probably be Skegness, or 'Skeggy' as it is usually called, which is a little further north along the coast and does carry the reputation of possessing healthy air, as promoted by the well-known slogan 'Skegness is So Bracing.' This highly successful piece of seaside promotion arrived in 1908 in the form of a Great Northern Railway poster that in turn made the resort practically world famous. This is quite something when you consider it was all down to a picture depicting a fat, jolly, camp fisherman prancing along the beach like a big girl's blouse, clearly revelling in the benefits of fresh air despite the fact that he is smoking a pipe which would surely have offset any healthy gains he might otherwise have enjoyed by prancing along the beach looking like … well … a big girl's blouse!

Be that as it may, back in Derbyshire its stunning scenery has over the centuries been a magnet for writers, artists and all manner of travellers, many of which have left their impressions. One of the very earliest comments on the Peak district came from Ranulph Higden who lived from 1280 until 1364 and was both a chronicler and a monk. He wrote a book referred to simply as *Polychronicum* for reasons which will become self-evident when I tell you that its original full title was *Ranulph Castrensis, cognomina Higden Polychronicum (sive Historia Polycratica) initio mundi usque ad mortem regis Edward III in septum libros dispositum* whatever all that means. Any good at Latin? No, me neither! He says of the Peak District, 'There bloweth so strong a wind out of the fissures of the earth that it casteth up again clothes that one casteth in.' Now at this point you have to ask yourself why would anyone let alone a monk want to be chucking their clothes into a hole in the ground! The interesting aspect of this multi-titled book is that as history books go it became a best seller during the 15th century and anybody who professed to be anybody had a copy.

James Croston a much later visitor to Derbyshire in the latter half of the 1800s who fortunately for us wrote in English states, 'We know no other district that better repays investigation than the Peak of Derbyshire' and goes on to enthuse over its, 'remarkable geologic structure, the quiet pastoral beauty of its romantic vales' along with the, 'rugged grandeur of the precipitous rocks that abound the course of its mountain streams.' Later on in this book I shall be following some of Croston's walking routes, for his detailed notes make fascinating and revealing writing and he did clock up some mileage during his rambles, despite his habit of arriving at some of the destinations rather late at night and in the dark, as was the case when he walked the Wye from Bakewell to Buxton. Another time he finished up walking the eerie Winnats Pass by moonlight and got a tad spooked; and there was also the occasion he arrived at Hartington just as the publican was about to retire to his bed.

Croston was certainly intrepid and must have been fitter than a butcher's dog! Another sightseer describes the Peakland rather fancifully as a place of, 'tender meadows, streams such as must have meandered through Arcady' with, 'fanatical hillocks and mountains that cut the skyline with dog-tooth edges.' Early writers tended to greatly exaggerate the steepness of roads, the heights of cliffs and the bleakness of the countryside. For example, take the description given by a traveller at the start of the eighteenth century who coming from Chatsworth into Bakewell, or 'Bankwell' as he calls it, descends a road from, 'a vast hill to which you would think it impossible to go down, by reason of its steepness and hazard.' Another early visitor standing beside the river Wye near Blackwell observed that ,'Down the precipitous and seemingly inaccessible sides of this stupendous cliff (Topley Pike) the Buxton road has been carried. As we looked up a carriage passed on, but so diminutive did it appear that with difficulty the eye could follow it along the fearful and giddy heights.' He makes it sound more like a horse-drawn carriage traversing the Eiger North Wall rather than what would later become the A6 descending into Ashwood Dale!

Early guide books tended to be unreliable and when *The Matlock Tourist Guide Through the Peak, embracing Matlock Bath, Haddon, Chatsworth and Castleton* to give it its full title was published in 1838, the author whose simply goes by the name of Henricus gave them a jolly good slagging. In his opinion all are, 'either unattainable to the many, from the high prices at which they are sold, or they contain fulsome and disgusting puffs, such libellous matter and low slander, that every reader must turn away in disgust from such offensive trash.' So, no beating about the bush and being overly judgemental there then! I can breathe a sigh of relief knowing that Henricus is not around to give this flippant tome of mine a severe slating! He does eventually calm down enough to concede that Ebenezer Rhode's *Peak Scenery* is a 'beautiful treatise' and also James Croston's *On Foot through the Peak* which had yet to be published was worthwhile. Well done Eb and Jim.

A soulful visitor once said that in Derbyshire it was possible, 'to escape farther from the footprints of other men than anywhere else in England.' He had obviously never stood in the bleak featureless hinterland of Dartmoor on a grey overcast day when nothing can be heard and there is not even a tree or a rock to break the emptiness. There you can feel as though you are the only person left on the planet. In Mee's county book he opines that Derbyshire is, 'Perhaps the most exquisitely English piece of England' and Lord Byron somewhat romantically announced, 'there are things in Derbyshire as noble as in Greece or Switzerland.' Another enthusiast was Thomas Fuller a churchman and historian who around the middle of the 1600s wrote of the county, 'God, who is truly thaumaturgus, the only worker of wonders, hath more manifested his might in this than any other county of England.' I have to confess that the word 'thaumaturgus' sent me fleeing to the dictionary, but if you need a clue, think Paul Daniels or David Copperfield. No, not the Dickens character!

Daniel Defoe on the other hand who travelled through the county in the first quarter of the 1700s said the place was, 'a howling wilderness' and continued to curl his lip at much of what he experienced almost from the first instance he clapped eyes on the 'frightful view' of the 'black mountains of the Peak.' However, to give him some credit he was complimentary about the beer stating the further north he travelled the nearer to perfection was the ale and intimated that he was in anticipation of some sort of alcoholic bliss by the time he crossed the county border into Yorkshire. Maybe it was the 'morning after the night before' that often put him in a sour state of mind with regard to his periodic scathing comments. An early lady traveller complained that Derbyshire was full of steep hills making, 'travelling tedious and ye miles long' and there was, 'neither hedge nor tree but only low drye stone walls round some ground.' I feel sure you are getting the general picture by now, and yet the simplest and most apt summation that really catches the essence of the county is an old maxim stating that, 'Derbyshire has everything except the sea,' although if you care to stand beside a limestone outcrop such as Hob's House in Monsal Dale and use your imagination, the fossilised shells and other remains of long dead marine life, evident in the rock are sufficient proof that a mere 280 million years ago you would indeed have been standing on the sea bed and possibly wondering just how much longer you are going to have to hold your breath before the tide goes out.

Despite its apparent remoteness Derbyshire has always had its inhabitants. Neolithic man squatted in the entrance of caves chuntering about the weather and whose turn was it to hunt for dinner. He left behind spear heads and domestic implements along with his earth-stained brittle bones in many tumuli dotted about the hills. He also erected stone circles which to this day still leave us scratching our heads in confused wonderment. The Saxons also threw up some piles of earth in the form of barrows for their dead along with knocking out numerous skilfully carved stone crosses that have been left sticking up here and there around the county. The invading Danes were also responsible for throwing up a few earthworks and also for calling Deoraby from which the modern name Derby derives.

However, in 917AD the local populace was getting a tad hacked off with these Nordic intruders swaggering about as if they owned the place, so King Alfred the Great's daughter Athelfled, the Lady of the Mercians who was clearly not a woman to mess with stormed the city gates of Derby and gave the Danes a damned good thrashing, which rather cleared the air somewhat. Maybe it was the constant smell of bacon frying that got right up her nose. The invading Normans also left many clues to their occupation including some fine churches with cleverly carved and decorated doorways and tympanums, which is an architectural term for the area within an arch and above a lintel and not as you might at first have thought anything to do with that bit you cannot quite reach when you stick your finger down your ear.

Probably the invaders that most people think of are the Romans (Veni, vidi, vici. I came, I saw, I conquered) who put up tourists sites like Hadrian's Wall and the grand palace at Fishbourne. In Derbyshire they set up camp at places such as Melandra (Glossop), Anavio (Hope) and Little Chester (Derby), from where they would march out and cause an occasional bit of 'aggro' with the locals. On the whole they were fearful of the wild hills and the wild folk of the Peak and found they were unable to come anywhere near to taming the feral population and consequently left behind only scant remains of their fortifications. The Peak was the last stronghold of the Celtic Brigantes and most invaders quickly realised they were better off not to truck with this fearsome bunch. However, the Romans were pretty clued up on things and quickly discovered the healing properties of the thermal springs at Buxton.

The original Roman baths eventually sunk without trace until discovered when digging the foundations for the now famous Crescent. The waters have continued to attract the ill and the ailing over many centuries. Many notables have tried its alleged curative powers, which I will detail later in the book, but one such person was the famous potter Josiah Wedgewood who took his rheumatic ridden wife Sally there in an effort to cure her. Interestingly, Wedgewood himself at the time was clumping about on a wooden leg the original leg having quite literally been sawn off in an operation which he insisted on watching. (Ouch! There was no anaesthetic.) I cannot help thinking that this example of the thirst for knowledge is pushing the 'Age of Enlightenment' a little too far and had he considered Buxton water for his own medical condition of osteomyelitis (thickening of his leg bone) then he might possibly have still been the owner of two legs and matched his wife by recovering as she did and living for a further forty-two years.

In spite of Derbyshire weather having been described as, 'Nine months winter and three months bad weather,' it has never deterred hordes of walkers, hikers, ramblers, call them what you will, descending on the Peak District from all points of the compass armed with greasy, dubbin smeared boots, waterproofs, a Thermos flask of tea and a Tupperware box of meat paste sandwiches. In 1928 when wandering about the Peak District, the travel writer H.V. Morton came across such a person, who he classed as an Amazon because she had very long legs, very long arms, khaki breeches, an old tweed jacket and a pair of stout walking boots. He goes on to say that, 'There are thousands of them, men and women,' which he splits into two types, the 'ordinary rambler' who plays it safe and only ventures out in good weather and the 'storm fiend' who apparently enjoys nothing better than to drop down off the moors in the evening looking like, 'he or she had been blown up, flung into a stream, dragged through wire netting, ending up with a triumphant victory over sixteen gamekeepers and a dog.' For all those factory workers and office workers and everyone else stuck in a nine to five job, the Peak District has proved to be a safety valve for the wage-earners of Derby, Sheffield, Manchester and all ports in between. They willingly forego a traditional Sunday roast at home in favour of striding out in the fresh air to congregate at the end of their walks in a country pub downing beers and heartily singing the chorus of the Rambler's Anthem;

> I'm a rambler, I'm a rambler from Manchester way.
> I get all my pleasure the hard moorland way.
> I may be a wage slave on Monday,
> But I am a free man on Sunday.

It helped them cope with the drudge of Monday morning and the working week that lay ahead of them. My father was one such rambler, who was never happier than when he was out walking the Peak District and it became a way of life for me, starting as a youngster in short trousers.

The thing was that during the fifties and sixties, prior to the county becoming swamped with motor cars, it was far easier to do a walk from A to B and not have to worry about how to get back to A, which now days of course is where you have parked your car. This was because there was frequent bus coverage of the area as well as good train connections, so it was simply a case of hopping onto a passing bus or train to get you back home or wherever you had started from. Today's bus services are not so numerous especially on a Sunday, which was always the day that the majority of walkers set out, whereas back in the fifties you could for example catch a bus outside the White Lodge tea house (long gone) at the end of Monsal Dale for Derby at thirty-five minutes past each hour, daily, and for Buxton at twenty past each hour, daily. Now that's what I call a service. As far as the trains go, nowadays beyond Matlock you are pretty much snookered due to the line being closed in 1968 and torn up shortly after. Apart from Peak Rail's intermittent, but nonetheless, excellent steam train operations from Matlock to Rowsley then I am afraid that waiting on any platform north of here means you will just get very lonely, very bored and eventually very hungry. Five or so decades ago it was a very different story. Back in 1959 for example there would be numerous train services to choose from and usually at a reduced price. In this same year the Whit Monday service from Derby to say Matlock Bath would have cost you the princely sum of three shillings and seven pence return which by 1963 the same journey had rose to five shillings. This would be second-class travel, as first class would cost you an extra fifty per cent or half price if you were between the ages of three and fourteen. Alternatively, on Easter Sunday in 1964, as another example, it was possible to travel from Derby to Hathersage by diesel no less (diesel still being a bit of a novelty) for eight shillings and all the way to Edale for nine shillings and six pence. You would then have just enough time to sprint up Jacob's Ladder, lie back and smoke a bowl of shag before heading back to enjoy a pint in the Nag's Head and catching the return train. The Sunday and Bank holiday services were usually run as cheap day specials in conjunction with the Rambler's Association, who could be pretty certain that all carriages would be full to capacity with both young and old. The young in particular took full advantage of the single compartment coaches to engage in noisy and no doubt salacious activities, while the older folk preferred a corridor coach, especially after a few drinks in a pub before catching the train home, for there is nothing like a couple of pints (or more) for seeking out a weak bladder and sending you fleeing to the toilet at the end of the coach. I recall as a lad once spending the entire journey from Derby to Edale sitting along with other walkers on the bare wooden floor of a freight wagon, which looked and smelt like a cattle truck that had been added to the train at the last minute in Derby to cope with the overflow of people. Now wouldn't Health and Safety have loved that!

Naturally in a county with a heritage as rich as Derbyshire there is always going to be another sort of populace which is that of the ethereal, make-believe, questionable truth and the figments of fertile imaginations. There are accounts of Lover's Leaps off which lovers have leapt (and survived), as well as sightings of phantom miners, ghostly riders, cursed skulls and boggarts, which can take the form of hair-raising, shadowy shapes like the ones that allegedly waft about the recumbent stones of Arbor Low; or the Lumb Boggart of Bradwell, said to be the spectre of a murdered girl who was eventually exorcised and turned into a fish. Quite whether she thought this was a satisfactory outcome for the afterlife is a matter for speculation. Despite Derbyshire being an awful long way from the sea it still manages to find itself with a Mermaid's Pool supposedly salty and allegedly, so legend would have you believe, connected to the Atlantic. Situated below Kinder Downfall it was the habitat of a Siren who in age old fashion lured men to their deaths and a watery grave. Normally to fulfil such criteria you would have to be standing on a shoreline by the sea or shipwrecked on rocks. Unlike her marine equivalent she was not all bad and on one occasion is said to have escorted a lost walker off Kinder to a nearby pub. Now that would really have been worth seeing. I mean putting to one side if possible the image of a walker descending the slopes of Kinder accompanied by a life-size, humanoid fish, awkwardly flapping and slapping alongside him, consider the following plausible scenario, because it sounds not unlike the opening lines of an awful gag. So this bloke walks into a pub with a mermaid and says to the barman,

"Two whiskies please. I'll take water with mine."

"And what about your friend?" asks the barman.

"She prefers hers on the rocks."

Please yourself. The mermaid was also very approachable and to glimpse her on Easter Eve meant she would confer upon you immortality, which depending on your circumstances in life (your wife has just run off with the milkman, you are six months in arrears with the mortgage, and the Inland Revenue is on your back), may or may not have been a blessing.

Well known characters like Robin Hood and his sidekick Little John pop up here and there around the county, as do reclusive bearded anchorites dwelling in hollowed out rocks, and of course the old lad himself; the Devil, who crops up showing us the dubious spectacle of his backside at Castleton and being blamed for twisting the spire of All Saints church at Chesterfield. There are ruined stately houses and castles where ghosts from the past flit around standing ominously by doorways in darkened rooms as at Bolsover Castle and guaranteed to scare the pants off you. The present castle was a rebuild that took place in the first quarter of the 1600s by Charles Cavendish after the previous Norman structure fell into an unmanageable heap. Cavendish was the son of feisty, 'don't truck with me,' Bess of Hardwick who in her lifetime had not been amiss to knocking up a few grand houses herself including Chatsworth and Hardwick Hall to name just two. Actually between them, Charles and Bess were a tad like Barratt Homes, but rather more posh as they built on an estate that was rather different to today's concept of an estate.

Tales of restless ghosts come thick and fast, with tradition normally stating that such apparitions are in dire need of appeasing before they cease annoying folk by clanking about in chains or moaning outside your bedroom door all hours of the night. A typical story is one recorded in Chesterfield where three ghastly, ghostly and somewhat off-putting spectres appeared on three consecutive nights knocking on the bedroom door of an elderly couple. The first night the old man got out of his bed, opened the door and found himself face-to-face with a huge slavering black dog that clearly was not there for walkies! Naturally he quickly closed the door and promised himself never to eat cheese ever again last thing at night. The second night the old boy is again wakened from his slumbers by the sound of knocking and opened the door to be treated to the apparition of a woman covered in blood and making a bit of a mess on the floor. The third night (I can't believe he is still there! I would have moved out by now, or sent the wife to open the door) he opened the door (he must have been getting more than a bit cheesed off by now) to find a giant of a man standing there who persuaded the old boy, by now quaking in his jim-jams, to accompany him to where he had stashed a heap of stolen loot asking him to return all the money to its rightful owners, after which his restless spirit would wander no more. The story was published in 1675 and seems to be only marginally longer than the title of the four page pamphlet called, 'Strange and Terrible News from Chesterfield in Darbyshire; being a full and true Relation of a horrible and terrible Ghost that was visibly seen on Sunday the 24th of January 1674. First in the shape of a Dog, then a Woman and afterwards a Man. Together with the discovery of some money that was hidden by Him in his lifetime.' Apart from the title almost certainly taking up one side of a page, it does pretty much tell the story without having to read on.

Another strange but not uncommon phenomenon was the keeping of an old skull in the house; an event which occurs in many houses throughout the country in various locations and Derbyshire is no different. The stories all bear a similarity, usually running along the lines of the skull belonging to some unfortunate soul who had been murdered, which even if this was not the case it at least added some clout and mystique to the tale rather than just saying Uncle Albert dug it up in the garden one day when he was planting a row of King Edwards. The best known Derbyshire skull was called Dickie who resided at Tunstead Farm and was said to be the head of the original owner of the farm, the best part of two hundred years ago who, surprise, surprise, was treacherously murdered. Again the general format is that should the skull be removed from its resting place (in Dickie's case this was a windowsill), you would be courting trouble which could be anything from your cattle dropping dead to the collapse of a nearby railway line. Consequently, most skulls had the reputation of being cursed and were best left undisturbed, especially so if the owner was still using it!

In many ways Derbyshire can be compared to a set of books comprising umpteen volumes that are continually being added to, for there is still much yet to be discovered, unearthed and learnt about the county's rich seams of history, folklore, people and places. Lifting the lid on some of this was always going to be a challenge, in particular knowing where to start and what to include. I gazed at an Ordnance Survey map of the county for ages before deciding to start with what the map did not show me, which was what lay beneath the surface and something I had first-hand knowledge of, namely its subterranean world. Holes, caves and mines hold gems of both myth and fact that has surrounded them for centuries, which in the past quite often made them places to fear. Today these stories are more likely to simply make you stick your tongue firmly in one cheek. Some tales are fact, some borderline, some elaborated on over time while others might once have held a grain of truth that is now almost impossible to substantiate, because of an exaggeration of the facts with the story having been passed on from generation to generation. I am afraid you can only decide for yourselves.

"To say more on this subject might be useless; to say less
would be ungrateful."

Ebenezer Rhodes

I.

The Hole Truth
... well almost.

Derbyshire is riddled with natural cave systems and extensive mine workings to the extent that Conan Doyle wrote in his novel, *The Terror of Blue John Gap*, if you were to hit the county with a very large hammer it would resound like a drum. What he failed to mention is that it would also cause an awful amount of damage. Frankly I find myself questioning this idea, for a drum is normally a void, a mass of emptiness beneath a taught skin, whereas mile upon mile of passages and holes all of varying sizes would surely make Derbyshire more akin an Emmental cheese or a sponge, which if hit with a large hammer especially after a prolonged period of rain, the latter would more likely produce a kind of muffled squidgy, squelching sound. Derbyshire is undoubtedly full of holes with many I suspect still waiting to be discovered. It is the holy land. Many holes at some time or other in the distant past have been inhabited by animals using them as dens or lairs. Remains of beasties such as the sabre-toothed tiger, woolly rhinoceros, bear, horse and hyena are but a few that have been unearthed in the layers of sediment that often forms the floor of a cave. Competition for occupation of a hole must at times have become keen for these holes were also much sought after by humans, like those spear-wielding Neanderthal chaps loafing about in reindeer skin underpants (Okay, so more loin cloth than underpants), who were in need of somewhere to shelter. After all the caves were rent-free, required no updating and there would normally be no chain involved, or if there was then the stronger of the two groups would simply club the weaker one to death and in all probability eat them; for cannibalism was not unknown. The group or family could then move in to their new subterranean home and peacefully settle down for the night, provided of course there was no ferocious animal lurking beyond in the dark depths of the cave just about to wake up and discover dinner asleep in the entrance.

Both early and more modern man have left behind a plethora of daily artefacts including pots, spears, arrowheads, knives, beads, and bones, in fact practically everything associated with living except the proverbial kitchen sink, which of course they did not possess. Many caves were also used for burying the dead, which presumably devalued it somewhat as a much sought after 'des-res' for I imagine few people would find living in what would be tantamount to a cemetery particularly desirable. Caves were also the haunts of robbers and general miscreants that plagued the countryside in abundance and as a result of this Derbyshire gained the reputation of being a great county in which to get mugged and possibly murdered. Fortunately things have changed for the better, for which the Peak District National Park Authority and Tourist Board must be truly grateful.

So what is it about holes in the ground that seem to either fascinate us or fill us with fear and dread? I suppose I could compare a cave to Marmite, you either love it or hate it. I personally hate Marmite but find holes truly compelling. Generally speaking you are either the sort of person who sees a hole in the ground and twitches like a dog nearing a lamp-post and immediately feels an overwhelming urge to disappear into it quicker than a ferret up a drainpipe, or else you take one look at a gaping black hole and your mind is instantly awash with images of a hideous end by drowning in a constricting watery tunnel or being buried alive beneath tons of collapsing rock. Holes come in all shapes and sizes from a yawning abyss like Eldon Hole where you can dangle in space during a descent, or something rather more confined like Lathkill Head Cave where your chest is flat against the floor and your rear end scraping the roof, with only the echoing drumming of your heart for company. Then there was always the old way through Waterfall Swallet that required as near as dammit for you to stand on your head in a constricted tube – the point of no return – before negotiating a tight ninety degree bend at the bottom. Derbyshire has an abundance of everything that constitutes a hole and with them come many tales that are very much a part of Peakland folklore.

Take Peak Cavern for starters (we may as well begin with something big) with its immense entrance that throughout time has drawn the curious and the inquisitive from far and wide, thus earning a place on the list of the Seven Wonders of the Peak. This short list is usually attributed to Thomas Hobbes around 1613 in a poem he originally wrote in Latin which I will not be bothering with here. This is a translation.

'Of the high Peak or Seven wonders writ.
Two Fonts, two Caves, one Pallace, Mount and Pit.'

These refer to St Anne's Well and the Ebbing and Flowing Well, Peak Cavern and Poole's Cavern, Chatsworth House, Mam Tor and Eldon Hole. Whether other people thought these were 'wonderous' wonders is another matter altogether as we will see. Peak Cavern is also known by the rather more indelicate name of The Devil's Arse i' t' Peak, a name coined back in the mists of time because of the sounds made by wind and syphoning waters 'which after heavy rain, is seen to boil up from underneath the rock' in and around the entrance that were comparable to the eruption of intestinal gases, or put another way, farting, but fortunately without the accompanying odious odours. The Devil gets blamed for many things and appears to have his parts distributed all over the place. The Devil's Footprint for example (obviously not wearing shoes or socks that day) lies near Hollingbury Hill fort in East Sussex, while the Devil's Elbow or at least one of them can be seen at Cairnwell Pass in the Highlands and another on the Stikine River in British Columbia. There are others to be found elsewhere but I feel I should draw the line somewhere, I mean, just how many elbows does he need?

The Devil's Nose (La Nariz del Diablo) can be found in Ecuador where he seemingly raised no objections to having a gang of Ecuadorians and Jamaicans crawling all over it as they blasted out an incredible feat of engineering in the form of a 'zig-zag' railway up the precipitous sides of his considerable hooter. Presumably it was thought they would be pushing their luck by considering the use of his nostrils as ready-made tunnels! Perhaps the most unlikely piece of the Devil on show is in Scotland and known as Bod an Deamhain which is Gaelic for the Penis of the Demon (Devil), which even in the depths of winter covered in snow and ice in sub-zero temperatures still stands solid and erect in the freezing air. You have to admire it for few men, if any could lay claim to such prowess in such near arctic conditions! It has even been gazed upon by Queen Victoria who was shown Old Nick's Nob by none other than John Brown (not Billy Connolly) who was sufficiently discrete not to inform her of the translation from the Gaelic. This was also the case when Victoria viewed Peak Cavern, where again she was not told that in essence she was entering the Devil's back passage to listen to a concert in an inner chamber or put another way, deep inside his colon.

The Devil is certainly well travelled as I have seen his marbles (this is not a double-entendre as there are many of them) lying about in an untidy heap off the Stuart Highway north of Alice Springs in Australia. The thing is with his bits and pieces strewn hither and thither, why is it that the beautiful county of Derbyshire should have drawn the short straw and end up with his yawning rectum that appears to be in readiness for an imminent colonoscopy! To my way of thinking it is very unfair and thoughtless given there are some particularly uninteresting places in the UK where the Devil could have displayed his butt. My theory is that Old Nick was a bit of an exhibitionist and had figured out that at some time in the future the popularity of the Peak District would grow to such an extent that millions would come, as indeed they do, to gaze and allow inquisitiveness to force them to venture in awe into the dark, damp cavernous innards beyond his rectal end.

When Daniel Defoe, who can sometimes be as dull as ditch water (he was far better as author of *Robinson Crusoe*), visited Peak Cavern in the early 1700s he was not at all impressed. With regard to the alternative name of the Devil's Arse he commented that, 'the grossness of the name given,' as far as he was concerned bore nothing, 'between the thing signified and the thing signifying.' Defoe did travel some distance inside the cave and concluded that in his opinion the cavern was not in the least bit worthy of being called a 'wonder.' In the same vein he did not think much of Poole's Cavern either, stating that if a good light was to be cast upon its roof then, 'there would be no more beauty on it than on the back of a chimney' and the supposed formations or, 'stones called Mr Cotton's, Haycock's, Poole's Chair, Flitches of Bacon and the like are nothing but ordinary stones.' Harsh words indeed. In short Defoe classed Poole's Hole as merely another example, 'of the wonderless wonders of the Peak.' Obviously not a man easily pleased, and definitely not the kind of man to find yourself sitting next to you on a Wallace Arnold week-long coach tour of the Peak District. Just imagine it.

"Mr Defoe isn't it?"

"Yes."

"Did you enjoy your excursion into Poole's Hole?"

"No I did not. There was nothing worth looking at."

"Oh. Perhaps you found the Devil's Arse more fun. I mean to say what a name, had me in stitches when I first heard it."

"No I did not. I find the name vulgar and there was nothing of any interest inside there either."

"But surely you have to admit that Mam Tor as hills go is pretty unique."

"Not at all it's just a hill. Seen one you've seen them all."

"Hmm … but the Ebbing and Flowing Well was quite something I thought, with the water going in and out like a dog at a fair. I reckon that's pretty strange don't you?

"No, it was not strange and neither was it interesting."

"Er … would you excuse me for one moment Mr Defoe, I just want to go up front and ask the driver to stop the coach so I can step off and stab myself to death on the roadside!"

Lord Byron along with Mary Chaworth (his latest romantic conquest) wrote an account of his adventure into Peak Cavern saying that when they reached water, 'the stream which flows under a rock so close as to admit the boat to be pushed on by a ferryman, a sort of Charon, who wades at the stern, stooping all the time.' Byron, true to form also admitted that despite being confined in a boat in a dark, watery underground world, 'he had long been in love (with Mary Chaworth) and never told it, though she had discovered it without. I recollect my sensations but cannot describe them, and it is as well.' So to use the expression 'whatever floats your boat' which in this instance was a floating boat, Byron seems to have found the entire underground experience a bit of a turn on, and we can but hope that the limited light from a candle was enough to hide his visible ardour! Byron referring to the ferryman as Charon in this particular instance is highly appropriate as Charon was the mythical ferry-man of Hades and the river in Peak Cavern had long been referred to as the Styx. Okay, so you knew that already.

Another literary fellow, Murray Gilchrist who visited the great cavern wrote, 'The first impression is one of curious weirdness', as he first approached the entrance where he spied, 'mysterious drums and poles that bear a mysterious resemblance to gibbets. The light is pale and sad: one can scarce believe that one is looking upon an English curiosity.' Obviously Peak cavern was not on his list of top favourite places to spend a day out with the wife and kids. An excellent detailed account of a trip into the cavern is given by James Croston during the latter half of the 1700s. He was given a miner's felt hat to wear in case he inadvertently, 'happened to raise his head the chances were in favour of it being caught against the sharp inequalities of the superincumbent mass', or put another way, if you stick your head up then you are likely to bang it on the roof and see stars, which until that particular moment in time you would have considered to be an impossible underground phenomenon. A certain M. St Fond writes of a visit into the interior of Peak Cavern saying, 'we stood some time on the brink; and as the light of our dismal torches, which emitted a black smoke, reflecting our pale visages from the bottom of the lake, we almost conceived that we saw a troop of shades starting from an abyss to present themselves before us.' Sounds to me like somebody was getting a bit spooked out and could not wait to, 'return to the light of day.'

About the year 1700 a woman was plodding around England riding side-saddle on a horse and having to deal with unimaginable rough, muddy and sometimes barely passable trackways and country lanes in an effort to get from one place to another. Her name was Celia Fiennes and during her grand tour she had passed through Derbyshire and had stopped at a place, 'they Call the Devills Arse.' She describes the entrance as being situated in a hill, 'on one End jutting out in two parts (buttocks to her way of thinking) and joyns in one at ye top, this part or Cleft between you Enter a great Cave.' She notes that only poor people lived in the entrance in, 'Little houses built of Stone and thatch'd Like Little Styes', who eked out a meagre existence by begging and, 'by Lighting the strangers into the Cave.'

Celia (yes I am on first name terms) was shown into the cavern and as far as the river. Here she called it a day on account of it seemed to her to be a somewhat precarious crossing. 'Some do go on it with a Little boate to ye other side, but I would not venture. There was one Gentlewoman

7

in our Company sd she had been Carry'd over on 2 men's shoulders', but our Celia was not in favour of such antics and returned to the entrance. Normally I would reckon this to be a tad wussy of her to baulk at a bit of water, but to confront the dangers and suffer the hardships that Celia had been exposed to on her journey through England make her nothing short of courageous.

At the other end of the 1700s yet another female adventurer sallied forth on a tour of England and Scotland and called at Castleton on her way. She went by the name of the Hon. Mrs Murray (Sarah to her friends and me of course) of Kensington who left a fine description of her visit to Peak Cavern. She advises fellow explorers of the cave to provide themselves with a change of dress so, 'they need not fear getting cold or rheumatism.' Women will also require, 'dry shoes, stockings and petticoats', along with, 'night caps and a yard of course flannel to pin on the head', to prevent drips of water from going down your neck. This list is also suitable for cross-dressers, but it is probably best not to venture into such uncertain territory. However, it does make me realise how much easier it is these days when all you need is a helmet, electric light and a tight-fitting, thrombosis inducing neoprene wet-suit. Sarah Murray also advises taking, 'some snuff and tobacco', to offer the, 'old witch-looking beings spinning in the dark mouth of the cave.' Spinning in this instance refers to the rope-making industry that went off in the entrance and not that they were all throwing themselves about like crazed dervishes. The colony of rope-makers along with miscreants and people of ill repute lived in huts, which another writer described as consisting of, 'houses, barns, animals, hay, turf and stink.' Then almost as an afterthought he states that the female guide he had employed was, 'Handsome enough and Girlie enough she was.' Sounds to me as though he was thinking along the lines of any port in a storm! The industry declined over the decades and finished up as a sight-seeing novelty for the tourists who in 1949 for example, had to pay an entrance fee of two shillings. The ropewalks eventually finished up producing cotton and hemp fibres for bell ropes, sash cords, ropes for small boats and clotheslines.

When I became acquainted with Herbert Marrison the last of the rope workers in the late sixties he was pretty much down to clotheslines and towing ropes. This is a bit of a come-down when you learn that at one time rope was woven here for the rigging of the English ships that sent the Spanish Armada scurrying back home with their tillers firmly tucked between their sterns. Sarah Murray also warns that once inside the constrictions of the cave, and should you be in possession of a long nose then, 'take care of it whilst you cross the Styx or the pointed rocks over your face may take away a bit of it', so you have been warned Gerard Depardieu, Barbra Streisand, Barry Manilow, Sarah Jessica Parker, Dustin Hoffman, Bette Midler, Pinocchio and of course the incorrigible and immensely loveable Miss Piggy. 'An old pair of gloves' is also recommended when holding a tallow candle which you should, 'take care you do not singe his (the guide's) beard', as he piggybacks you across the river. The account of her trip is quite thorough, and of the party she was with she states as being, 'the most ludicrous scene imaginable;- a long string of uncouth figures, with each a candle in one hand, creeping knees and nose together, in the bowels of a mountain.' Similar strange apparel was noted by Rhodes when he visited the cavern around 1824 where the visitors had, 'prepared themselves with proper habiliments for the occasion – loose gowns were thrown over their travelling dresses, and the ladies had covered their heads with a species of shawl, that came over the shoulders and was fastened across the bosom. Monks with cowls, and nuns with hoods, seemed to make up the whole party.' Unlike Defoe who said there were far better caves than Peak cavern abroad that could be termed a wonder, the Hon. Mrs Murray of Kensington found, 'the cave at Castleton an astonishing natural curiosity.'

The thing about the Hon. Mrs Murray and I can never leave this unsaid, is the mind-boggling length of the title of her book of travels called, *A*

COMPANION and USEFUL GUIDE to the BEAUTIES OF SCOTLAND, to THE LAKES of WESTMORELAND, CUMBERLAND, AND LANCASHIRE; and of the curiosities in THE DISTRICT OF CRAVEN, in the West Riding of Yorkshire. To which is added, a more particular DESCRIPTION OF SCOTLAND, especially that part of it called THE HIGHLANDS. BY THE HON. MRS MURRAY of Kensington. Now you have to admit that that is quite a mouthful, yet quite acceptable at the time, and she is not alone for later in 1864 along came James Joseph Sylvester with a book on a totally different subject entitled, *Algebraical Researches Containing a Disquisition on Newton's Rule for the Discovery of Imaginary Roots and an Allied Rule Applicable to a Particular Class of Equation together with a Complete Invariative Determination of the Character of the Roots of the General Equation of the 5th Degree etc.* The 'etc' alarmingly implies that there should be more, but thank goodness we are spared any extras. It did occur to me that if only Sylvester had been able to add the word 'supercalifragilisticexp ialidocious' (thank you Mary Poppins) then it would only marginally have rendered the whole thing barely more incomprehensible than it already is!

The obvious difference between Sarah Murray's title and James Sylvester's is that there is unlikely to be anyone living today who has the foggiest idea just what the hell the latter book is all about, for if you understand the full meaning of that title then you are a better man than I Gunga Din! It would not be difficult for you to have a stab at which of the two books graces my bookshelf at home, especially when I tell you that my teacher at school told me not to waste my time taking GCE 'O' level Maths because according to her the only thing likely to be correct on the paper would be my name at the top of the page. Subtle she was not. However, it occurred to me that had I been writing this book around the same time as the above authors I could perhaps have titled it; *Some Perambulations, Observations and Whimsical Interpretations of Topographical Inclusions and Natural Phenomenon occurring within the Peak District of Derbyshire, encompassing Legend, Folklore and Mythical Events with Historical Tracts from Literary Bygones.* Doubtless this would ensure an immediate facetious and discouraging e-mail from my publisher along the lines of stop being such a silly arse.

Contrasting somewhat with Sarah Murray's account is a visit by Henricus who describes the entrance to Peak Cavern as, 'Within this shadowy gulf are several rude huts, formerly the abodes of some of the manufacturers of twine combined with a multitude of machines, and with the sublime features of the spot produce a strange and singular effect.' He goes on to describe his trip inside as, 'After proceeding about thirty or forty yards, the roof becomes lower, and a gentle descent conducts, by a detached rock, to the interior of this tremendous hollow.' Now in spite of admitting that Peak Cavern is indeed a worthy wonder, Henricus manages to summarise his own wondrous underground experience in just one very uninspiring sentence! In the year 1772 a visitor James Ferguson wrote of a trip into Peak Cavern saying, 'Toward the further end from the entrance, the roof comes down with a gradual slope to about two feet from the surface of the water fourteen yards across the rock, in that place, forming a kind of arch, under which I was pushed by my guide across the water in a long oval tub, as I lay on my back in the straw with a candle in my hand and was for the greater part of the way on the river so near the arched roof that it touched my hat, if I had raised myself but two inches from the straw on which I lay in the tub (called the boat) which I believe was not above a foot in depth.' By now you will probably have realised that this account of his underground experience has been related in one very long uninterrupted sentence, and if you have read it without pausing for breath then in all likelihood you will not be reading this line as you will have passed out some time ago! It certainly flies in the face of todays cosseted 'elf and safety' regulations which, of course would never allow a lighted candle in a boat full of straw. Even I can see that it was a cremation just waiting to happen! What really beggars belief during the early days of cave tourism was the fact that although the entrance fee to most show caves was somewhere around the two to three shilling mark in the late 1800s (not cheap), it seems that extras in the form of 'blasts and Bengal lights' could be purchased. A blast was the ignition of a small quantity of gunpowder, thus giving a brief if somewhat smoky impression of the caves interior while a Bengal light was basically a flare comprising of a mixture of sulphur, saltpetre and orpiment, the latter being a form of arsenic. One can only imagine what the caverns must have been like at the end of a full day of showing visitors around who were letting off blasts and flares. It must have been thick with toxic fumes that would certainly have cleared anyone's sinuses prior to an early death!

Meanwhile back at Peak Cavern an account of an entirely different nature unfolds that is guaranteed to put you off your dinner and related in ballad form (altogether now …) of a notorious Elizabethan rogue called Cock Lorel, which is a weird name if ever I heard one and sounds to me like a play on the word cockerel. Anyway, the story goes that Cock Lorel was said to have invited the Devil to dinner in Peak Cavern. Now this needs a bit of careful thought, because given the fact that Peak Cavern is the Devil's Arse, could he really eat there? I mean Old Nick really would have had his head up his own arse on this occasion! The ballad tells of how the good for nothing miscreant Cocky Lorel served Old Nick a truly scrummy meal of a, 'rich, fat Usurer (Wonga.com springs to mind) stewed in his own marrow and a Lawyer's Head (Haven't we all at some time in our lives wanted to boil a solicitors head after an unnecessarily prolonged wait, only to receive a grossly expensive bill?) served up in a green sauce.' I have to say that in keeping with the meal 'green sauce' smacks of some ghastly concoction consisting of mucous and bile. Come on now, you know you were thinking exactly the same! I have to confess that as menus go this would not see a crowd of diners beating a path to the door particularly as there was no mention of a pudding. Michelin Star, no chance!

Finally, and to finish on a cheerier note there is a very early story from around 1212 of a swineherd who on a winter's day managed to lose a sow about to farrow that belonged to one William Peveril. After a fruitless search 'pig-man' decided that it must have wandered off into Peaks Hole. Now despite the evil reputation of the cave he thought it to be a lesser threat than the wrath he would incur from his master, who in all probability would fly into a blind rage and beat the living daylights out of the poor fellow before handing him his P45. Bill Peveril was not amiss to having the occasional mega-strop so it was imperative that piggy be found pretty promptly. The swineherd entered the cave probably calling out, 'Here piggy, piggy. Where are you?' but piggy had scarpered and was nowhere to be found. After a while 'pig-man' suddenly spied daylight ahead and found himself overlooking a verdant plain where the sun shone, the air was warm and reapers were busily getting in the harvest; and here snoozing beneath a thorn tree was naughty Miss Piggy surrounded by some squealing piglets. Somehow the swineherd was able to cajole the porcine party back through the dark cave to emerge again into a cold winter-bound Derbyshire. I cannot help thinking that 'pig-man' was a bit of a rustic clod for not staying in the summery world he had wandered into, which, wherever it was sounds like a great place to take a winter holiday. I think it is almost time I left the Devil and his Hole and moved further up the road.

Before I do so and while on the subject of the Devil and things demonic, I feel I should include a quick diversion into the dark, shadowy, gloomy and malevolent atmosphere that inhabits Demon's Dale and its cave. Here the writer Nellie Kirkham 'first sensed evil' by the gaping hole in the hillside. Another writer refers to it as, 'a weird little ravine known as Demon's Dale; a dark and narrow place where one would scarce go o'nights.' Demon's Dale cave has sometimes been referred to as a 'rock shelter', which given the fact that it is a resurgence cave often gushing forth torrents of water, would strongly suggest it as somewhere you would not wish to seek shelter from a cloudburst unless you were a fish, a duck or a complete half-wit. Demon's Dale is probably little noticed or even known by the countless motorists passing along the A6 as their attention is no doubt drawn to the riverine landscape of the end of Monsal Dale and the precipitous sides of Fin Cop. One William Worcestre born in 1478 was very aware of Demon's Dale, Dimmins Dale, or as he called it, Dymyneysdale, as he wondered about Derbyshire in his old age (his wife probably wanted him out of the house and not getting under her feet all day long) and had this to say of the place. It was a spot, 'where spirits suffer torments. Where there is a marvellous entrance into the earth of the Peak where souls are tortured.' Not much of an incentive to go poking around there then, but it does sound like an ideal place to send the mother-in-law for a day out. There is a sinister air about the cave and the dank dale especially on an overcast drizzly day when the clouds hang low in the valley. Apparently there was a local saying:

The Old Woman of Demon's Dale,
The Pipes of Shacklow,
The Fiddler of Finn,
Gather them all in.

This rhyme is of course self-explanatory. Well actually, that is a big fib, for it seems that nobody knows how old it is and neither does anybody have the faintest idea what it means, but I thought I should mention it and suggest it as a conversation piece to try out at your next dinner party, when one of those awkward pregnant pauses presents itself. It is many years since I last visited the place, but I recall that the sombre mood was only slightly lightened by a discarded empty packet of Walker's Salt and Vinegar crisps and curiously, a pair of sopping wet, faded pink knickers laid out on a mossy rock, an invitation for ripe speculation if ever there was one. The question in my mind is how is it possible for someone who was presumably previously knickered, to then walk away completely knickerless? Unless, of course, the unfortunate female had been witness to something so diabolical and so unspeakable that it had quite literally 'scared the pants off her.' I think all this demoniacal dabbling is having an effect on me. I really am going to head off up the road.

Up the road in this instance from Peak Cavern literally means up the steep, narrow road that winds its way between high overhanging towers of limestone that is the Winnats Pass. In the past this was a wild and remote place and not somewhere you would be wise to linger. James Croston came this way and described it as, 'rent asunder by the convulsions of nature' and that, 'a feeling of awe took possession of the senses and the mind, conscious of the deep solitude that prevailed, became oppressed with melancholy.' His narrative would give anyone the willies, but in all fairness he was walking through the pass on a moonlit night where everything looked decidedly spooky, and he sure was ready for a stiff drink when he finally crashed through the door of the Bull's Head in Castleton. Croston would have been well aware of the murder that would have fuelled his angst that night of the two lovers in the mid-1700s that were set upon by five miners in the Winnats Pass.

The unfortunate couple, Henry and Clara were returning, so it is rumoured from having got married at Peak Forest (a sort of Gretna Green in those far off times) when the miners violently relieved them of their money. Poor Henry had his throat slit and Clara was unceremoniously whacked on the head with a pick-axe (shades of Leon Trotsky here), which rather put an end to their honeymoon plans. However, history relates that in actual fact the five 'Mr Nasties' did not come out of it quite as they had expected. One apparently fell off the Winnats and died on the spot and another suffered a terminal headache after being crushed by a falling rock near where the couple had been murdered. Another, who by now had possibly cottoned on to the fact that things were not going too well for his mates and rather than hang about waiting for the unexpected to happen opted for suicide, while a fourth one died 'raging mad' after several attempts to destroy himself. I mean how hard can that really be? He should have taken some tips from his mate. I am afraid this is a 'red ink' case of 'Must try harder.'

The last miner lived in torment and was consumed with remorse and despair and unable to die on his 'sinner's bed' until he had disclosed all the gory details of the heinous crime he had committed with his mates in Winnats Pass. I think it would be fair to say that for those five miners crime really did not pay. They should have stuck to digging holes and looking for lead. Just to compound the general air of gloominess that often prevails in the Winniates Pass as it is sometimes called, in 1937 a man standing on the Lions Rock fell and bounced seven hundred feet where his limp and battered body finally came to rest on the roadway. The unfortunate man never made it to the hospital alive. This tragedy inspired the Rev A.G. Jewitt to later compose a doggerel ballad that finished with the lines;

'Christians, I have told my ditty,
If you shudder not with fear,
If your breasts can glow with pity,
Can you now withhold a tear?'

Not quite what you could call a great poetical work, and as for 'glowing breasts' … well that is certainly something I have never come across, but I can see they would be useful for finding your way home on a dark night. But do not be put off by these stories of Winnats Pass. They are not everyday occurrences!

The head of the pass joins a road that wanders over a bleak landscape and here among the hills lies the great abyss of Eldon Hole, or Helldon Hole as it was once called. Over the centuries it has initiated numerous tales mainly about it being bottomless and therefore a direct entrance into hell. (No surprise there then!) Proof of this theory was provided way back in the form of someone chucking a goose down the chasm where it disappeared only to emerge some two miles away in Peak Cavern. After what was presumably a subterranean journey through the very fires of hell itself it finally emerged featherless and seriously singed. Naturally this story takes a bit of believing. Eldon Hole is certainly not noted for being hot, as I once bottomed it one year after first having squeezed myself between the wall of the chasm and a massive ice plug wedged in the bottom, and this was in early August! Neither is it known how long it took the goose to get there. Bearing in mind that the eternal fires of hell are going to be pretty hot and that the average cooking time for an average size goose is around three hours at gas mark five, then it could not have been too long a trip as it only got a scorching. This is merely a passing thought, but if the goose had flown in first from the Peak Cavern entrance and become well roasted en-route, then on entering the bottom of Eldon Hole flown slap-bang into the ice plug then it would have become the very first 'ready frozen goose dinner.' Like I said, it was just a passing thought. It does put me in mind of another strange bird story which this time involved a duck. It is said that a duck flew into an ash tree on Sheldon green and subsequently disappeared. The hypothesis is that the silly duck flew into a hole in the tree and was unable to extricate itself, having become irretrievably wedged and the tree simply grew around it. This tale is based on the fact that many years later the tree was eventually felled and sawn into boards, two of which revealed the shape of a flattened bird. I wonder if this is where the term duckboard originated ... probably not. Anyway, this is a true story with photographic proof apparently in Buxton museum. Few people who have lived through the 70s will have failed not to have experienced the dubious delights of that gourmet pub meal 'chicken in a basket' but 'duck in wood'... I can't see that catching on, can you?

Anyway, back to Eldon Hole or the Bottomless Pit as it has also been called. The bottom of the hole actually contains a massive heap of rocks most of which have been thrown down by passing visitors. Perhaps the most famous descent is that of the hapless peasant who was persuaded (for persuaded read, the promise of gold, yeah right!) to do the deed of being lowered into the chasm by the Earl of Leicester. The victim was lowered on a rope and after seven hundred and fifty feet (presumably they had run out of rope) he was duly hauled back to the surface, a raving loon and completely off his trolley. He died eight days later without speaking a word about what he had experienced. Now given the fact that a couple of hundred feet of rope as we now know would have seen him on the bottom, I offer the theory that the prospect of a premature burial beneath the additional and unnecessary five hundred and fifty feet of weighty rope piled on top of him was sufficiently traumatic for him to utterly lose it and emerge a gibbering lunatic. We will of course never know and presumably the Earl saved himself a few pennies in the process by deciding it was pointless paying gold to a peasant who was now completely cuckoo and, as it transpired, on a one-way ticket.

This gaping gulf in the past has been described as 'a place full of horror' and 'a gulf wide, steep, black and a dreadful one' according to Cotton. After Cotton had finished lobbing rocks into the hole he decided to test its depth with a rope and lead, coming up with the amazing answer of eight hundred and eighty-eight yards, which is wildly inaccurate, and the best that can be said of this is that he made a complete pig's ear of the task. As a result of this he remained in awe of the place and was sufficiently inspired to put pen to paper and write; '… who dare, look down into the Chasm, and keep his Hair

From lifting off his hat, either has none,

Or for more Modish Curls cashiers his own.' … so no problem for baldies, or to use a word more apt for the time this was written, those with a pilgarlic bonce.

It seems that the overwhelming desire to throw something, anything into deep holes is inherent in almost everyone including some particularly silly people who have been known to throw themselves in by error of judgement. The overwhelming urge to throw something into Eldon Hole accounts for why fences put around the periphery according to local farmers almost disappear overnight, and stone walls never last more than a few years at best. Most of us are unable to stand on the edge of a chasm without feeling compelled to chuck in the nearest stone, fence-post, tree branch, live dog (I have seen this happen in the Picos mountains in northern Spain) and the occasional human. Hobbes says that he and his fellow companions rolled an enormous rock, 'to the mouth of the cavern, and then thrust it into the aperture.' Along with an obvious inordinate tonnage of rocks lying in the bottom of the hole there are the bones of sheep, cattle and the body of at least one traveller who was forced to the edge by two villains until he reluctantly, 'stept at once into eternity', which is quite a poetical and somewhat understated way of saying they dragged him yelling and screaming and wetting himself with terror to the edge of the drop then shoved him over, where he no doubt continued to yell and scream and wet himself for a few seconds (well you would, wouldn't you!) before hitting the bottom after which all went quiet.

Sarah Murray on her travels stopped off to take a peek and said, 'you may look into Eldon Hole; a tremendous place', while Defoe said it was a place (and surprise, surprise), 'we may justly call a WONDER.' Well how jolly condescending of him. He finally found something that impressed him. The thing is though, he based his comment on the depth recorded by Cotton, which Defoe writes, 'he (Cotton) let down eight hundred fathoms of line into it, and that the plummet drew still; so that, in a word, he sounded about a mile perpendicular.' The alleged depth of the hole obviously put the wind up Defoe as he goes on to comment, 'What nature meant in leaving this window open into the infernal world, if the place lies that way. There is something of horror upon the very imagination when one does but look into it.' So who's a bit of a scaredy pants now? And who was well and truly conned by Cotton's grossly incorrect measuring?

The depth of Eldon Hole grew ridiculously deeper with the passing of time culminating with a Dr Plot (who seems to have totally lost the plot) claiming in the year 1700 that the correct depth was sixteen thousand and eight hundred feet. If it carried on like this for much longer getting deeper and deeper it was only going to be a matter of time before some barking mad individual claimed he had peered into the hole and spotted the Sydney Opera House! Clearly things were getting out of hand, so in 1770 a courageous John Lloyd descended the chasm and gave the depth as two hundred and twenty-eight feet, which is much nearer todays differing figures of between two hundred and forty-five feet to two hundred and seventy-eight feet. Take your pick.

In 1767 two horses belonging to a gentleman and a lady were found without their riders and in close vicinity to the abyss. Fearing the worst that the two riders had been set upon by robbers, murdered and then tossed over the edge lead to some miners being lowered down into the depths to search for the bodies, but none were found. Then around the year 1800 a similar situation arose of a riderless horse being found wandering around the periphery of the hole and once again some miners were sent down to look for a body, and once again nothing was found. Such are the mysteries that surround the dark, yawning abyss. Only a few years ago a young woman fell over the edge and died after losing control of her dog, thus sadly illustrating that Eldon Hole remains to this day a dangerous place.

If you drive along the A515 south of Buxton and take the left turn signposted King Sterndale you can park near where the Midshires Way crosses the road and follow it through a couple of open fields. Almost without warning the ground drops away in front of you and suddenly you find yourself standing on the lip of a very steep-sided gorge called Deep

Dale. Descend into its depths on a still grey day and it has the feel of a primordial wilderness about it, as though it is a place time forgot, remote, barren and sequestered. I have walked this dale many times and have often thought how it would not surprise me to turn a corner and come face to face with a munching Leptoceratops, or catch the fleeting shadow from an Archeopteryx swooping overhead from a bare limestone buttress. Actually that is a complete lie. I would be surprised. In fact I would be so surprised I would turn and scarper for cover at such speed it would make Jessica Ennis look like she was doing the hundred meters hurdle pushing a Zimmer frame!

The feeling of isolation you can encounter down in the confines of the dale has given rise to the belief that it is inhabited by fairies, or the 'little people' and allegedly many years ago a miner returning home from work was passing through the dale and managed to capture an elf which he promptly put inside the bag he was shouldering. Now not unreasonably the elf got a tad hacked off about being stuffed into a smelly old bag and kicked up such a stink, kicking, yelling and screeching that the miner felt compelled to let it go. He probably thought that as pets go this had been a really bad choice and has he went on his way his thoughts no doubt turned to something quieter along the lines of a goldfish or a tortoise.

The very 'hard-to-miss' cave entrance in the dale is Thirst House Cave, Hob's Thirst House Cave and sometimes Deep Dale cave. In the past it was probably inhabited in Neolithic times, as a couple of skeletons – assumed to be of this period – were discovered in a shallow grave just outside the entrance and fragments of Romano-British pottery (some people are just so untidy), have been excavated from the silt within the cave itself. Also discovered in the cave by an archaeologist with the suspiciously mineralogical sounding handle of Micah Salt were bones once belonging to a Great Brown Bear that growled its last growl a few thousand years ago, for which present day cavers should be grateful. Let us not make any bones about it (groan), the last thing you would want to pick out in the beam of your torch would be the sight of thirteen hundredweight of snarling bear carrying on like ... well, a bear with a sore head heading swiftly in your direction and hell-bent on giving you a terminal hug. Such an unexpected surprise (for surprise read heart-stopping, pant-soiling, open-mouthed bombshell) would without a shadow of doubt stop you dead in your tracks, make you drop your Pifco rubber torch, transform you into a simpering wet Nellie putting in an urgent request for your Mummy!

Similarly, had you been unfortunate enough to be poking around at the bottom of a shaft in Dream Cave near Wirksworth at the wrong time, then this too would have turned out to be very hazardous. In all probability the very last thing you would have heard would be the sound of a drawn out 'whooooosh' as the best part of three tons of Woolly Rhinoceros that had mistakenly gone over the edge of the hole plummeted down to pancake you into eternity. The Woolly Rhinoceros died out a very long time ago, but looked not unlike our present day African rhino, only clad in the equivalent of an angora sweater. Very nice. Very chic.

If you really wanted to live on the edge then Thor's Cave in the Manifold valley would certainly accommodate any suicidal desires you might have been contemplating, for at one time this hole harboured three different types of bear (but no Goldilocks) along with a bison, cave lion and a rhinoceros. This would be comparable to a day out at the zoo; the downside being that none of them were in cages and you would be down on their menu as 'Todays Special', which in hindsight would hold little appeal.

If that does not provide enough action then Victory quarry at Dove Holes could top that collection, for in 1901 a cave was broken into by workmen that contained masses of bones and more teeth than you would find in a dentist's waste bin. These were identified as the remains of mastodons, sabre-toothed tigers, elephants, rhinoceroses, horses, deer and hyenas, but not in the cave together at the same time or it would have been hell on earth with the hyenas getting the upper hand as their teeth marks were found on many of the bones. At the time of discovery it was said to be the oldest collection of animal remains as well as the most found on one site in the whole world. Those hyenas must have been well pigged –out! Anyway, back in Deep Dale the only hairy things you are likely to encounter in the vicinity of the cave now days would be a group of bearded ramblers being led by Arnold a self-professed expert on most things. He would be the stringy one wearing the cheapest National Health spectacles, sporting a knitted woolly hat with a silly purple bobble and continually ordering everyone to 'keep up please.' Arnold would eventually position himself in the grand entrance of the cave and launch into a pontificating account of the finding of a skeleton of a Great Brown Bear in a chamber behind him; an account it must be said delivered with such conviction that you could be forgiven for thinking he had discovered it himself. By the finish a restlessness of shuffling boots had set in within the group and only sixty-something spinster Enid Barroclough, she of the pleated skirt, hairy top lip and Aran-style bobble hat would be hanging on Arnold's every word. The remainder of the group's thoughts were leaning heavily towards actually hanging Arnold and wished so very much that his spell-binding saga (or so he thought) would quickly come to an end before their thoughts became a reality. Arnold finally moved off along the dale continuing to rabbit on about Deep Dale being a fine example of landslip formation and Permian-Carboniferous igneous activity, while the rest of the group taking no notice of him discussed the merits of the anticipated pint of ale in the Church Inn at Chelmorton.

A somewhat friendlier inhabitant of Hob's Thirst House Cave was the goblin Hob himself, who it turns out was a bit of a DIY fanatic. On the downside he had a reputation for being a tad tetchy and easily upset and would vent his anger by souring all the milk in the neighbourhood. Today of course, his services as a repair man would possibly prove too much for him. He might very well emerge from his cave one morning and find himself gazing out over a heap of broken and discarded junk, such as several dead computers, a rusty fridge, numerous defunct televisions, a conked out petrol lawn-mower, a 2CV with its wheels missing and a severely punctured Miranda (no doubt due to over-excitement) all of which would guarantee to put old Hob in a really nasty mood, thus assuring that many folk that morning would be staring unhappily into breakfast bowls of dry cornflakes and tea without milk! However, despite his unpredictable mood swings it is said that Hob had blessed the spring that bubbles out of the ground below his cave, which should you care to drink its water on a Good Friday, will apparently cure you of all your ailments. I presume this is perhaps a bit of wishful thinking for if it really was true, and bearing in mind the state of today's National Health Service, then on every Good Friday Deep Dale would be thronging with more people than you could pack onto Blackpool beach on an August Bank Holiday weekend and all hoping to be cured of anything ranging from chronic halitosis, a flaccid todger, to an in-growing toenail. It hardly bears thinking about.

There are rumours suggesting that Thirst House Cave once had more chambers than the two accessible today but no one has been able to locate them, or hear the supposed waterfall mentioned in an old account of an early exploration. I recall many years ago dropping through a hole in the floor of the second chamber and wriggling down between rocks to a puddle where my light went out. I spent a mindless fifteen minutes in the pitch black silence, which is precisely the length of time it took my mate who had already left the cave to decide I was not coming out and that he had better come and find me. I had no wish to become the last inhabitant of the cave, that role still goes to a batty old woman who took up residence around the year 1870 and was known locally as Straw Legs. This refers to her fashion conscious practice of binding straw around her legs as stockings to keep out the cold (little wonder she lived alone in a cave) and earned a meagre living carrying crocks around to sell, along with begging and hurling abuse at anyone who refused to give her alms. I think I am safe in saying she falls short of being your ideal choice for a neighbour and was best left to her troglodyte lifestyle.

In case you had not realised, I have been down-sizing in caves since leaving Peak Cavern and my final three are very small holes that very much suit the theme of being inhabited. They are part natural and part man-made. The first of these lies in south Derbyshire and is called Anchor Church, a name it has had since at least 1658. It lies beside a backwater of the river Trent near Ingleby and is hollowed out of a sandstone buff with a doorway and windows. Charles Cox in his book *Derbyshire* describes it as, 'doubtless once occupied by an anchorite or recluse, but much altered in comparatively modern days', which is all he had to say about the place. Equally, Arthur Mee simply refers to it as, 'a hermit's rude shrine cut in the rock centuries ago', so not much going for it from these two writers. In *Bemrose's Guide to Derbyshire*' Anchor Church was presumed to have had a resident who is somewhat adversely mentioned as one of those 'idle people' and human bones were said to have been dug up by the cave, but 'tradition, however, has failed to give us any clue to his identity' so obviously he left no forwarding address or an unpaid gas bill lying about. Much nearer the mark with his description was William Woolley writing around 1715 who observed correctly that 'Anker Church' was, 'an anchorites cell, and it really is a most solitary, pleasant place', an opinion shared by Sir Francis Burdett of nearby Foremark Hall. It was he who made several later additions to the cave in the form of some steps leading to the re-shaped doorway and a window or two (he decided against parquet flooring and a home-built drinks cabinet) where he and his family used it as a cool summerhouse on hot sunny days when picnicking by the riverside. But there is more to the cave than this for legend has it – although like most legends it is open to contradiction – that it was originally home to a friar or a monk called

Bernard (Bernie the monk. I like it!) who was doing penance for a misdeed. The story tells of Sir Hugo Burdett who had a wife called Johanne that by all accounts was a bit of 'all right' and had caught the roving eye of dastardly Baron Boyvill who lived in Castleton and had fancied her something rotten for some time. It seems that the beastly Baron caught hold of Bernie the monk and involved him in some monkey business whereby he had to persuade Sir Hugo to take a holiday abroad to do a bit of sword bashing with the Crusaders.

After Sir Hugo had left, surprise, surprise, but who should turn up on Johanne's doorstep but none other than bad-boy Baron Boyvill, who informed her that hubby met his Waterloo in the Holy Land and would not be coming home. He then claimed the Burdett estate for himself and eventually arranged to marry a reluctant Johanne, who quickly realised that if she refused to marry him she would shortly be sleeping in a hedge bottom. Anyway, the night before the wedding Sir Hugo turned up out of the blue and bumped into bully boy Boyvill who taunted him with alleged tales of his wife's infidelities (what a rotter) which naturally put Sir Hugo in a pretty foul mood. He was not a happy bunny, and to prove the point he lopped off Baron Boyvill's head, thus rendering him speechless, which served him right for being such a blabbermouth and a downright cad! The following day Sir Hugo met his wife who was overjoyed to see him alive. However, before she even had time to plant a smacker on his lips, or ask him what he fancied for tea, Sir Hugo still believing Boyvill's taunts of his wife's promiscuity, cut off Johannes hand, which was a tad harsh and presented her with a life-long problem when it came to carrying home bags of shopping. Sometime after all this had blown over Sir Hugo received a message requesting him to go to Anchor Church where a dying man (Bernie the monk no less) sought his forgiveness after confessing to his part in the fiendish plot hatched by the now headless Baron. So there you have it, a tale of dastardly deeds and daring-do which does not really have much of a happy ending.

Still in the same vicinity and not too far away is a similarly looking cave, also in a sandstone outcrop known as the Hermitage which lies in woodland behind the church at Dale Abbey. The first thing noticeable here is the remaining massive arched window of the former Abbey of Le dale which was inhabited by the order of Premonstratensian monks (they must have been very devoted. I can hardly pronounce the word) and although it is rather old being founded in 1160, it has to be said that they really have not looked after the place very well. The tiny church of All Saint's attached to Church Farm, which had once been a pub called The Bell had a connecting door so those wanting to quench a hymn singing thirst could nip through with ease and have a pint. The farmhouse according to Jack Helyer in his 1948 book *Rambling Round Nottingham* is where, 'hot water may be obtained for those carrying their own rations, and also the key to the church.' I feel sure that if you banged on the door now days asking for hot water you would probably be told in no uncertain terms to clear off! The cave is a hole that has been greatly enlarged by the hand of man, and it has even been suggested that one of those hands could be that of Robert Burdett. Those Burdett's certainly liked a bit of rock hacking.

This area was also known as Depedale and at the time was, 'a marsh exceeding dreadful and far from any habitat of man.' When Arthur Mee visited the site he described the hermit's cave as being, 'hewn out of the rock and measures six yards by three, with a doorway, two windows, a peephole (What was there to peep at? It's not as if he was expecting the postman or the milkman to call.) and a niche for a light.' The hermit was, so the story goes, a pious baker from St Mary's street in Derby who was noted for his generosity, for he would buy as many clothes and gather together as much food as he could afford then give it all away to the poor.

After years of running his one-man charity outlet he was supposedly summoned in a dream by the Blessed Virgin Mary to give up all his possessions and go to Depedale. This in itself created an immediate problem as he did not really get out much and consequently had not the foggiest idea where Depedale was. However, he did as BVM had instructed and fortunately managed to set off in the right direction – without the aid of an OS map – and came across a farm where an old woman was ordering a young lass to herd some cattle to Depedale, so she showed him the way. He found the beginnings of his new home (for new home read very small hole in a cliff; draughty, dank with damp walls and a wet earth floor), which he enlarged over a period of time, and as instructed in his dream he, 'served God by day and night, in hunger and thirst and cold and nakedness.'

Now I do not wish to appear irreverent here, but what on earth possessed the baker to bake his last loaf of bread, and his last batch of buns, give up his home and his belongings to suffer a life of denial, hardship and deprivation in a hole in a rock? If I had ever acted on some of my dreams with such conviction, then I would either have had to quickly flee the country, serve a life sentence in gaol, or be wearing one of those not very fashionable jackets that strap-up at the back. The man must have been a sandwich short of a picnic, or else he ate far too much cheese than was good for him before going to bed at night. After several years of going about his business, whatever that might have been with a constantly rumbling stomach and round the clock goose pimples, he was suddenly confronted one day by the owner of the land Ralph Fitz-Geremund who had nipped over from Normandy on a long weekend for a spot of hunting in the woods. It was here that Fitz-G came across the ex-baker and initially he was a tad miffed to find a squatter on his land. The outcome was that Fitz-G took pity on the scrawny hermit and told him he could go on living in the cave and even assisted in the hermit's welfare to the extent that the hermit was eventually able to abandon his cave and move to a nearby house he had built along with an oratory. Didn't he do well?

The final word on Dale Abbey Hermitage must go to Crichton Porteous who suggests in his county book *Derbyshire* that, 'a modern hermit might find peace here' and the, 'original hermit's cave in a cliff of sandstone is still available!' I can just picture this unique residence being advertised in the window of a local estate agent: Quiet countryside residence with no near neighbours. A distinctive two-roomed character home with original features, situated in remote woodland and in need of modernisation. Would suit someone with a Zsa Zsa Gabor complex. Vacant possession. No forward chain.

Finally, the subject of hermits in holes brings me to a very small cave, or rock shelter barely the dimensions of your average sized garden shed that lies at the base of a, 'precipitous rock called Cratcliff Tor', where an ancient dwelling can be found. Croston writes, 'At the foot (of the rock) a rude archway admits to a cave or recess, said to have been excavated by an anchorite, who made it his abode. Perhaps some gloomy recluse, with mistaken zeal may have made it his retreat, or perhaps some good and holy man.' Inside can still be seen the remains of a well-executed carved crucifix, said to be aged about the time of Edward I (latter half of the 13th century) alias Edward Longshanks, alias Hammer of the Scots, which in Latin is Malleus Scotorum and not to be confused with Malleus Scrotorum which would bring tears to your eyes! But I digress. Another source describes the interior as having, 'a humble seat and a niche that might contain some domestic utensils are hewn out of the rock: and it seems probable that some melancholy man once made this solitary and cheerless cave his dwelling.' It seems that no one thought the hermit was ever going to be a laugh a minute. A very tatty 1949 edition of A Guide to Black Rocks and Cratcliffe Tor gives climbing routes on the gritstone around the hermit's cave. The cave is described as, 'a once beautiful spot that has long since been disfigured by vandals.' An earlier writer had observed that the carved effigy's 'legs were broken off above the knee' otherwise it was 'little defaced.' Having no legs sounds like major vandalism to my way of thinking, not to mention inconvenient. 'The ugly railings are a fallen guardian against cheap little people (or as we would call them these days, complete half-wits) whose initials mar many of our Peakland beauty spots.' The writer then speculates on whether the hermit, 'was an enthusiastic gritstoner', as an, 'ingenious guttering and channelling round the cave show at least that he did some climbing.' I think the old hermit would be rather miffed at having his seclusion interrupted by today's hairy-legged climbing fraternity clambering over the rock face. He might however, have had second thoughts if it happened to be a young Catherine Destiville or Isabelle Patissier dangling precariously above his cave wearing little else apart from a scant pair of shorts, a vest and a bag of chalk. This vision could unexpectedly but not unpleasantly have distracted him from his pious devotions!

The reality is that little is actually known about the old hermit, but apparently he would trade for money and kind, pray for people's souls, alongside giving guidance and advice to the many who travelled the great Portway, an ancient prehistoric trackway which was the motorway of its day. This lengthy track had already passed by the Hermitage at Dale Abbey before passing Robin Hood's Stride, the jumbled outcrop of rocks next to Cratcliffe, so it is unlikely that our hermit would go short on customers for very long. I suppose in his own humble way he was a bit of an entrepreneur, not that I am suggesting for one minute that he should have branched out into cream teas and 'I've seen the CRATCLIFFE HERMIT' cart and saddle stickers, but with such a constant stream of folk walking past his rocky abode he did manage to work the situation to his own advantage. I guess being a hermit meant he just wanted a quiet life and selling the occasional rabbit, as was stated in the kitchen records of Haddon Hall two days before Christmas in 1549, where ten rabbits were supplied by 'Ye harmytt' plus the fourpence (daylight robbery) he received as an early tourist guide pushing people in the direction of Haddon was enough for him. The thing is, the whole truth will never be known, which is probably for the best as it may otherwise ruin some rather good lore and legends.

2.

The Great, the Glorious
... and some others.

Over the centuries the splendours of Derbyshire – although not everyone saw them as such – have been visited by a list of notable persons as long as your arm, encompassing the good, the great and the glorious along with a few who probably wished they had stayed at home. For example there was Izaak Walton the fanatic fisherman who wrote an all-time best seller *The Compleat Angler* and Sir Richard Arkwright whose inventive mind spun with ideas for a cotton-spinning revolution as did Jedediah Strutt, another mechanical genius and inventor of the ribbed stocking frame (I do so love a good ribbed stocking come the winter). Erasmus Darwin (Charles' grandad) who lived at Breadsall Priory (I used to play around there as a kid) was a co-founder of the Lunar society, which had nothing to do with astronauts or moon-gazing, and Thomas Cook who quickly twigged that hiring a train and filling it full of people was a jolly good money-making idea and in no time at all he was sending tourists by boat up the Nile.

There were authors like Alison Uttley whose book *A Traveller in Time* based loosely around the Anthony Babington plot to free Mary Queen of Scots from Wingfield Manor becomes, historically speaking, a tale whereby Babington undergoes a sex change as his role is played by a 20th century time-travelling girl (think along the lines of *Dr Who* meets Mary Queen of Scots) and George Elliot who based *Adam Bede* around Wirksworth. Jane Austen also based *Pride and Prejudice* on various Peak locations, while D.H. Lawrence produced his infamously raunchy novel *Women in Love* centred around the coal mining district in the eastern part of the county, and his even raunchier book *Lady Chatterley's Lover*, which if nothing else took the innocence out of the simple childhood pleasure of making daisy chains!

Florence Nightingale turned nursing on its head and Barnes Wallis caused more than a few headaches when his hair-brained invention, but ultimately successful 'bouncing bomb' made a very large hole in the Mohne Dam in Germany's Ruhr Valley and no doubt wiped the smile of Hitler's face in the process, not that Hitler was much of a one for smiling. As a former pupil of the Joseph Wright school of Art it would be remiss of me to leave out Wright the painter who was well known for the chiascuro effect he created in his paintings like *A Philosopher lecturing on the Orrery* and *The Alchymist*, or to be more precise, and here Wright is as guilty as the authors of long titles I mentioned earlier on in the book, *The Alchymist, in Search of the Philosopher's Stone, Discovers Phosphorus, and prays for the successful Conclusion of his operation, as was the custom of the Ancient Chymical Astrologers.'* I think I'll stick with *The Alchymist* or *The Alchemist* to update the spelling.

There are far too many Derbyshire worthies to be included in this chapter, but I will relate the connections that a few of them have made with the county. I am sure that every one of my generation for example, who is still in possession of sufficient marbles to harken back to their history lessons at school will remember the name James Brindley being hammered into their non-receptive skulls as the man who built the Bridgewater canal. This enabled the coal magnate, the Duke of Bridgewater to get his bags of nutty slack from his pits at Worsley to Manchester and on to Liverpool. Brindley was born in 1716 in a cottage by Tunstead, some three miles slightly north-east of Buxton. According to Cox's *Derbyshire* he showed early on an aptitude and quickly, 'gained much reputation as a repairer of machinery', where he proved his skills among the complex apparatus in the mill industry as opposed to just sticking to repairing the broken kitchen mangle, a spout that had snapped off the kettle and re-hanging the door belonging to the 'thunder box' at the bottom of the garden. This boy was going places.

Later in life he also engineered and constructed mills for the grinding of calcined flints (whatever they are) to glaze Wedgewood pottery, but ultimately he became a respected authority on the design and construction of canals, his greatest work being the Trent and Mersey canal also known by the pachydermatous title of the Grand Trunk. It is said that when Brindley was confronted with a difficult problem he simply took himself off to bed where he sorted everything out in his mind. Initially this might be viewed as somewhat odd, but given the fact that again according to Cox he was illiterate, unable to spell and barely able to write, I guess this was the only option open to him. However, despite lacking these basic fundamentals he was a brilliant man and if nothing else it does give all those people out there who struggle trying to put together an Ikea flat-pack kitchen cupboard some sort of hope.

James Brindley died in 1772 after standing about too long in the pouring rain while surveying a branch canal between Froghall and Leek and getting a thorough soaking. His B&B at the time proved to have inadequate drying facilities (no tumble drier or even a radiator to drape his soggy clothes over) which resulted in him catching a serious chill that sent him to his grave. An almost unpardonable epitaph appeared in the *Chester Courant* which attempted to condense his life's achievements into eighteen painfully written lines finishing with;

But while busy with Pit or Well,
His Spirits sunk below Level,
And, when too late his Doctor found,
Water sent him to the Ground.

See what I mean. Whoever wrote this was no Tennyson or Shelley and should definitely consider an immediate career change.

Intrepid travellers like Daniel Defoe, Celia Fiennes, James Croston, Sarah Murray, Ebenezer Rhodes, J.B. Firth and many others all courageously pitted their wits against the perils and trials of early exploration in Derbyshire. But how did they go about it and what were their biggest problems? It was not simply a case of leaping into the saddle of your trusty four-hoofed transport and galloping up the A6; for lanes and tracks were generally in an unbelievable state of neglect, through over use and nil maintenance.

Hooves and narrow wagon wheels were massively contributory to churning up the earth surfaces especially in winter and the best that can be said about riding anywhere on horseback was that it was cheap. Uncomfortable, but cheap. After all, you only needed to shove hay in at one end to make it go, and it was probably far speedier than the first recorded long distance motor car journey undertaken by Bertha Benz in 1888, who took around fifteen hours to complete fifty-six miles and wearing what turned out to be an impromptu repair kit comprising of a hat pin and a garter. The only respite from the tedium of travelling the highways and byways of England would be on reaching a section of turnpike road where you would have to pay for the privilege of riding on a decent piece of surfaced road, but it would prove to be a welcome relief from hours of bone-shaking, stomach-churning and haemorrhoid inducing soreness of the crutch.

Turnpike roads normally consisted of a surface of well-laid stone chippings, which had been laboriously produced by unfortunates who more often than not were roaming itinerant workers employed cheaply by the parish and whose job it was to sit by a roadside, day in, day out, bashing pieces of rock with a hammer into suitably sized smaller pieces. If ever there was a case for 'repetitive strain injury' along with 'can there be anything more boring as a career' then this must surely be it. William

Cobbett in *Rural Rides* comments somewhat facetiously that the labourers were employed by the parish, 'at the expense of half-ruined farmers, and tradesmen and landlords, to break stones into very small pieces to make nice smooth roads lest the jolting in going along them should create bile in the stomachs of the overfed tax-eaters.' No mincing of words there then. Some idea of this mind-numbing task has been captured in the paintings of John Brett's *The Stonebreaker*, Gustave Courbet's *The Stonebreakers,* and Henry Wallis's (yes, you've guessed it) *The Stonebreakers,* which were slated in their time for depicting the taboo subjects of 'misery and poverty' thus making them highly unacceptable for the walls of Victorian drawing rooms. The clients of the day wanted bucolic scenes of contented rustic life as painted by the likes of Helen Allingham (a Derbyshire lass and Victorian watercolourist born in Swadlincote) and Birkett Foster to name just two who portrayed cosy thatched cottages (for cosy read damp, overcrowded, earth floor hovels) and rosy-cheeked children at play who in reality were undernourished and likely to succumb at an early age to consumption (tuberculosis) or dropsy (edema) and consequently have a short life.

In the south of England particularly breaking stones was called 'knapping' which involved splitting flint, chert and other hard obsidian rock and had nothing to do with taking 'forty winks', on a grassy verge. It would not be a job taken by choice, but more a case of necessity (no weekly dole cheque here) to stay alive and feed a family in the absence of any alternatives. A true portrayal of such desperate circumstances, poverty and destitution, has been evocatively captured in Herkomer's well-known painting *Hard Times,* which shows just such a family, and his studies were genuine itinerants grouped forlornly by a roadside. Okay, I promise to finish my history of art lesson for today.

Back on the road, undertaking any journey of any length on rubbish roads required a considerable degree of tenacity, determination and an awful lot of luck. Folk drowned crossing fords and in winter perished in snowstorms, or spent endless hours well and truly stuck in glutinous, claggy, slippery mud; akin to wading across a field at the Glastonbury Festival to get to the toilet block. Lord Macaulay wrote in his *History of England* that, 'often the mud lay deep on the right and the left; and only a narrow track of firm ground rose above the quagmire. At such times obstruction and quarrels were frequent with carriers blocking the way for hours as neither would give way.' Hands up all of you who thought road rage was something new! Ralph Thoresby the antiquary who frequently travelled between London and Leeds noted that on one occasion, 'passengers had to swim for their lives and a higgler (fore-runner of a Betterware or Kleeneze salesman) perished in the attempt to cross.' Another time Thoresby was all but, 'swept away by the inundation of the Trent' and was afterwards detained in Stamford for four days due to the 'state of the roads.' J. Brown in his *Tour of Derbyshire* in 1662 says that, 'on the roads of Derbyshire, travellers were in constant fear for their necks, and were frequently compelled to alight and lead their beasts.' All in all it is obvious that touring about the countryside centuries ago was exciting, risky, slow, tiresome, fraught with danger, with a real threat to life and limb, something which, it has to be said is noticeably lacking on today's journeys by National Express coach which really could do with livening up a bit.

Early chroniclers exploring Derbyshire normally left the impression that it was a wild and remote place inhabited for the most part by unintelligible heathens who you would not even trust your mother-in-law to. Despite the sometimes disagreeable and dour Defoe I should in all fairness allow him to have his say. His account of Derbyshire, which he entered after crossing over 'the fury of a river called the Derwent' is a mixed bag of likes and perhaps too many dislikes, as we saw previously regarding his opinions on the 'wonderless wonders' of the Peak. In Derbyshire Defoe desires you the reader, 'to travel through this howling wilderness (everything seems so over-the-top dramatic) in your imagination, and you shall soon find all that is wonderful about it.' Sarcastic or what! It is almost as if he had set his mind on not enjoying himself as he wandered through the county. However, he comments that the ale exceeded all else, but the rigours of travel left him more than a tad peevish. By way of a change he reported quite encouragingly on entering Derby saying it had, 'a fine bridge, well built, but ancient and with a chapel upon the bridge (Our Lady of ye Brigg) now converted to a dwelling house.' This subsequently became a carpenter's shop, a sort of early 'Furniture Village' before it was claimed back by the church in 1873. The silk mill on an island in the Derwent, erected in 1715 by John Lombe (Lambe), seems to have had a lasting impression on Defoe if only for the curious tale he relates concerning Soracule, who appeared to be a rather over-enthusiastic tour guide to a group of visiting gentlemen when he came to show them the large waterwheel of which he was immensely proud. Throwing his arms about like Magnus Pyke he overbalanced and fell into the water and was swept along at a great rate of knots towards the rapidly turning water wheel. When his body, with a kind of dull, wet, thud hit the wheel it became momentarily jammed. The water pressure built up and became so great that one of the plashers broke and the wheel turned once more dragging Soracule beneath it. Just when everyone had given him up for dead and decided to go to the pub he unexpectedly spewed out from under the wheel and was subsequently hauled to dry land by the gentlemen observers, an experience from which he 'received no hurt at all.' Unbelievably lucky, or what! Now there is no denying that it was a pretty impressive, albeit impromptu stunt that certainly grabbed the attention of the guests and to which Defoe strangely described as 'a very odd experiment' which seems to imply an element of showmanship about the entire performance. I have to say that the idea of Soracule (I mean just what sort of a name is that anyway?) or for that matter, anyone in their right mind suddenly throwing themselves into the path of a rapidly revolving water wheel to be dragged underneath as 'an experiment' beggars belief, but it is certainly one for extreme sports enthusiasts and adrenaline-seeking junkies to consider!

After leaving Derby Defoe's next port of call was 'Quarden' where he found only, 'wretched lodgings (take note all B&B's in this area) and entertainment.' Travelling on to Wirksworth he states that, 'the inhabitants are a rude boorish kind of people, but they are a bold, daring, and even desperate kind of fellows in their search into the bowels of the earth.' He is referring of course to the lead-miners or Peakrills, as they are sometimes known. In the vicinity of Brassington he came across one of these 'subterranean creatures' as he called the poor wretch, who was in the process of hauling himself out of a narrow shaft. Defoe was somewhat taken aback at what he saw and goes on to describe the miner as, 'lean as a skeleton, pale as a dead corpse, his hair and beard deep black, his flesh lank, and as we thought something of the colour of the lead itself.' I think that even with the addition of 'non-smoker' and 'GSOH' as an advertisement for a Lonely Hearts column it would leave his mailbox decidedly empty. Defoe endeavoured to engage the miner in conversation by asking him how deep the shaft was from which he had just emerged, but was completely unable to understand a word the miner said as his dialect was beyond any known English, so obviously not great at dialogue or dinner party chit-chat. However, it turned out the miner had a wife and five children living in a 'hole in a rock' where the miner had been born and his father before him. Their troglodyte existence led Defoe to note that, 'she lived in a den like a wild body' (makes her sound like a bit of a 'goer') and it is little wonder that the miner's appearance was so ghastly when you consider he spent all day in a hole and then came home to another hole. Apparently on a good day he could earn five pence, which seems a mere pittance, yet his children were 'plump and fat, ruddy and wholesome' and his wife 'tall, well-shaped (well fit in today's parlance) clean' and a 'comely woman.' So outwardly they all appeared in better health than the dreadful, ashen-faced breadwinner who was forced to spend his days crawling around in the underworld picking at lumps of lead. If you think about the circumstances of his working day, it makes being employed in a call centre seem not quite so naff!

Defoe continued on his journey to Buxton which as a spa town he thought to be rather down-market, but did concede to the virtues of the famous waters insomuch as 'wonderful cures have been wrought by them, especially rheumatic, scorbutic and scrofulous distempers, aches of the joints, nervous pains, and also in scurvy and leprous maladies.' The very thought of masses of people sploshing about while suffering from such disorders, coupled with Defoe's account of the baths being more akin to, 'a prison than a place of diversion' that barely gave the health seekers, 'room to converse out of the smell of their own excrements' and the whole place was said to, 'stink like a common-shore' is somewhat off-putting. It sounds very much like an odious human soup created by an unsavoury populace, where you might possibly leave with something more ghastly than whatever ailment drove you there in the first instance! Given the choice I would personally have preferred to stay at home, wait until it rained then rush outside in the nip and take my chances with a bar of coal-tar soap and a scrubbing brush.

Leaving all this behind Defoe crossed to Castleton and as we have already witnessed, did not enjoy himself at Poole's Cavern, nor did he enjoy himself at Peak Cavern and said the Ebbing and Flowing Well was, 'a poor thing to make a wonder of.' He was more favourable towards Eldon Hole, and when he arrived at Chatsworth House, the Duke of Devonshire's stately pile built in 1687 by William Talman, this definitely put a smile on his face. Chatsworth dubbed the 'Palace of the Peak' lives up to this title and Defoe called it 'a most magnificent building' and rather sweepingly the 'most beautiful palace in the world.' Wow! Derbyshire finally came up with something that bowled him over. Next he visited Chesterfield 'a populous town, well-built and well inhabited' before turning his back on the Peak to wend his way to the rigours of Yorkshire. I can only add that Derbyshire did its best to charm, but Defoe seemed to be a hard man to please. Of course I would not dream of letting my love of such a stunning, bewitching and diverse county cloud my judgement of the man and his opinions. Curmudgeonly old b.....d!

With Chatsworth still in mind this brings me to one of Derbyshire's royal visitors even though it was not by choice. The captive Mary Stuart, who was not only Mary Queen of Scots but also Mary Queen of freebie B&B's, spent several of her years of confinement in Derbyshire, but sadly not enjoying the lifestyle she was compelled to live, being banged-up in often less than desirable (not even one star) accommodation. This was because her cousin Elizabeth I was sitting comfortably upon the throne of England and was not only a tad jealous of Mary's apparent beauty, but also knew that given half a chance Mary would be sitting comfortably upon the throne of England instead of her and that would never do, so for many years she had her incarcerated in various castles and households well out of harm's way. Chatsworth was one such place and whereas today we have to pay the best part of twenty pounds entrance fee Mary was allowed in for free and stayed for a considerable time.

She first came to Chatsworth in May 1570 and liked it so much she could not keep away from the place returning again in 1573, 1577, 1578 and 1581, and it never once cost her a single penny. Unlike Sarah Murray a couple of hundred or so years later who complained it was necessary to pay, 'the housekeeper and gardener at least five shillings each, or you will hear grumbling.' She then adds somewhat sourly that, 'When noblemen have the goodness to permit fine seats to be seen by travellers, what a pity they suffer them to pay their servants wages.' I reckon the housekeeper and the gardener were in collusion and simply on the make for some extra pocket money. But in truth, our Sarah was not overly enamoured of Chatsworth House for she called, 'the building heavy, the river is spoiled by being shaven and shorn; the fountains are children's spouts, the cascade which cost so many thousands of pounds, is an affront to the understanding.' Do we, I wonder, see a touch of the 'green-eyed goddess' here? Mary was originally transferred to Chatsworth House from South Wingfield where she was being held under the watchful eye of the Earl of Shrewsbury who had the thankless and harrowing job of preventing Mary, who was a bit of a Harry Houdini on the quiet, from escaping every time he turned his back to go to the loo or have a nap.

The reason for the change of scenery was because while Mary was staying at South Wingfield she came over all peculiar and felt a little queer, which her two physicians put down to the highly unsanitary state of her rooms while pointing an accusing digit in the direction of Shrewsbury. He quite naturally was a bit put out and rather miffed (well you would be wouldn't you?) and replied by saying, 'the very unpleasant and fulsome succour in the chamber hurtful to her health' was a result of the, 'continued festering and uncleanly order of her own folk.' Not an unreasonable retort when you consider that Mary was accompanied by a retinue estimated at two hundred and thirty and still counting. Shrewsbury rapidly tiring of the situation packed them all off to Chatsworth while he had Mary's quarters thoroughly cleaned with whatever the sixteenth century equivalent was of Mr Muscle or Cillit Bang. Chatsworth according to Lord Burleigh in a letter to Shrewsbury considered it to be an ideal place for the imprisonment of Mary for in his opinion it was, 'a very mete hous (he was really naff at spelling) for good preservation of his charge, having no town or resorte wher any ambusher might lye', so I guess that scuppered any plans Mary might have been hatching of sneaking out for a tasty treat at Ye Olde Bakewell Pudding Shoppe, or a quick pint at the White Horse Inn or the Rutland Arms Hotel as it is now called.

In reality of course, she would have been out of luck regarding a pudding, as the happy scrumptious baking mistake did not occur allegedly until around 1820. However, as there is decidedly no place for pedantry in this book I will continue to resort to equally questionable anomalies throughout its pages. Mary was not totally confined indoors for at Chatsworth there is a small structure by the river Derwent surrounded by a moat reached by a flight of steps known as Queen Mary's Bower. It is generally accepted the bower was constructed especially for Mary, for at the head of the steps is a stone archway bearing an iron plate depicting the arms of Mary Queen of Scots. This high-level garden is of some architectural merit and far removed from some old wooden shed hastily knocked-up at the bottom of the garden where Mary could do a bit of knitting. The description given by Gilchrist in his book *The Peak District* is of, 'an airing place for the unfortunate prisoner, filled with rich soil in which grow ancient trees.' This 'melancholy little enclosure' can be viewed from a locked wicket gate and it was here where Mary would sit among her ladies at work with her needle, probably having to sew on the odd button or two as I am sure the dire circumstances imposed upon her would have instigated a 'mend and make do' policy.

Mary's only other perk after much deliberation and finally permitted by Elizabeth I were a few outings to Buxton to take the waters, where she lodged in Shrewsbury's old house which is now the site of the Old Hall Hotel. Little if anything of the original building exists, although some of the old house is said to have been incorporated into the present hotel. There exists a pane of window glass that is reputed to have been recovered from the original house, which has engraved upon it the somewhat poignant couplet; 'Buxton, whose warm waters hath made thy name famous, perchance I shall visit thee no more – Farewell' which is supposed to have been scribed by Mary Queen of Scots with the aid of a diamond ring, thus making her the culprit behind an early form of graffiti. She called at the baths several times in the hope of easing her rheumatism brought on and constantly exacerbated by being exposed to damp and unhealthy conditions in castle prisons. I can only assume that Mary's bathing sessions were conducted with some degree of privacy, as I cannot envisage her waiting her turn with the hoi-polloi, standing in a queue with a rolled up towel under one arm, a bar of Camay in one hand and a bottle of Head and Shoulders shampoo in the other.

These bathing trips proved to be one of the few joyous moments of her captivity as well as being one of the few times when she would have been relatively clean. The thing is, life was never ever going to be plain sailing for our Mary and just to pile on the agony on 28 July 1580 she was riding over to Buxton when her horse shied and tossed her onto the ground where she sustained a back injury. She then began bathing twice a day in an attempt to ease her condition. So what with a bad back, arthritis and constant captivity, poor Mary must have been pretty hacked off with life.

An interesting account of Buxton baths is given by Celia Fiennes when she took the water around 1700, and says of the experience, 'its not so warme as milke from ye Cow, and not a quick spring, so its not Capable of being Cleansed after Everybody has been in. (Yeuk!) Its warme Enough just to Open the pores of ones body, but not to Cause sweat, I was in it and it made me shake.' I am even more convinced that attending the baths was not unlike slopping about in a giant bowl of well-used dishwater. Celia goes on to describe the interior which consisted of, 'a pavement of Stone on one side at ye brim to walk on, with benches of Stone to Sitt on. You must have a guide yt Swims with you, you may Stand in some places and hold by a Chaine and ye water is not above yr Neck, but in other parts very deep and will turn you down.' It sounds like an unforgettable experience, but for all the wrong reasons.

Mary Stuart left Chatsworth and returned to South Wingfield, then back to Tutbury, then back to Sheffield, then back to South Wingfield (it's very exhausting all this 'toing and froing.' I hope you're keeping up with it) with her growing entourage in tow much to the chagrin of Shrewsbury, for it was he who had to foot the outrageously massive grocery bill each week. The initial arrangement with Queen Lizzie was that Shrewsbury would be compensated by her to the tune of £52 a week which it seems she rarely paid. Then to add insult to injury she later dropped the amount to a piddling £30 a week. Now either there was a recession on and nobody had informed the distraught Earl, or else Queen Lizzie was getting just a touch crabby at having to continually fork-out money from the royal coffers to keep her captive cousin and her merry band of sponging parasites. Whatever the reason she was certainly not as miffed as poor old Shrewsbury who in fact was coughing up £30 a day out of his own pocket to feed this motley crew, which included as records show 'four officers in the pantry' (sounds suspicious) three more in the kitchen including a master cook and a potager, grooms for Mary's chamber, a physician and numerous others who quickly cottoned on to the idea that if you professed to share Mary's faith and discretely promote her bid for the throne of England, then free board and lodgings was a very cheap way of living. It really was becoming a case of 'Old Uncle Tom Cobley and all' and they were really on to a good thing for the chaps were eating eight dishes at every meal and the ladies five.

At the end of a year poor Shrewsbury was feeling pretty pooped and thoroughly stressed out to discover that all this gluttonous scoffing made him £10,000 out of pocket to Morrisons or wherever he did the weekly shop. To compound his misery he was having to suffer the constant rowing, and nagging, and taunting from his wife Bess of Hardwicke who was horribly jealous of Mary and accused her husband of having dalliances with his prisoner, spending too much money on her (When did you last buy me a bunch of flowers … eh?) and practically anything else she could find to carp on about. Thank goodness tubes of toothpaste had yet to be invented, for committing the heinous crime of leaving the top off has been responsible in more modern times for instigating more than a few divorce proceedings, along with leaving the lavatory seat up and kicking your soiled underpants under the bed at the end of a day. In short Bess was domineering, nit-picking, stroppy and a bit of a Tartar, who could start an argument at the drop of a bonnet; eventually wearing old Shrewsbury out to the point where they decided to throw in the towel and part company.

Mary's attempts to escape wherever she was being held tended to be rather hit and miss affairs, but she did succeed when being held on an island at Leven with the help of a young lad called Willie. Now Willie who was only sixteen was merely carrying on the plot, which his father had begun, but who had been discovered planning Mary's escape and promptly bumped off. In a curious old book written in 1846 entitled *Evenings at Haddon Hall* one of the listed entertainments for an evening was the recital of a poem called *Queen Mary's Welcome* which begins with the lines;

'O'er dark tow'r the young May moon has risen,
And our Queen, our bright Mary, has 'scaped from her prison.
God speed to the shallop, that bears o'er the waves,
The fortunes of Scotland, the fair and the brave

This would, of course, be performed with appropriate dramatic intonations and grossly exaggerated theatrical gestures. This may not seem particularly exciting for an evening's amusement by todays' standards, but I would not mind betting it could knock the spots off gawping at yet another suicidal episode of *East Enders*. Anyway, the thing is that the poem goes on to mention 'Willie the landless, or orphan' and Mary never forgot her obligation to him, and at the hour of her death she wrote his name in her will on her last night in captivity before her execution the following day. For those of you who might still be wondering what a 'shallop' is, well it is a small rowing or sailing boat. Okay, so I had to look it up in a dictionary. I mention this savour of Mary because Willie's success story tends to be overshadowed in history by the failure of one Anthony Babington –who was not the brightest bulb on the Christmas tree – with his plan to abduct Mary and escape with her to Matlock. (See what I mean!) I suppose there is just the outside chance that no one would think of looking for her there among all those bikers on a Bank Holiday weekend. The story goes that Babington, who lived at nearby Dethick was somewhat smitten with our Mary and had the habit of sneaking into her chambers (the bounder) at South Wingfield. These clandestine visitations saw him allegedly smearing his face to avoid detection with green walnut juice which probably gave him a complexion somewhere mid-way between Des O'Connor's fake tan and a performer off the BBC's *Black and Minstrels White Show*. (Remember them? Yes you are getting old.) From these antics stems a tale that the large walnut tree growing by Wingfield Manor came from a seed dropped by Babington during a session of 'putting his face on.' The story turns out to be apocryphal due to the tree having been proven to be of insufficient age, but it still serves to strike a note of pathos with today's tourists if you are lucky enough to get in.

Anyway to continue the story of Babington the blunderer (I just know you're going to love the gory finale), he was discovered up to his skulduggery by Walsingham's famous spy network, which kept a close eye on Mary's conspirators and was duly arrested. He was given a free admission ticket to the Tower of London which on the face of it sounds like a good deal until you realise that it was a one-way ticket. He was finally taken out for what would have been a day to remember, had it not been for the fact that it was his last day in the land of the living. Before a baying mob, he along with some of his fellow conspirators were hauled through the streets to Holborn strapped to wooden sledges (yes, you can bet your life they were not on their way to see Santa's Grotto), after which they underwent the entertaining ritual (at least the crowd thought so) of being hung, drawn and quartered. They were hung until nearly unconscious, then brought down to have their genitals hacked off (Ouch!! I bet that made their eyes water.

It's making mine water just writing it down), cut open and disembowelled, the heart yanked out after which they were beheaded and their body cut into four. To put it another way, Babington went for a short stretch, became a castrato, was turned inside out, had a heart-stopping experience before finally becoming an easy-to-assemble, but extremely messy five-piece jigsaw puzzle. I bet he wished he could have stayed in bed that particular day.

Mary Queen of Scots did not actually fair a great deal better after she bade farewell to Derbyshire and some eighteen years of imprisonment, found herself in 1587 at Fotheringay Castle where she was tried and told the night before that the following day she would be headless. How thoughtful of them. As it was February and possibly a bit nippy outside the scaffold was erected inside Fotheringay's Great Hall so the select few hundred, by invitation only to witness the event, would not get a chill hanging about in the cold air. That was even more thoughtful of them. Mary full of dignity went to the scaffold, calmly and elegantly attired in silks and velvets and duly placed her neck on the block. Now the executioner named Bull turned out not only to be Bull by name, but Bull by nature carrying out his job like … well, a bull in a china shop and managing to miss and hit the back of Mary's head by mistake. (It makes you wonder how he got the job!) At this point Mary was heard to whisper the words 'Sweet Jesus' which may well have been uttered as a religious plea, or a polite cover up for 'You clumsy arse.' After this hiccup the fatal blow was finally delivered and Mary's severed head thumped to the ground. Bull then held high Mary's head for the spectators to behold, when it unexpectedly hit the deck for a second time with a dull thud. It seems that the very last vestiges of her beauty and femininity had been stripped away for Bull was left holding a wig which unbeknown to anyone Mary had put on at the last minute to hide her grey hair. (Wouldn't we all have had grey hair if we'd lived her life?) As you can imagine this rendered everyone speechless except Mary, whose lips continued to move for a further fifteen minutes, which begs the question, was it merely a muscular twitch, or as I like to think, it was the stoic Mary Stuart actually having the last word! We will never know.

With the show over the assembled mass slowly shuffled away home leaving the housekeeping staff to move in with buckets and mops to clean up the bloody awful mess. I cannot help feeling that whichever way I was to present this final scenario it would always come out as a touchingly heart-rending finale to the beguiling and sadly tragic Mary Queen of Scots. Perhaps the final comment should go to Henricus who exclaims, 'Mary Queen of Scots!—Hated be the memory of England's maiden Queen Elizabeth. The cruel death of Mary is an indelible stain on her reign, which can never be effaced.' He continues in his outrage by writing, 'this deed of blood will tell as a damning record of vindictive cruelty and savage barbarity worthy only of the haughty daughter of one of the most arbitrary and capricious monarchs that ever wielded Britain's sceptre.' So, clearly a big fan of Mary, but definitely 'nil points' for Elizabeth the first.

Someone who truly left an indelible mark particularly in the form of 'stones and mortar' was Elizabeth Hardwick or Bess of Hardwick as she was more commonly known. She was born in 1518 and by the age of twelve was already married to Robert Barlow of Barlow. He only lasted five minutes before dropping dead and leaving his vast estate to young Bess. Now she was smart for her years and immediately embarked upon a fruitful career of gaining great wealth. In 1549 she once again pitched herself into the marriage stakes by coupling up with Sir William Cavendish and introduced the name to Derbyshire by persuading him to sell all of his estates in Suffolk and buy some land in Derbyshire namely around Chatsworth where she built a grand mansion for a mere eighty thousand pounds. This project was only completed after Sir William had also dropped dead, so he never even got the chance to put his feet up with pipe and slippers inside the place. Time for Bess to go hunting again and this time she hauled in Sir William St Loe, who after a short spell of matrimonial antagonism (yes, you know what's coming next) also dropped dead. (Ye Gods, she must have had an insatiable appetite in bed to have husbands dropping like flies.) I am surprised that carrying this reputation before her anyone in their right mind would want to get hooked up with our Bess, but she must have had some beguiling ways for next up was George, Earl of Shrewsbury who fell for her wit and beauty. Bess however, was not so easily had and being a wily old bird insisted that her eldest lad Henry (she had obviously been busy procreating in the bed chamber in the past) marry Grace Talbot, Shrewbury's youngest daughter at the same time as Gilbert Talbot, Shrewsbury's second son should marry Mary, Bess's youngest daughter. (Are you keeping up with all this match-making?) Only after this alliance had taken place did Bess marry Shrewsbury who finally got her into bed to enjoy her legendary beauty and wit, as no doubt she told him a few jokes during the breaks in their sessions of carnal lust.

In 1574, Bess was again playing the role as a one-woman dating agency by managing to get another of her daughters married off to Charles Stuart the Earl of Lennox (bad move), which now posed a very real threat to the throne of England. Understandably this went down like a lead balloon as far as Queen Lizzie was concerned, so to show her appreciation of the situation Queen Lizzie gave Bess free board and lodgings in the form of a three month stay in the Tower of London. Upon her release and not in the best of moods Bess set about accusing poor old beleaguered Shrewsbury of hanky-panky with his charge Mary Stuart. Apart from all this disharmony Bess still managed to get on with her hobby of building big houses and succeeded in knocking up Bolsover Castle and another pad at Worksop as well as Chatsworth House, then decided to build a grand hall at Hardwick. She was banging out houses at such a rate it would have made Barratt and Taylor Wimpey look like a bunch of amateurs. In 1608 at the grand old age of eighty-nine she was at it again with another building project at Oldcotes when she suddenly chose to throw down her mortar trowel and call it a day.

Despite her long and vigorous life she had not been overly popular with the people, yet was still able to wangle a costly resting place at All Saints in Derby where she lies to this day. For a time her remains in an unexplained broken coffin were on display as the source of a cheap peepshow laid on by the sextons of the church. They were plainly not ones to miss out on an entrepreneurial opportunity to swell the church coffers and help pay towards those extortionately high candle costs and cassock cleaning bills. Time to move on I think to a character familiar to all of us who was as inspirational, at least to young boys, as was the burning desire to become the driver of a steam locomotive.

A close scrutiny of any number of maps of Derbyshire will soon reveal the traces of a bow-wielding hero who was allegedly afoot in the county many moons ago in the shape of none other than Robin Hood himself, part man, part myth, but famous beyond all doubt for his swashbuckling exploits in favour of the underdog. You will find, for example, two Robin Hood's caves, one at Cresswell Crags and the other at Stanage Edge. There is Robin Hood's Stride at Cratcliff Rocks, Robin Hood's Well, Robin Hood's Cross (which is a place and not a comment on his temperament), Robin Hood's Picking Rods, Robin Hood's Farm, Robin Hood's Hill, Robin Hood Village and Robin and Maid Marion's Yew Tree at Tutbury; all of which clearly indicate that someone called Robin Hood was around at some time in this neck of the woods.

Robin Hood's grave however, is said to be in Kirklees Park in south Yorkshire, although some would beg to differ. The thing is, in medieval times Robin Hood, or Hude, or Hode was a fairly common name, which I feel sure has contributed greatly to the general confusion and varying tales concerning the traditional historical figure of Robin Hood, or Robin of Loxley as he was sometimes called. The surname Hood, Hude or Hode refers not surprisingly to a person who wears a hood, so to all you 'hoodies' out there, I am afraid it has all been done before. There are also ballads and rhymes mentioning Robin Hood as far back as the 15th century and beyond, claiming he was causing havoc in Nottinghamshire, Yorkshire, Leicestershire, Warwickshire and Derbyshire. This is, understandably a grey area, as is the supposed number of 'Merrie Men' he had who crop up in differing versions of Robin's life, thus compounding the virtually impossible task of attempting to separate fact from fiction. Consequently, I for one will not be bothering to try and unravel the mess here and will stick conservatively to the popular image of the Robin Hood I was indoctrinated with as a child, with of course, some speculative additions.

Robin Hood (alias Douglas Fairbanks, Errol Flynn, Kevin Costner and Russell Crowe, to name but a few who have played the role) was to me and thousands of kids of my generation memorably played by Richard Greene who starred in the BBC series The Adventures of Robin Hood and lived in Sherwood forest. This series which hit those giant cathode tubes in the late fifties was memorable for the catchy song (for catchy read, a mind possessing, irritating, jaunty tune that circulated your brain during every waking hour of your day and night pushing you to the very edge of insanity) that introduced each programme.

'Robin Hood, Robin Hood, riding through the glen,
Robin Hood, Robin Hood, with his band of men.
Feared by the rich, loved by the poor,
Robin Hood ... Robin Hood ... Robin Hood.'

No self-respecting kid at the time could ever contemplate refraining from galloping along the pavement, belting out the song at full-lung capacity, slapping their right buttock with gusto (long before ASDA cottoned on to the idea) and finishing with a clenched fist held to the mouth to simulate a hunting horn, thereby producing an excruciating sound that normally came out as a cross between a cow having birthing difficulties and a noisy outburst of flatulence! Ah yes … they don't write tunes like that anymore. Actually, now I come to think of it the theme to Captain Pugwash had a similar mind-invading effect. 'Diddly-dee. Diddly-dee, di-di, di-di dee. Diddly-dee … STOP that right now!!

Robin Hood, so legend would have us believe wedded Maid Marion, or another woman called Clorinda, or perhaps he was a bigamist and married both of them, or else they were the same person, for legends abound with contradicting accounts; and was he really married beneath a greenwood tree at Tutbury? In those far off days of childhood the popular concept was that Robin married Marion and they set up home in Sherwood Forest.

"So, where's our home?" asked Marion looking around.

"Here it is sweet one," enthused Robin pointing to a nearby spreading oak.

"But that's just a tree," answered Marion somewhat bemused.

"No, no, no, honey-bunch, it's not just a tree, but a fine English oak that will give us shelter and protection and what's more it …"

"STOP!" yelled Marion with her hands placed defiantly on her hips. "Stop right there. It's a tree Rob, trust me on this one, I've seen some before."

"But dearest one I …"

"Look at me Rob," demanded Marion angrily. "It's a tree, Okay. Squirrels live in trees. Am I a squirrel? Do I look like a squirrel? If you think for one minute that I am going to live in a tree cracking nuts between my teeth all day long, then think again sunshine. This is not my idea of a 'des-res'. I want a proper home with stone walls and a roof." This was not looking like a good start to marital bliss.

"I just thought," stuttered Robin "that …"

"Don't think anything Rob. You're not good at it. And another thing, I want you at home putting up shelves and assembling that new flat-pack wardrobe I've just ordered off 'Tree-bay' not poncing about in the forest all hours in your natty Lincoln green jacket, wrinkled tights and 'Hush Puppy' bootees with that bunch of reprobates shooting arrows at anything and everything."

"I say, steady on Marrers old girl," chipped in Robin. "They're my mates."

"Mates," she retorted. "Take a good look at them Rob. Little John is more big girl's blouse and as for Will Scarlet, well, he looks as if someone has dropped a tin of red pain over a garden gnome; and Friar Tuck, I wouldn't trust him as far as I could throw him, which would be hardly any distance at all given the fact he's always drunk and grossly obese."

"But he's a good man," interrupted Robin.

"You think so?" snarled Marion. "Then try swopping the first letters of his name around then you might think differently."

She was one smart cookie that Marion and would have been great on Countdown. (Surely you've worked it out by now!) Rumour has it that Robin was eventually able to claim back his land and property and forsook the outdoor life beneath a tree. Of course the whole Robin Hood story in its many forms is always going to be a matter of conjecture, but we all love a good tale and this one has certainly stood the test of time, well maybe not this particular version.

As much is based on hearsay, then it is only fair that the other popular version should be given an airing which is that Robin hood actually married Clorinda who was sometimes known as the Queen of Shepherdesses (easily recognised by her fetching hand-knitted woolly tiara) who was out hunting in the woods. It was here that Robin witnessed her bring down single-handedly a buck, which as far as he was concerned was tantamount to love at first sight. This story is related in a 14th century ballad written and performed by none other than the King of the Fiddlers himself at a wedding in Tutbury, which was said to be the union of Robin and Clorinda. Meanwhile back in the forest, Robin is busily ogling Clorinda who was apparently dressed in a long green velvet gown and a pair of lace-up knee length boots (sounds like a real babe to me), when suddenly she is set upon by eight yeomen who fancied a buck (be careful how you interpret this). She told them in no uncertain terms that they would not get a buck from her. Predictably a scrap followed with Robin joining in and all eight buck-happy yeomen were seen off which only served to further inflame Robin's passions having now witnessed Clorinda's fighting prowess. In a very short space of time they nipped off to Tutbury, hired a vicar from Doveridge and did the deed. In that case was it Clorinda who went back to the forest with Robin looking all around saying "So where's our home?"

"Here it is sweet one," enthused Robin, pointing to a nearby spreading oak.

"But that's just a tree," answered Clorinda somewhat bemu …"

Hang on a minute we've gone through that already. The thing is we will never know for certain just what the truth was and the same goes for some of his merry men. Rob's merry men seem to number from a mere handful to a few hundred depending on which of the dozens of different accounts you care to read. Alan-a-Dale for example, has been strongly connected to Derbyshire for he was married at the tiny church at Dale Abbey near to what now remains of the one-time abbey, namely the graceful and enormous east window. Anyway, just to be awkward Alan-a-Dale also appears to have got married at Steetley church near Worksop, so from this we can conclude that either there were two Alan-a-Dale's, or somebody is lying through their teeth. Sadly there is no real hard evidence to back-up either claim and as Alan-a-Dale failed to leave the equivalent of a *Mrs Dale's Diary* (of course you remember it on radio. You just don't want to admit it) then like so many of these stories it will never be substantiated.

Whichever of the two places Al was wedded, the tale goes that his long-time sweetheart was being forced to marry a knight who turned out to be a wrinkly old duffer who was old enough to be her father. Understandably, she was not at all enthusiastic about her wedding night with a decrepit knight. However, help was at hand in the form of (a blast on a hunting horn is called for here) the gallant Robin Hood and his motley band of men, who took it upon themselves to dispense with the knight and the bishop who was to conduct the ceremony (it's sounding like a game of chess), whose clothes were then worn as a disguise to conduct the wedding of Al and his sweetheart. Quite who carried out the clothes swop is a matter for conjecture as different stories say they were worn by Robin Hood, Little John or Friar Tuck, take your pick. Now at this point in the story it has to be said that the apparent versatility of the bishop's robes is something to be wondered at given that Robin Hood was of average build, Little John was a giant of a man and Friar Tuck a man of great girth. I can only assume that when the bishop ordered his gear he must have gone for a 'fit all sizes' outfit like socks you see advertised today in the Saturday newspapers.

While on the subject of clothes, it seems that Alan-a-Dale also dressed in scarlet as did Will Scarlet who was in fact a bit of a fashionista (or a big Jessie as rumour has it), yet it does not seem to have occurred to either of them that bright red would not be the first colour choice of an outlaw wishing to blend in with life in a greenwood. They would both, quite literally, stick out like a sore thumb! Then again the band of merry men I suspect were far from being the cream of medieval England's intelligentsia, as no doubt many were on the same level as Midge the Miller's Son that history has down as an outstanding example of, 'the lift doesn't go to the top floor' and youth was no excuse. The thing is with preposterous names like Wat O Crabstaff, Gamble Gold, Arthur the Bland (I bet he was a laugh a minute) and Gilbert with the White Hand (I wonder what colour his other hand was) who would leap to the rescue from nowhere on hearing three blasts of Robin's horn, it begs the question of just how did such a miscellaneous mob of misfits, or put another way, whackos, manage to find themselves in the same piece of forest. Robin Hood certainly had a talent for attracting fruitcakes.

Robin Hood's side-kick Little John, famous for whacking Robin about the head with a quarterstaff (an elongated broom handle) on their first encounter that ended with Robin taking an unexpected bath in a river, is said to have been born and bred in Derbyshire and buried in the churchyard at Hathersage. In this very same churchyard according to Clarence Daniel in *Pinnacles of Peak History*, 'the chemicals of its churchyard soil, and that of the neighbouring moorland, was found to possess amazing properties of petrification whereby buried bodies were congealed into stone.' In essence this means you could dig up one of your relatives after a few years and have a unique piece of garden sculpture! After Little John was done burying his master at Kirklees it is said he returned to Hathersage weary of life and promptly dropped dead in his rather small single-roomed cottage. I say rather small because his corpse was said to touch the walls on either side when laid out (I've heard of wall-to-wall carpets, but a wall-to-wall corpse, now that really is original), so it was definitely a 'Band A' council tax rated cottage. According to Mr Spencer T. Hall in his book *Rambles in the Country Surrounding the Forest of Sherwood* written around 1840, 'the tiny cottage at this time was occupied by one Jenny Sherd who was seventy years of age and well remembers Little John's grave being dug-up in October 1784.' She says that after two shovels had been broken in the process a thigh bone measuring thirty two inches which had been accidently broken in two by a third shovel (obviously the result of a cack-handed enthusiast who would not be eligible for a stint of delicate tooth-brushing archaeology on the *Time Team* programme) was unceremoniously dumped on her kitchen table. The story of this outsized thigh bone seems to have entered into the annuls of history, as though Little John never had any other bones that ever get a mention, this giant of a man consisting merely of just one leg, well only half a leg in actual fact. Involved in the excavation was Captain James Shuttleworth who subsequently commandeered the bone as a macabre souvenir and took it home to display on his mantle-piece or some such place. However, a series of misfortunes convinced him that the bone was cursed and he had it re-interred in Little John's grave, thus lending credence to the prophesies of an old huntsman who happened to pass by during the removal of the bone who uttered the warning that no good would come of it, 'as long as ye keep dead man's bones above the ground.'

There is another school of thought proffered by Ebenezer Rhodes in his 1824 book *Peak Scenery,* which alludes to a tall man from Offerton who because of his stature assumed the name of Robin Hood's right-hand man and that this grave at Hathersage was his. Because the original exhumation of the bones had revealed an oversized thigh bone then the two gravestone markers were moved further apart to enhance the tale. And just to confuse things even more an Irish author claims that Little John dangled from the gallows having been executed for a robbery on Arbor Hill in Dublin. It really does start to make your head spin trying to make some sense out of all these conflicting stories. The thing is that Little John has become a bit of a scene-stealer for although little mentioned, Hathersage was the inspiration for 'Morton' in Charlotte Bronte's novel *Jane Eyre,* the title coming from the tomb of Jane Eyre which can be seen inside the church. Anyway, some years later along came another raiding party, this time from Yorkshire, re-exhumed Little John's grave and again the famous thigh bone was carted off to Barnsley (it certainly gets around a bit for only half a leg!) along with his natty, but tatty green hat and aged wood-wormed bow that had hung for many a year in the nearby church in Hathersage. Over the years it seems that everything has just disappeared and will never be seen again, unless of course, they mysteriously turn up one afternoon on the *Antiques Roadshow.* As Fiona Bruce would say at the end of the show, 'If you think you might have Little John's cap or bow tucked away in your attic, then bring it along to the Roadshow as we would love to see it.'

Little John and Robin Hood share an unlikely connection with Robin Hood's Stride by Cratcliff Rocks, so named because the distance between the two towers of rock measures the length of (yes, you've guessed it) Robin Hood's stride, which is a tad far-fetched as the towers are sixty-six feet apart. Ranking alongside this figment of some ones questionable mental state are the rock towers themselves, with one being known as Weasel Pinnacle, and the other Inaccessible Pinnacle. The fact that the former looks nothing like a weasel, while the latter is totally accessible seems to be of no consequence and it does make you wonder just who dreamt up those names. Because these two towers apparently give the clump of rocks the look of a castle or similar, when viewed against the sky at dusk, it has earned itself the alternative name of Mock Beggar's Hall.

Equally bizarre is the cock and bull story alluding to Little John who according to a past farmer stood with a foot on each pinnacle and proceeded to empty his bladder which is now responsible for the stream that runs from between the two heaps of rock. Now this image takes a bit of swallowing, if you will excuse the expression, with Little John coming over as an exhibitionist by displaying his 'Captain Winkie' for all and sundry to see. A local farmer way back has been quoted as saying, 'I dunna know 'ow he did it though. He mun abin bigger than Goliath.' A further version of this story states that it was Robin Hood as a giant who relieved himself astride the rocks which was witnessed unfortunately by seven maidens who promptly turned to stone, or as was more likely the case stopped dead in their tracks and rendered speechless. The sight of such a gigantic member would have kept the poor girls awake for many a night had they survived the spectacle!

So there you have it, and although there have been many occasions in the past when on a hot summers day I have resorted to drinking from a Derbyshire stream, I must remind myself never to be caught out in the vicinity of Robin Hood's Stride without my Thermos, just to be on the safe side. I mean it's not as if I believe in any of this stuff, after all it's only a tale …

3.

The Wye and its
many Wherefores.

The bleak and often wind-swept, rain-lashed moorland of Axe Edge is situated south-west of Buxton and gives rise to several springs that in turn become well-known Derbyshire rivers, in this particular instance the Wye. When James Croston in the latter half of the 1800s climbed to the pathless summit he came across a small cairn left by some Ordnance Sappers who claimed to have seen from this lofty height two signals simultaneously displayed at night, one on the top of Snowdon and the other on Lincoln Cathedral some one hundred and fifty miles apart. They must have had binocular vision. Quite what the signal signified is not stated, but thankfully the sappers did not act upon on It by going ahead and blowing Axe Edge to smithereens as was there particular speciality. The surface water from this peaty upland quickly percolates through the ground to dribble, drip and gurgle into the many sink-holes on the lower levels of Stanley Moor where they gather to form the headwater of the fifteen mile long river Wye. I can personally account for the tight constrictions of some of these holes, as a descent of one when I was a young man with a group from college resulted in having to extricate a fellow female student from a vertical fissure. Gravity enabled her to drop down with ease, whereas climbing back up was a different matter altogether. Even for me, comparatively slim at the time it was rib-crushingly tight, but she had to contend with a pair of womanly attributes that rather impeded her progress. After a considerable amount of pushing, squeezing and coaxing of various parts of her body in an operation that took far too long (this was out of pleasure rather than necessity), I was eventually able to haul her out of the unforgiving cleft. Such incidents are what memories are made of!

Looking down on this area is the twenty feet high round tower of Solomon's Temple, or Solomon's Pimple as it is sometimes known. Apart from providing first class views from its top, it serves no other purpose for it is merely a Victorian folly, erected in 1896 by Solomon Mycock (I bet he got ragged at school with a surname like that) purely to provide employment for the locals during dire times. Given today's unemployment figures, if such a philanthropic gesture was to materialise now then there would be more follies springing up all over the countryside than you could shake a stick at. The area called Grin Low near the tower is now given over to parkland, which is a far cry from the days according to Croston in his book *On Foot through England,* when he walked this way, things were very different. He recalls that, 'A great portion of the summit of Grin Low is covered with dross and slag, the refuse of the neighbouring limekilns.' He also remarks that the many small hillocks to be found the area had rather curiously been excavated and at one time been lived in by the lime-burners, with a hole in the side for a window and another hole in the top to let out smoke. It would be hard to imagine anything more squalid to live in than a hovel like this, which would even make living in a tenement in the one-time notorious district of the Gorbals in Glasgow seem strangely attractive. The lime-burners were eventually moved on and re-housed in comfortable dwellings in nearby Burbage. Close by is Diamond Hill, so called for the celebrated 'Buxton Diamonds' that have been found here lying about in an area of loose mining debris. These often-large diamonds are in reality clear quartz crystals so forget any ideas you may have been harbouring about hiring a mini-digger and becoming a billionaire overnight!

Until quite recently it was assumed that the Wye started its journey somewhere in the darkness of Poole's Cavern, but as we now know Axe

Edge is its proper source, yet only in Poole's Cavern does it begin to look like a river on a mission. The cavern is around two million years old, which by anyone's standards is very old indeed, but did not open as a show cave until 1854, by the then owner the 6th Duke of Devonshire who probably wanted a bit of extra pocket money. Prior to this it has been proven that primitive man had inhabited the cave entrance and in all likelihood squatted in a huddle in hairy loincloths, scratching themselves and uttering unintelligible grunting noises, as they tore at raw meat from bones, which they chucked onto the floor, not being the slightest bit cave-proud. A few thousand years later someone in the name of archaeology came along and bashed a deep hole through the layers of sediment forming the cave floor to discover these very same leftovers. This can be classed as an extreme case of turning up late for dinner! The thing is that a final summation of all the finds, which included cow, goat and pig bones along with pottery fragments and charcoal (they were clearly up for having a few friends around for the occasional barbeque) that the troglodytes had left behind constituted what Danish antiquarians labelled, according to Croston, as a 'kjokkemodding' or put another way a refuse heap which is much easier to both spell and pronounce. There is also evidence that the Saxons hid inside Poole's Hole to avoid the Roman legions that were tramping past who in all probability would be looking for some local Brits to beat up and make into involuntary road workers to finish building Icknield or Ryknild Street. (They had only got as far as laying it just north of Breadsall and needed to get to Chesterfield in time for the shops.)

The most well-known resident of Poole's Hole was the infamous Poole himself who is remembered as an outlaw, a robber and an all-round bad egg. He lived in the cave for many years hiding from his pursuers as well as stashing away his contraband and a host of 'black market' goods along with not paying his council tax. Although to be fair this was back in the time of Henry IV who no doubt had more important things than tax collecting on his mind, like what to do with Richard II whose throne he had purloined while Richard was away having a bit of a punch-up with the Irish.

As a show cave Poole's Hole became very popular and in time a cute little Swiss cottage was built by the entrance where Francis Redfern, who was a stonemason and custodian of the cave lived. I have hanging on the wall at home a tinted and delicately engraved picture published by J.C. Bates of Buxton showing the entrance to Poole's Cavern and the delightful Swiss cottage that would have been executed somewhere around the 1860s, which I bought at an antiques fair in Buxton over fifty years ago. Being a public show cave brings disadvantages insomuch as it attracts the flotsam and jetsam of society, and this included the guides who in general were a disparate and often untrustworthy bunch that would lead you into the darkness of the cave then sometimes threaten to abandon you in the pitch black unless you handed over more money. Understandably, this was a very effective ultimatum. Contemptible but effective! In its early days visitors were at the mercy of these guides who in all probability were local cottagers, mostly female and often described as 'weird women, witches, who are in eternal squabble with each other' so great was the competition. An 18th century traveller commented, 'our guides were all female who by their dress and looks recalled to memory every picture of the midnight hags in Macbeth', so no 'page three pin-ups' there then, and definitely not the kind of woman you would want to take home to meet mother. Whether Mary Queen of Scots was subjected to this rabble of partly-demented women when she visited the cave is not recorded, but it is known that she gamely ventured far inside to a stalagmitic column which was imaginatively named 'Queen of Scots Pillar' after her trip. Being in awe of the moment she is said to have embraced and kissed the crystalline column. Charles Cotton who rated Poole's Hole in 1883 as one of '*The Wonders of the Peak*' proved to be a game but cautious visitor, unlike Defoe who as we know from earlier on in this book cited the place as a 'wonderless wonder' and continued his attack by saying the cave, 'brings fools a great way to creep into it' and that they, 'generally go away, acknowledging that they have seen nothing suitable to their expectations'. Cotton was transported into the cave no doubt attired in fine clothes by a, 'Peak-bred Convoy of rude Men and Boys, all the Way wooting with that dreadful Noise' whereupon coming to a steep section he was supported by his arms by two 'Hob-nailed Peakrills', who lowered him down onto the shoulders of another. This ghastly experience left Cotton of the firm opinion that how could Poole or anyone else for that matter, apart from the Devil himself have possibly dwelt there. Back then it did not sound like the sort of place to take the wife and kids to for an outing, unlike today where it very much caters to the family needs.

In 1860 Francis Redfern had the cavern fitted out with gas lights which at the time was a novel innovation. Previously the cavern had been lit by raised candelabras, but now he was able to advertise it as being, 'illuminated at all hours of the day with one hundred and thirty gas lights' (I wouldn't mind betting his face was a picture when the quarterly gas bill dropped through his letterbox), along with a band playing inside twice a week. Evidently Poole's Cavern was the 'in place' to hang out if you fancied some light entertainment coupled with a bit of an underground 'knees-up' on a wet afternoon. In his book *The Peak District* Gilchrist says of the cave's interior, 'there are more or less appropriately christened stalactites, and the cavern being smooth of path (advertised as suitable for wheelchairs) and well-lighted with gas, is without terrors even for the most nervous'. The names given to the formations are something to be wondered at and one visitor suggests that they could only be the result of a 'pregnant imagination'.

Over the centuries the paying public has been subjected to the dubious delights of the Flitch of Bacon, Poached Egg Chamber, Lions, Haycocks, the Font, the Rhinoceros, the Beehive, the Oyster Beds, and as Celia Fiennes noted on her underground trip, 'one Looks Like a Lyon wth a Crown' and another, 'Lookes just Like ye shape of a Large organ wth ye several Keys and pipes' while yet another, 'Rock Looks like a Chaire of State wth ye Canopy.' Her exploration terminated at Queen of Scots Pillar after which she was shown, 'St Annes Needle after wch is only sand', but she was an enthusiastic visitor who enjoyed greatly all the, 'great white Stones or Large jceickles.' When Ebenezer Rhodes paid a visit to Poole's Hole he was none too impressed as, 'The entrance into this dreary cavern is narrow and forbidding; and the air even in summer has a cold and chilling effect that creeps through the whole frame.' Like all other visitors before and after him, a variety of formations were pointed out and, 'in one place we were shown a *petrified turtle;* (highly suspect) in another, a *flitch of bacon;* (this ubiquitous formation is almost mandatory in any self-respecting show cave that calls itself such) in a third, *Old Poole's saddle;* and still further on there are other calcareous incrustations, called *wool-packs; a chair, a font, a ladies toilet, a pillion',* all of which caused Rhodes to comment that not in any shape or form did they feature an uncouth resemblance to the objects they were said to represent. Clearly a fertile imagination could and did run riot when it came to conjuring up weird and wonderful names for oddly shaped formations. Redfern himself acting as a guide was only too keen to point out to the explorers in his charge all manner of formations including, 'lion couchant guarding the entrance to my lady's chamber', which seemed so far-fetched that apparently it sorely taxed the imagination to find anything on the mass of crystal that remotely resembled anything near a lion. On one particular occasion this description of his caused the ladies to giggle and one ready wit (isn't there always one comedian) asked in a facetious manner if the lion ever showed its teeth, to which Redfern, who was clearly quite nettled replied, 'Only when it hears a braying ass.' Touchy or what! I think the time has come to follow the river Wye, head for daylight and the town of Buxton.

Black's *1872 Tourist's Guide to* Derbyshire describes the town of Buxton as, 'pleasantly situated on the river Wye' and its, 'principal employments are the manufacture of spar ornaments and burning lime', which on the face of it would not encourage you to leap out of bed to visit the place. The town is situated the best part of a thousand feet above sea level, protected by a circle of hills and has certainly changed for the better since those days. The Derby physician, Dr Jones wrote in 1572 of the benefits of the, 'Auncient Bathes of Buckstones which cureth most grievous sicknesses', but to go, 'well-clothed', for although the air is pure and wholesome it is, 'farre colder and more sharpe than many parts of the earth.' Better not forget your thermal underwear and aunty's knitted Christmas jumper the one with the prancing reindeer with snowflakes and matching snowman mittens.

Because of its fine architecture Buxton has always had an air of elegance about it and consequently the town was graced by the landed gentry, royalty and the wealthy which once included the likes of the Grimshaws of Errwood Hall that, 'gentleman's Italianate style shooting lodge', an oasis of fine living, rare books, classic sculptures and valuable paintings perched on a ledge on a hillside surrounded by wild rhododendrons among the even wilder moorland of Goyt valley. The ladies of the house often rode into town in a horse drawn carriage to buy gifts and take refreshment at the former Cavendish Coffee House in Terrace Road.

Long before all this took place it was the Romans who first placed Buxton on the map, or Aquae Arnemetiae, which for those of you who are a little rusty with your Latin, or if like me never knew any in the first place, apparently means Spa of the Goddess of the Grove. I think Buxton is a far better name to cope with and what a headache the post office would have with Spa of the Goddess of the Grove! The Romans built their spa baths (inconveniently as it turned out where the Crescent was to be built later) sometime after AD40 when they first set sandal on the shores of Britain. It was an awful long time after AD40 before the Crescent was built in 1780, the Romans by this time having scarpered long ago on account of it raining too much, it was sunnier in Italy and you could not get a pizza for love-nor-money.

It was during excavations for the Crescent that the old Roman baths were first discovered and found to be made of bricks as hard as stone with walls covered in a reddish-pink plaster as hard as the bricks. Analysis according to one person proved it to be 'a mixture of lime and powered tile, cemented with blood (whose I wonder) and eggs, which if you think about it, makes it half-way to being a black pudding. In those far off days a Roman chap called Lucas recorded the bath water as being extraordinary hot, so either it has cooled down considerably or else Lucas was a bit of a wimp when it came to bath time, for the water is now known to be a constant all year round 82 degrees Fahrenheit. The water is said to be effective in curing rheumatism, gout and Tic-doloureux which is a spasm of the face and apparently so painful that you would give anything to find a way of continuing to live without a face.seful as a means of ftence!nce n is indeed a worthy wonder, Henricus manages to summerise y a detached rock, to the i The water is also alleged to be radio-active, so if you emerged glowing this could have been useful before street lighting was common place.

Accounts of the baths in and around the 18th century inferred they were little better than an unhealthy looking human soup. This is not surprising when you consider that the baths were inundated on a daily basis with multitudes of unwashed bodies suffering from all manner of ailments and skin diseases (with the odd bit no doubt occasionally dropping off), cavorting cheek by jowl in a bath whose inflow and outflow was insufficient to cleanse the water. The word soup is perhaps an apt description. It has to be said that it does tend to conjure up a ghastly image in the mind which is not easily dismissed. It is therefore, interesting to note that when Crichton Porteous visited around 1950 he states in his county book that the waters were brilliantly pure and harebell blue in colour.

Clearly the water had been changed and someone had been busy with a bottle of Harpic and a damp cloth. At the time Porteous was not suffering from any of the ailments the waters were said to successfully treat, so he was unable to comment on their curative properties, but found nevertheless, the bath very agreeable to swim in and was guaranteed a sound night's sleep after taking the plunge. As a rubbish sleeper myself this has appeal if it was not for the fact that wandering around nowadays clad in only a pair of swimming trunks would make me feel like a fish out of water, for the baths are now a shopping arcade with only the original shiny Minton wall tiles lining a drained plunge pool being surviving evidence of its former glory.

Perhaps the most agreeable description of the baths was by that popular travel writer of the 1920s and 30s, H. V. Morton who defied anyone to see the effervescent blue water and not be overcome with the desire to strip off and leap in, as indeed Morton did. He reported that, 'the nitrogen bubbles burst and tickle you. It is like bathing with invisible goldfish.' How wonderful and relaxing does that sound? His opinion of Buxton was, 'It is a very quiet place. There is practically no sound but the bursting of nitrogen bubbles on blue water.' If that truly was the case then sadly the roar of today's town traffic would have certainly put paid to that. A certain Mr Page (surgeon to the Bath Charity) recommended the waters for sufferers of, 'gout and rheumatism; in many nervous disorders such as epilepsy, paralysis, St Vitus dance (a category yet to be included in *Strictly Come Dancing*), palpitation of the heart, etc' and listed certain rules to be adhered to when bathing one of which was, 'To go in with the feet first', so clearly no showing off with a half-pike, double twist, triple back somersault. As a footnote, 'All the baths are supplied with douches which can be used at pleasure' and if you are thinking what I am thinking then I guess this is truly a case of whatever floats your boat!

Of course all this splashing and sploshing about came at a price and the treatments cost money, as someone had to pay the wages of the attendants who sadistically hosed you down as part of the course. In the 1930s for example, a resident of Buxton could get into the baths at the cheaper rate of one shilling as opposed to the half-a-crown charged to a non-resident. However, in 1572 it was a different story altogether. An archbishop, for example had to pay five pounds, although I cannot for one moment think that many archbishops frequented the spa. It stretches the imagination a little to visualise of a group of them standing about in Speedos, leaning on their croziers and chuntering about the low return on the Sunday collection plate, as being barely enough to pay for a bathing session and a cold water douche to bring the colour back to one's cheeks! A Duchess would have to pay two pounds at the pay office, a Duke three pounds ten shillings (I'm sure the Duke of Devonshire was allowed in for free seeing as how he built the pool in the first place) and a Yeoman a mere twelve pence.

If you take into account inflation then these charges were not cheap. In Elizabethan times apparently swarms of people descended on the spa to the extent that an act of Parliament passed a motion that all persons wishing to enter the baths must first be in possession of a licence, which had to be signed by an official magistrate, or alternatively, you had to prove you had sufficient funds in your piggy bank to keep yourself, otherwise you were out on your ear. In the absence of the original baths, a way of getting around this problem now – provided you have the time and patience – is to arm yourself with a heap of plastic bottles which you can fill up for free at nearby St Anne's Well and take home to empty into your very own bath.

St Anne's Well was spoken of by Charles Cotton in his 1682 *Wonders of the Peak* because of there being two streams within six feet of each other, one hot and the other cold, a true geological conundrum. However, in his description Cotton tends to get a bit carried away for he says if you should cross from one side of the bath to the other where these two streams were once harnessed then the effect of passing from cold water to hot would immediately force you to, 'endure, at once an ague and a calenture.' Given that the definition of ague is a malarial fever, and a calenture is a feverish delirium associated with sailors in the tropics, it would appear that either Cotton has grossly over-exaggerated the effects of this bath water, or you are going to be a lot worse off than when you entered! Personally, I would ask for my money back.

In the distant past an area close by St Anne's Well was once littered with discarded sticks and crutches left behind by the cured who came as cripples and left 'leaping and rejoicing.' Over a period of time the area became such an unsightly mess that one day someone came along and made a bonfire out of the whole lot and blamed it on some of Cromwell's cronies. The instigator of the clear-up was one William Basset who sent a sycophantic, brown-nosing letter to Cromwell (a notorious spoilsport and party-pooper) saying how he, 'did take away crutches, shirts, and shifts, with wax offered, being things that allure and entice the ignorant to the said offering.' He then, 'locked up and sealed the baths and wells of Buckston, that none shall enter to wash there till your Lordships pleasure be further known.' Bassett finished off by stating he had written the letter at Langley, 'with the rude and simple hand of your assured and faithful orator, and as one and ever at your commandment, next unto the King's, to the utmost of his little power.' A bit of a toady if ever there was one.

Early visitors to the baths complained bitterly about the lack of accommodation in Buxton as there was little choice for the bathers, so apart from one or two lowly lodging houses it seems that the Duke of Devonshire's old house which originally stood on the site now occupied by the Old Hall Hotel was the only place recommended and even that had a questionable reputation. Defoe who in general had little to say about Buxton did pass the comment that Buxton would do much better if more accommodation was available to the many visitors and consequently attract a better class of person. The Duke's grand house simply referred to as the Hall and built for the 'reception of visitants' was described by Dr Jones of Derby in 1572 as being 'four storeys high' and with a, 'great chamber and other goodly lodgings to the number of 30. Yea, the poorest shall have lodgings and beds hard by for their use.' Jones who was possibly a bit of a health freak or a keep-fit nutter suggested that in the event of anyone finding themselves at a loss as to how to fill their time between bathing sessions should try exercises like, 'bowling, shooting at butts (which I presume has nothing to do with taking pot-shots at peoples rear ends, fun though that may sound) and tossing the wind ball.' Make of that what you will! Another way to pass the time if the weather was inclement writes Jones was that you, 'maye have in the ends of a benche eleven holes made, into the which to trowel pummets or bowles of leade, bigge, little or meane, or also, of copper, tynne, woode, eyther violent or softe, after their owne discretion, the pastyme, Trowl in Madame, is termed.' Basically, this riveting game of Trowel in Madam (which could be misconstrued as a sexual innuendo) involves sticking objects made of different materials into holes in the end of a bench. Now what you have to ask yourself is, what pastime today could possibly complete with the 'edge of the seat' (or in this case bench) cut and thrust of this most intellectually electrifying game! Stumped for an answer? Me to!

Macauley quotes a piece from Thomas Browne's *Tour of Derbyshire* who mentions that the gentry of Derbyshire were, 'crowded into low wooden sheds, and regaled with oatcake and a viand which the hosts call mutton, but which guests strongly suspect is dog.' Oatcakes have been the staple diet of Derbyshire miners (bearing the same role as a Cornish miner's pasty) and quarrymen for decades and resembled a pancake, slightly smaller in size than an old 78rpm Bakelite record, made of oatmeal and water and cooked on a hot plate. Depending on your particular taste they could be spread with butter, honey, syrup or black cattle treacle, which is black molasses that is put into cattle feed. Another recommendation especially on a winter's morning is to fry them and serve with bacon with a fried egg on top. My mother would buy oatcakes every Friday from a small stall which operated in the draughty archway of the clock entrance to the market hall in Derby. Mee tells a humorous anecdote relating to oatcakes that were bought by a Cockney who came to work at Chapel-en-le-Frith where he was served them by his landlady. Such was his enthusiasm for the fare he sent some back to his family and six months later when he returned home for a break he was somewhat surprised to see the oatcakes he had sent home laid out on the sideboard with vases of flowers placed on top of them. It seems that when his family first received the oatcakes they caused a degree of confusion, but after a discussion it was decided they must be place mats! Wasteful, but innovative. As for the other part of the meal where dog might have been on the menu, well I think I will give that one a miss. Even Heston Blumenthal's wacky recipes have not included oatcake and dog … yet.

Anyway, back to the inadequacies of Buxton's B&Bs. Celia Fiennes wrote that her stay was, 'overshadowed by having to pay for so much a piece for ye dinners and suppers and so much for our servants besides: all ye wine and ale to be paid – besides, the beer they allow at meals is so bad yt very Little Can be dranke.' After that things went from bad to worse for, 'ye lodgings so bad, 2 beds in a Roome, some 3 beds and 4 in one Roome so that if you have not Company Enough of your own to fill a Roome they will be ready to put others into the same Chamber and sometimes they are so crowded that three must Lye in a bed.' It all sounds rather cramped, but to look on the bright side if I found myself in that situation and sharing a bed with a couple of young serving girls then I am sure I could put up with the discomfort. However, there would be no appeal at all if the other occupant of my bed was an obese, flatulating old fossil who snored and scratched himself all night long. As a result of the sleeping arrangements Celia Fiennes says that few people were willing to stay more than two or three nights, because it was inconvenient and noisy. I think I can see her point of view.

The Right Honourable Sarah Murray was also cheesed off about the poor facilities for her visit to the Hall in 1790 required her to pay one shilling and sixpence per person for dinner, supper was a shilling and breakfast ten pence with another eight pence for tea. I think a branch of McDonalds or Subway would have gone down well at this time, although whether a line in 'Dog Burger and Fries' would have been popular is a matter for speculation. Evidently she is still steaming angrily as she goes on to say that, 'Both at Matlock and Buxton liquor of all kinds, at dinner and supper, must be paid for besides, and procured by your own servant at the eating houses.' As a subtle hint that your meal and the time at your table was over, 'a person comes round the dinner and supper table, and the cloth is taken off to collect from each person for the meal.' This sounds very much like an eighteenth century version of 'I'm closing up now love. Haven't you got a home to go to?' Bed chambers were let from fourteen shillings to a guinea a week which is nowhere near what you will be paying at today's prices for just one night's stay at the Old Hall Hotel, which also boasts of being the oldest hotel in England.

In 1780 the Crescent, also known as the 'Jewel of Buxton' cost the princely sum of £120,000 to build, which again fell to the Duke of Devonshire as he was responsible for its construction on a design by Carr of York and modelled on the more famous one in Bath. Built from limestone quarried on the spot it was then clad in gritstone from a quarry a couple of miles away. The most impressive feature of its palatial interior was the Grand Assembly Room measuring some seventy feet in length by thirty feet high (I bet nobody got up there very often with a feather duster) and became a natural gathering place for elegant Georgian society who came to take the waters. It originally comprised of two hotels called The Crescent and St Anne's that provided much needed accommodation. However, if your pocket did not run to being able to stay or dine in either of them then at least you could keep warm for free on a cold day by standing over one of the vents in the continuous colonnade that runs the length of the Crescent that were an outlet for the warm air from the thermal baths. Little compensation I admit, but probably enjoyable in its own way for it would be not unlike a low budget sauna, except the last thing you would want to do would to take off all your clothes, unless of course you were either foolhardy, a masochist or an exhibitionist, any of which would get you promptly arrested for scaring young children and frightening old ladies of a nervous disposition.

And what of the poor old river Wye you may ask? Where has that disappeared to? Well the fact is that barely has it got over blinking from the daylight after emerging from the dark of Poole's Cavern and serenely passing through the Pavilion Gardens before it is suddenly bunged into an underground culvert to ignominiously vanish beneath the streets of the town. In that brief airing the serpentine water just has time to reflect the Victorian splendour of Joseph Paxton's glass pavilion also referred to as yet another 'Jewel in the Crown of Buxton', which was opened to the public in 1871. Tagged on a bit later in 1903 is the wonderful Opera House where in the 1960s I once watched a back-projected screening of the film 'Irma la Douce'. Because there was no projection it seemed odd not seeing the all-to-familiar cigarette smoke curling up through the beam of the projector light above the heads of the audience.

In the past the beautiful ornamental Pavillion Gardens was where 'important tennis tournaments' were held and 'during the summer months orchestral concerts are given twice daily in the Concert Hall of the Pavilion' while the Theatre Festival in late summer and early autumn saw plays performed by the Old Vic Company. In the gardens themselves some two miles of walks and five bridges had been constructed, for which there was an admission fee of three pence for one person a day. Only licensed bath chairs were allowed to enter at seven shillings and sixpence per year, and dogs on a string for three pence a day.

The Wye does not seem to get properly released until after flowing in a culvert beneath the town, starts its open-air journey in Spring Gardens, but even this turns out to be a temporary affair. Here it is overlooked by the dominating eighty feet high, thirteen arched viaduct that carries the LNWR line over the bleak hills to Ashbourne from Buxton Station, which still displays a lone window, yet again another creation by Joseph Paxton. On entering the very treed Ashwood Dale the river Wye once again finds itself ingloriously confined in a constrictive concrete channel that in essence is little better than a gutter sandwiched between the A6 and the Buxton to Miller's Dale railway line that runs along a limestone shelf as it criss-crosses the valley on high viaducts.

The river gurgles and chunters and mutters discontentedly at the indignation of being controlled in a vale where it once ran free, but where it is now quite literally, stuffed in between the retaining wall of the A6 and a bank which separates it from the large circular tanks that sort and sift the waste products discharged from the front and rear ends of the population of Buxton. The Wye suffers ungraciously at the hands of man, but in *The Peak District Homeland Guide* the tenacity of the river is captured in the sentence, 'Such a beginning may well have daunted the spirit of many a stream, but the Wye was begat inside a stout Derbyshire hill and that stoutness of heart enables it to suffer such indignities and lose nothing of its spirit.' The problem with Ashwood Dale is that the first couple of miles or so of its natural features of bosky hillsides and limestone crags has been visually degraded by gas works, sewerage tanks, quarrying, the railway and the almost unceasing drone of heavy traffic on the road, to the extent that most guide books suggest this section as being a place best avoided with any river walks beginning at the turning to Blackwell.

This well-founded advice does have a drawback in that you miss out on the little visited limestone canyon called Sherbrook Dell and its Lover's Leap that appears within trolley pushing distance of the useful, but incongruous Morrisons supermarket. Ebenezer Rhodes in his book *Peak Scenery* written in 1824 waxed lyrically about the gorge for here, 'a little dell opens its craggy portals to the road' and goes on to describe it as no finer place on a winter day, or in summer when the waterfall at the far end splashes down between rich foliage. Gilchrist said, 'it is like the scene of some old story of gnomes and fairies', which to some it might be until your imagination focuses on the demise of some desperate lover plummeting down from its rocky heights to land among the ferns and mossy boulders in an unappealing crumpled heap and bloodied mess. Actually, that is my imagination getting the better of me for legend has it that the couple were on horseback when they took the leap and made it to the other side and to church after which they presumably lived happily ever after. I tend to be in favour of Gilchrist's view of Sherbrook Dell for it is a spectacular magical ravine clothed in rich, luxuriant green moss and everywhere is the sight and sound of rushing water and if this ravine was anywhere else in Derbyshire it would be declared a truly beautiful spot even though it is difficult to negotiate without a pair of wellies.

Regrettably, because it is tucked off the busy A6 few visit the place, with the exception of the mindless morons who are responsible for the entrance being a tip for plastic bottles, beer cans, black bin bags bursting with waste, and on my last visit a discarded electric circuit board and a sizeable plastic double-glazing window frame. And almost as bad is the top path that winds through the wooded hillside above the rocky ravine for even here a miscellany of rubbish including a discarded plastic garden chair is strewn everywhere you care to look. What sort of mentality do these dim wits have that they wish to litter such a wonderful spot?

Derbyshire is not short of Lover's Leaps which might normally be considered as a depressing thought if it was not for the fact that the majority of them seemed to have survived the experience and were no doubt the wiser for it. The best documented story along with the inevitable variations of a lover surviving a leap is that of Hannah Baddaley who lived in Stoney Middleton and had the 'hots' for one William Barnsley who being a bit of a reprobate did not return her affections, but was not amiss to an occasional bit of slap-and-tickle with the unfortunate Hannah. He mainly preferred to spend his time downing pints of ale with the lads followed by a bit of night-time poaching, simple pleasures that satisfied young Billy Barnsley. Unfortunately, the same could not be said of the rather misguided Hannah who over a period of time became very moody, sultry and thoroughly worked-up about the whole situation. She just wanted to be married, have a few kids and live in a nice cosy cottage. She was clearly born at the wrong time, for a few centuries later she could have got herself 'up the chuff' and been found a house with all expenses paid courtesy of Social Services! Anyway, one Sunday in 1762 and dressed in her best clothes (I do so admire a girl with a sense of occasion) Hannah stood poised on the lip of a 'fearful precipice' took a deep breath and launched herself into space. What happened next is a matter for conjecture as one account relates how her clothing became caught in some brambles which helped to break her otherwise rapid descent resulting in her hanging unceremoniously in the undergrowth in a battered, bruised and lacerated state, pondering no doubt on just how badly wrong it had gone.

If you are now overcome with a sense of disappointment because you were anticipating a gory finale then I will quickly sate your appetite by mentioning Carlswark cavern a little further down the road. It was here a couple of hundred years ago that a flood washed a silver buckled shoe (we are talking Loakes here) out of the entrance and into the dale. Nothing much untoward about that you will be saying to yourself until I tell you that the shoe still had a soggy decomposing foot inside it and the remainder of the body was found later inside the cave. Both the foot and the body belonged to a wealthy Scottish pedlar who frequented this area and had been murdered then dumped in the cave. So how's that for a macabre, dastardly deed! And if you think that hurling yourself off the top of a cliff despite being love-stricken is daft, then further down the dale is a tall pinnacle of rock which the foolhardy would climb and then stand on their head! Just don't ask.

Anyway, another version of Hannah Baddely's leap into Derbyshire folklore according to Norman Price in his book *The Derbyshire Dales* says she fell onto a 'cushion of rubble and dust in a woodman's saw-pit.' I cannot help thinking that the words 'cushion' and 'rubble' is an odd combination to use implying that it somehow softened Hannah's landing. Just how much more uncomfortable could you get than lounging about on a settee among a heap of rubble-filled scatter cushions? Luckily she had been snagged on the way down by brambles and a few rocky projections before hitting the deck where she was discovered in a dazed and dishevelled state by some passing locals. This was obviously not her day for her antics had all been to no avail, besides which she had missed out on Sunday dinner back home. She lay there overwhelmed with depression as she reflected that not only had her love been rejected, but it seemed to her that even her failed attempt at suicide meant that death itself had jilted her. At this point Hannah was picked up, brushed down and taken to the nearby pub the Ball Inn (long gone) and in the absence of a tube of Germolene was given first-aid treatment in the form of a posset (not to be confused with a posser, which was for bashing your laundry with in a Dolly tub), which is said to be a Derbyshire remedy consisting of spicy bread soaked in milk and ale. Well that sounds really yummy and certainly worth throwing yourself off a cliff for. Miraculously Hannah survived her injuries and despite being sadly crippled lived the rest of her short life unwedded. In actual fact poor disillusioned Hannah only survived another two years and died in December 1764 leaving a £180, which at that time would have been thought of as a more than reasonable fortune.

The thing about this tale along with many others of a similar ilk is that they all have one thing in common, which was that the broken-hearted victims had jumped of cliff-tops (and even Clifton suspension bridge) wearing some form of full, flouncy dress which acted as a sort of Heath Robinson parachute by considerably slowing down their descent. It could be seen as the fore-runner of bungee jumping where the elasticated rope is swopped for a voluminous skirt. On reflection, I guess for blokes it would rather spoil the macho image if they had to dress in a crinoline first before throwing themselves into space.

Meanwhile back in Ashwood Dale the river Wye, now finally released from any further restrictive bonds, runs on passing a public house called The Devonshire Arms that closed down many years ago. I recall passing it many times and thinking how dismal and forlorn it looked situated right on the edge of the A6 and constantly sprayed by the filth from passing traffic. Given its remote location, it is puzzling how it ever came into being, as its catchment area must have been scant at best, coupled with walking out of the door at night with a beer-addled brain must surely have been an open invitation to be instantly wiped out by a speeding lorry. Croston who a few centuries ago walked the Wye from Bakewell to Buxton in one day remarked on seeing in the fast failing light a group of labourers outside The Devonshire Arms, 'lounging about the doorway, some engaged in friendly chat, while others are lying by the side of the way in a state of divided allegiance between Bacchus and Morpheus.' I love Croston's summation here of the drunkards being, 'in a state of divided allegience', which in today's parlance would be described as wrecked, ratted or bladdered, and others completely blotto, wasted or zoned. Of course in Croston's time the road was not the A6 as we now know it, yet even wandering blind drunk into the path of a galloping horse and wagon must surely have been a not uncommon occurrence.

Further on down the road past the steep little road that leads to Cowdale, a neglected track climbs to the hamlet of Kings Sterndale, which despite being a mere handful of dwellings actually boasts a fine Hall. This was the residence of William Pickford, or Baron Sterndale to give him his proper title. The Pickfords now known nationwide by their fleet of removal vans, began life hacking out stone in a quarry in the Goyt Valley some of which ended up paving the streets of London. William Pickford apparently was a noted lawyer, but a lawyer who was not too proud to roll up his sleeves and lend a hand in gathering in the hay, as he did in 1923 after which he suddenly and unaccountably dropped dead. That must have been some mega-bout of hay fever! The Pickfords also turned their hand to a bit of lime-baking to enrich the land to which purpose they constructed a huge kiln, and true to form they did what they were best at, removals, which in this instance saw them removing many stone walls to provide building material and in so doing reduced the surrounding area to a barren waste. This great kiln was described at the time by an eye witness as a 'pudding pie' being two hundred yards in circumference and twenty yards in diameter, 'the like of which has ne'er been seen, nor e'er again will be.' The location of the great 'pudding' is not known for there are no longer any clues to its whereabouts. It has completely disappeared. There are no second helpings.

The Wye continues hugged closely by the road crammed in between one bank of the river and steep limestone buffs until the vale opens out where a track leads off on the left to Blackwell. This side of the river is easy on the eye, whereas opposite lies the entrance to the dusty, white world of Topley Pike quarry where buildings, trees and verges seem to be coated with powdery flour. Whether travelling from Buxton or Derby, in my day it would be here that you would alight from the bus having been conveyed to this spot courtesy of the Trent Motor Traction Co. Ltd. There was normally a choice of buses and passengers tended to be treated with more respect, with far more tolerance being evident in those far off days as the following tale proves.

In my early teens a friend and I took a bus to this stop and went off to spend a day grubbing about in the many holes to be found just around the corner in Deep Dale. It was a good day apart from a crawl into Churn Hole that was infested with ghastly, bulbous-bodied, intimidating spiders that suggested in no uncertain terms that this cave was theirs and we were trespassing. It quite put us off for a while. Anyway, in those days our meagre pocket money was insufficient to allow us to obtain even the cheapest of wet-suits, which came as a 'do-it-yourself kit comprising of pre-cut pieces of Neoprene, a roll of yellow rubber tape and a tin of Evo-Stick glue. Consequently we were reduced to caving in thick woolly sweaters and thick corduroy trousers both of which got weightier by the minute the wetter and muddier we became.

Returning late in the day we waited by the roadside for the red bus and as a 'coup de grace' rain began to hammer down with unabated fury. The powers that be had not considered erecting a bus shelter here at this lonely outpost on the A6, so we rapidly became water-logged. Finally the welcome headlights and the illuminated destination board spelling out DERBY hove into sight and stopped. The door of the bus opened and a pale light fell upon two completely saturated mud spattered figures who sheepishly mounted the steps, sodden, drenched to the skin and dripping water everywhere. The driver leaned forward, looked us both up and down, checked our return tickets, then stating the obvious cheerily remarked. "You look a bit wet lads." When we left the bus at the Central Bus Station in Derby the rear seat with its patterned moquette upholstery where we had sat bore two very wet, telltale patches that hopefully the next set of passengers would not interpret as the aftermath of two incontinent adolescents. The point of this anecdote is that in today's world we would have been thrown off the bus, or to be more accurate, we would not even have been allowed onto the bus to get thrown off.

Heading for Blackwell the river Wye flows between lush verdant banks and passes beneath lofty viaducts until the vale opens out a little at Blackwell Mill where a corn mill once operated, but now only a weir remains to bear testimony to its one time existence. The short row of eight cottages on the far side of the river were originally built by the Midland railway about 1866 (costing £142:17s each to build, which will now cost you some £265,000 to buy) to house railway men and their families. It is a sequestered spot despite its location in a triangle of railway lines, its remoteness no doubt exemplified by the fact that initially a train only stopped there only once a week on a Friday to allow the occupants to shop in Buxton in the morning, returning later on an afternoon train. This was clearly a rubbish service so after some protestation by the residents it became a request stop for the railway families. Blackwell Dale Halt consisted of a couple of incredibly short platforms with a platelayers hut for shelter (no expense spared here then) and closed in 1976. It was thought to be the smallest station in the country, excluding some sleeper constructed halts like Bonwm for example in the Welsh Dee valley erected solely for the purpose of picking up two schoolchildren on school days. Another contender would have been Ingra Tor Halt on the spectacular but now sadly defunct Princetown line that wound its way around the rocky tors on Dartmoor. This was also a short wooden platform that originally served the workers from an adjacent quarry and was the only station in the country having the dubious distinction of a sign warning passengers who alighted here of a real danger of adders!

However, all was perhaps not as bad as it might at first appear living at the remote Blackwell Dale. According to my late uncle Bert who drove steam engines along this section of the line from Miller's Dale to Buxton, the innovative cottagers had surreptitiously constructed a chute down the hillside from a siding above the cottages where apparently 'stray' lumps of coal from passing tenders kept mysteriously rumbling down the chute to the coalhouses at the back of the homes. This was obviously a puzzling perk and a well-kept secret (at least from the railway company) for which the residents were truly grateful! This once isolated hamlet is now frequented by tourists, for here you can now leap onto a saddle and gallop away on two wheels provided you have legs fit to meet the demands of pedal-pumping power. The route is the newly opened Monsal Dale Trail which allows walkers and cyclists, and I have both walked and cycled, following the track, tunnels and all, of the former Midland railway. It gives onto some of the most spectacular views to be seen anywhere in this country and I found it both exhilarating and hugely nostalgic to see vistas of the river Wye that I had last seen from a carriage window over four decades ago; and what I would not give to be able to do so again by recapturing the wonderful age of steam and watch the passing panoramas of the dales from the windows of a railway carriage.

As A.G. Bradley wrote in *The Rivers and Streams of England* in 1909, 'It would be preposterous to deny that there is both poetry and sentiment in the corner seat of a railway carriage – everyone with a spark of sensibility must have felt it.' He goes on to say that should you lack this requirement in your character then, 'Such a man would be a dull, unimaginative soul indeed.' Hear, hear!

Because I travelled the line scores of times as a child it would be a sort of mantra for me to remember all the station names along the line. Okay, so it sounds a bit lame now, but I fancy it was more useful than what other kids were doing, which was reciting all the player's names of their favourite football team. So just to irritate you here they are (the stations names that is not the football teams) from Derby Midland Station, Nottingham Road (really a workers stop, but I did get off here once on probably the only occasion a Sunday Rambler's train ever stopped there), Duffield, Belper, Ambergate, Whatstandwell, Cromford, Matlock Bath, Matlock (this section of course is still open from Derby), Darley Dale, Rowsley (this section runs steam trains to Matlock), Bakewell, Hassop, Great Longstone, Monsal Dale, Miller's Dale, Blackwell Dale and finally Buxton; and having in the past relied heavily on the Rambler's train I have got off at every one of these stations at some time or another to begin a walk, with the exception of

Blackwell Dale where just once a Sunday train briefly stopped for some reason, for nobody got on, and neither did anyone get off. On reflection it bore shades of Edward Thomas's famous poem *Adlestrop*. 'The steam hissed. Someone cleared his throat. No one left and no one came.' And like the platform of Adlestrop today, Blackwell Dale is pretty much overgrown.

From here the Wye becomes quickly hemmed in and dwarfed by the towering three hundred feet face of Chee Tor rearing up out of the trees, while at its feet the river is forced between the spectacular overhanging walls of a limestone canyon, perhaps one of the most dramatic scenes in Derbyshire. Rhodes wrote a wonderful description of Chee Tor and aptly compared it to Sir Walter Scott's poetic description of Lock Katrine in Scotland, which I recommend you read. Passage through here for walkers has been made possible by the addition of some sizeable man-made stepping stones in the river bed which has rather taken the edge off the original challenge. Gone are the days when it was necessary to remove ones boots, tie them together by their laces, sling them around ones neck and with rolled-up trouser legs wade merrily through the freezing cold water. It is here that the Midland Railway is transported through the four hundred yards long Chee Tor Tunnel No1 beneath the tor, then bursts out of the sheer rock to leap across the gorge on a single span bridge and immediately disappear into the ninety four yards long Chee Tor Tunnel No2. When Crichton Porteous followed the Wye in the late forties to early fifties, he was obviously not inclined to getting his feet wet and solved the problem by scrambling up to the railway line passing the worst parts of the dale by walking through the tunnels, something he does not actually recommend. Now days this is no longer a problem as all the tunnels are accessible to everyone and illuminated throughout. Porteous however was well aware of possibly finding himself, rather alarmingly, sharing the dark confines of the tunnel with a London to Manchester express that was not going to be stopping for anything or anyone. On a rather calmer note, Gilchrist strongly suggests seeing Chee Dale by moonlight when, according to him it is at its best, so if you are up for a bit of night-time rambling then this is the place to go. Somewhere among the treed valley is the start of Miller's Dale and the scene of a brutal murder.

It is said that the young squire Bagshawe of Wormhill Hall situated above the dale came across five poachers one dark night filling their creels with fish from his bit of the river. A melee took place in the river itself as the poachers set about the squire where a watery scuffle took place as they gave squire Bagshawe a severe thumping leaving him dead on the bed of the river. All five poachers were later arrested then acquitted by pleading in their defence that it had been the squire who had started the fight first. This tenuous plea sounds like a school playground excuse considering squire Bagshawe was outnumbered five to one. Nevertheless, they got away with it and no doubt with the poached fish as well. This tale sounds very fishy to me in more ways than one.

Flowing on into Miller's Dale village the river is made to work in a landscape now dotted with mills producing cotton, corn, meal and even distilled peppermint. Croston notes the 'old fashioned whitewashed building' that in his day was a corn-mill where the Tideswell road joins the path along the river bank. The station at Miller's dale, despite its remoteness among the dales was a particularly important and busy railway junction catering not only for passenger trains but also for a vast amount of quarry traffic at work on its numerous sidings. The station was substantial enough to have its own subway between platforms, thus placing it in the posh category by the locals, and why not for its fame was widespread having been popularised in 1963 in a song called *Slow Train* which lamented the closure of so many wonderful rural lines and stations. It had been written and performed by the world famous duo Flanders and Swann with the opening line 'Miller's Dale for Tideswell' and each stanza finishing with 'I won't be going again, on the slow train.' Well, they just don't write catchy, toe-tapping songs like that anymore, now do they? Although to be perfectly honest, probably few people know the song anyway and the very mention of Flanders and Swann is more likely to bring on a chorus of the *Hippo Encore* 'Mud, mud, glorious mud, nothing quite like it for cooling the blood' and so on. There were sidings for coal, limestone and cattle and for a time the station did sport a signboard stating it was the Junction for Buxton Station and Tideswell before reverting back to plain old Miller's Dale. (Blacks 1872 guide has it down as Miller's Dale for Wormhill.) Another claim to fame was that it was the last station in England to have a post office on the platform. Today it is a popular rendezvous for day trippers, walkers and cyclists who years ago would have enjoyed the services of the corrugated tin shack opposite the station entrance and known as the Wriggly Tin café. It was built around 1897 and had to be lifted and moved from its original location a few yards downhill to its present site when it was realised that a railway line was planned to cut through the rear garden, thus putting an end to any thoughts of a lazy summer afternoon being spent snoring in a deckchair. Sadly it was closed in 2002 after serving its last cup of tea. Today there is in its place a mobile van in the station yard where visitors gather prior to their day of outdoor activities and also avail themselves of the revamped station toilets. These toilets are not what I would rate as a truly great nostalgic experience, but alas, it is pretty much the best there is on offer of what remains of the old Miller's Dale station.

One of the many firms in the past operating out of the sidings was the Miller's Dale and Oldham Lime Company (which because of enormous demands for limestone amalgamated with other quarries to become part of the Buxton Lime Firms Co. Ltd.) that had a siding adjacent to the lime kilns situated below Priestcliffe quarry. I mention this quarry in particular as it ceased working in 1930 after a humongous landslip caused the entire face of the quarry to slide downwards and forwards immediately halting any further production. This happened after the face became unstable due to it resting on a layer of compressed volcanic ash, which had formed into a kind of slippery clay that was incapable of supporting the weight of the exposed rock. Now that collapse would have created quite an ominous rumble that no doubt arrested the heartbeats of more than a few quarry workers at the time that probably thought the end of the world was nigh.

Veering away momentarily from the hard facts, I cannot help thinking that it would surely have been an unmissable opportunity if for example, somewhere on the hillside above an amorous couple just happened to be enjoying the freedom of the outdoors, fortuitously reaching a climactic crescendo that simultaneously coincided with the event in the quarry. The all-to-familiar question of 'Did the earth move for you, darling?' would certainly have brought forth an encouraging 'Phew!! I'll say it did!' as indeed it would have as half a hillside moved forward several yards. A large deep gash is very much in evidence above the quarry even today as a lasting testimony to man's meddling with nature and coming a bit of a cropper.

Continuing for a moment in the same vein of calamitous collapses Mam Tor or the Shivering Mountain as it is sometimes called near Castleton, is continually disintegrating of its own free will to the extent that it has destroyed and swallowed the original main road. The precipitous side exposed to the action of rain and frost continually detaches fragments of rock that slide down which according to the Right Hon Lord Avebury in *Scenery of England* will over a period of time eventually cause it to bury itself beneath its own debris. Evidence points to man having foolishly built an ancient camp on the top of Mam Tor, some of which has long since gone over the edge. This would have taken place long after they had abandoned the place so I guess they were really not too fussed about the inevitable demise of their labours. The summit area is notoriously wind swept, the strong winds having been responsible for more than a few mishaps with carriages and horse riders having been blown to oblivion. A recorded tale of a lesser event tells how a greyhound pursuing a hare on the lofty height chased it to the very lip of the precipice, whereupon the hare, who should have known the terrain better, leapt over the edge followed by an enthusiastic dog hot on its heels. Not surprisingly both were found dead several hundred feet below. Anyway, either the weather was much better a few thousand years ago or else they were a very hardy race of people inhabiting such an exposed hilltop. The only upside of living on the top of Mam Tor as far as I can see apart from the view, is that they would never have to worry about getting the washing dried.

The Rev John Magers Mello both curate and rock hound states in his *Handbook to the Geology of Derbyshire*, published in 1866 that during the many falls of rock, 'it is said that fields, trees, and even cottages were overwhelmed.' Considering its history of serious instability it almost beggars belief that someone came up with the barmy idea of building a road across the face, the remains of which now contributes to the general mess of rubble and stone lying heaped about the base of Mam Tor. There was another notable incident of the 'moving of earth' at Dove Holes due to the careless hand of man. One night in April 1933 a large, and as it turned out unstable 'Mont Blanc' mountain of lime waste shed with a terrifying rumble five hundred tons of slag that avalanched over the road almost reaching the height of the cottages. Clearly this was not conducive to a good night's sleep, which was fortuitous as a quick-thinking woman hung out of her bedroom window madly waving a light to alert the Buxton Royal Mail van from crashing into the debris. To say it caused an inconvenience would be a bit of an understatement for it required copious amounts of dynamite to clear the road, which is possibly the last thing you want to hear if you have been up all night and have a thumping head through lack of sleep.

The cluster of houses, cottages, church and inn that comprises the hamlet of Miller's Dale proper sit either on the hillside, or alongside the river as it continues to curve its way towards Litton Mill. The Angler's Rest, which has been a pub since 1753 to which the adjacent Angler's Cottage was once said to be part of (present day deeds still carry a ban on selling liquor from its two rear ground floor rooms) nestles cosily by the riverside, its only one time competition The Railway Hotel having been demolished in the 1970s. I can recall many a riotous evening spent drinking in the Angler's Rest in the late sixties when someone might wander in, have a pint or two then bash out an impromptu performance of *Classical Gas* on the piano after which, and given time, the evening would degenerate into a bawdy all-time singing session which you would not want your mother to witness, especially when some person three parts cut would balance on a table and have to be stopped from acting out the one-eared elephant gag. Should you not be au fait with this particular piece of entertainment then let me assure you that not knowing will in no way inhibit you either socially or intellectually in life, and I am not about to explain it in this book. Often in an inebriated state I would stagger outside into the black night, cross the footbridge over the river Wye and claw my way through the hidden hazards of Priestcliffe quarry to an isolated cottage perched high on the very brink of the hill.

When Croston walked from Bakewell to Buxton he called at the Angler's Rest in the hope of getting some refreshment to fuel him for the journey still ahead. He records how he was, 'refreshed on oatcake and cheese, the only fare the humble larder could afford.' So, no recommendation for them in the Good Pub Food Guide. It is here that the river gets a small, if somewhat intermittent top-up from a stream coming in from Monk's Dale where foundations of a monk's chapel remain along with some evidence of small-scale tilling of the land where they might have grown a few tatties or some other useful crop. The land was owned by Lenton Priory and some of their income came from the flour mill on the bank of the nearby Wye. Porteous on his travels veered off into Monk's Dale in order to get home to Peak Forest and records that he was trespassing at the time and describes the dale as having, 'the silence of a deserted world' much as he imagined the old Peak to have been in the time of wolves, bears and wild cats. Had this still been the case then I think he would have thought twice about taking Monk's Dale as a route home and stayed at the pub for the night. In the distant past Monk's Dale bore the brunt of glaciation and still has plants that have valiantly soldiered on for the last ten thousand years thus marking out this dale as rather a special place.

Once again the valley closes in as the 'freakish meanderings of the Wye' take it past the intimidating overhanging rock face of Ravenstor, a natural magnet for skilled climbers as indeed is much of the dale from now on down to Cressbrook Mill. Perched on the very top among the trees of this leaning cliff is Ravenstor House the former residence of Matthew Dickie, the one-time owner of both Litton and Cressbrook mills. His house is now owned by the YHA. Litton Mill and the few cottages pressed hard against the sheer hillside was once a very isolated and difficult place to get to which contributed greatly to the problems of the mill in its early life. It was erected in 1795 and run by a senior partner Ellis Needham who lured orphans and pauper children from the streets of London and Bristol on the promise of a healthy country life. The exact opposite turned out to be the case for these poor child slaves found themselves in a living hell. Because the aim of this book is to present interesting information wherever possible, yet keep it on a humorous and entertaining level, it would be both unfitting and inappropriate to relate any accounts of what these grossly mistreated wretches were subjected to, which were some of the most appalling punishments and torments imaginable, often resulting in death and suicide. Should you wish to learn more on this subject then I suggest you read the harrowing chronicle of life as a child labourer by Robert Blincoe. Litton Mill finally closed in the 1970s and has since, rather ironically, been converted into luxury apartments and upmarket holiday homes. Although the buildings you see today replaced the original mill after much of it was destroyed by fire in 1847, I bet the tormented souls of those brutalised children still wander somewhere within the walls; and I met a man very recently whose dream was to buy a house in Miller's Dale if ever he could afford one, but he was adamant that he would never live in Litton because of its past associations with the mill.

On a slightly lighter note, years ago there was a grocer's shop in the hamlet that not only sold the necessary provisions for day-to-day living, but also served excellent tea in pint sized mugs. However, had you been around in the year 1818 the last thing you would have wanted with your mug of tea would have been one of Hannah Bocking's special cakes. Hannah was a sixteen-year-old servant girl who had applied for a job and was turned down on account of her having a bit of a temper and being not altogether agreeable in her mannerisms. Instead the job was given to her friend Jane Grant with whom Hannah continued to foster a friendship, albeit a false one. One day they were both out walking in the neighbourhood of the Wardlow gibbet which I can only assume was due to Hannah's bizarre sense of occasion, given the beautiful countryside elsewhere that was at their disposal, when feeling a tad peckish Hannah offered Jane one of her special cakes. Fortunately it was a cake that even Mr Kipling has not followed through on for it was laced with a poison that quickly rendered poor Jane dead, thus proving that it was nevertheless, an exceedingly good poisonous cake! Hannah was arrested and despite trying to incriminate other members of her family in the crime she was found guilty and hauled off to Derby gaol where in March 1819, a mere four days after her trial she swung from the gallows a victim of her own recipe. Public hangings were always a popular crowd-puller and although not overly sympathetic to her crime, the assembled crowd were, nevertheless, rather horrified that someone so young could be that insensitive as to take another's life for no other reason than jealousy. On the face of it she did seem to go a bit over the top just because she failed to get a job, her extreme actions ensuring that she never got a job ever again! Anyway, the popular pint mugs of tea could be quaffed while watching the famous trials on the hill called Litton Slack, where years ago on a Saturday in May, as part of the Six Days Motor Trials, cars of all descriptions were put to the test on the one in three road gradient out of the dale. It is hard to imagine the tranquillity that exists today around the cluster of cottages outside the mill gates being shattered by the roaring of revving engines, clouds of choking exhaust fumes, the smell of overheated tyres and all round mayhem. It all sounds very back-to-front cloth driving caps and goggles accompanied by a babble of spiel about RPMs, torque, thrust and other equally boring banter.

Having been harnessed to provide power, the river Wye continues gliding past this melancholy mill that in more recent times produced Nylon and Terylene, into a bosky dale and a world of quiet serenity, flitting kingfishers, gliding trout and craggy overhangs that eventually make up the euphonious Water-cum-Jolly Dale. This stretch is very much a fishermen's river for it harbours a population of rare Rainbow Trout that was introduced here from North America in the 1890s and apparently flourishes nowhere else. Free access is permitted through Litton Mill yard where in the past a fee was payable, which was given to charitable causes. From here on a track hugs the river for just over a mile linking Litton Mill to Cressbrook Mill where surprisingly the dale opens out from its rocky confines to verdant riverside pastures. Walking along the road towards Monsal Dale the recommendation was to take tea on the loveliest of riverside lawns at Riverside farm. Close by at the footbridge crossing the Wye, 'On a hot day this is a good spot to bathe the feet in the river, in fact a bathing costume and towel on this ramble would be very useful when the weather is right.' The key words then as they are today are, 'when the weather is right!'

Back in Water-cum-Jolly Dale the scenery is particularly sylvan in spite of being at one time marred by the 'ruthless tree felling' of beeches in particular of which a writer once said in a somewhat vitriolic manner,

'I like least of all to see a fallen beech, especially considering the ignoble use to which most of the timber is put, to make heels for women's fancy shoes!' It does seem a little incongruous, as indeed it would be to spy a female walking the muddy and often flooded track in a pair of fancy high-heeled shoes. Boots or wellies yes, fancy high-heeled shoes, I think not. And certainly not the route that Rhodes took through the dale in 1824, which seems to have been along little more than a sheep path above a rocky ledge that pretty much scared the pants off him for, 'I now looked back upon the path I had passed and trembled at my own temerity.' A change of underwear needed here I fancy. Some way along the dale tucked into the bank of the river is the rusting remains of a small waterwheel that drove a pump which Porteous fondly recalls, as he came upon, 'the waterwheel placidly pumping, chug, chug, chug.' He concluded that here was a place, 'in which to dream of old romances.' It chugs no more for it is seized solid with rust and neglect but is still a fine place to sit on the wall and enjoy the peaceful surroundings.

Just before you come upon Cressbrook Mill complete with its Italianate style rooftop bell chamber – the very bell that once rung the workers to their machines in the morning – is a quirky building at the end of a row of cottages originally known as Apprentices Row, then Pancake Row, but now a more acceptable Dale View. This strange house seems almost to be stuck onto the sheer rocky buttress. The Gothic style building is part castellated with pointed arched windows presenting the idea of a castle with a hint of the ecclesiastical, but as an architectural oddity it serves as a welcome stop where you can quench your thirst and satisfy a grumbling stomach, as you sit outside admiring the waterside view. However, life for the young children who worked at the cotton spinning machines was far removed from the present bucolic scene that we enjoy today.

The mill was built in 1779 by Richard Arkwright and conditions here were only marginally better than those endured by the unfortunate poor creatures who worked at Litton Mill. The children once again either orphans or from poor and destitute workhouse families were still subjected to horrendous mistreatment at the hands of sadistic overseers as well as by the owner William Newton. He was not amiss to drawing blood with beatings by a hazel switch despite being known as the Minstrel of the Peak. This dubious title was bestowed upon him by a well-known poet Anne Seward, known herself as the Swan of Litchfield (where do they get these titles from?) who encouraged Newton in his poetical endeavours and who seems to have had a bit of a crush on him. To my way of thinking it seems absurd that a man who is capable of beating a defenceless child senseless can be sufficiently calm in his mind to create poetry, even though he was not really very good as a poet.

Perhaps he knew this in his heart and took his frustrations out on the child workers. Then again, man's inhumanity towards his fellow man has throughout the ages come easily. I think it is time to get back to the more acceptable splendours of the area. Apart from a mill close by here that once distilled peppermint from wild mint that grew abundantly on the nearby hillside, there was also at one time a lucrative trade sending bunches of Lily of the Valley to the Manchester market.

The dale of Cressbrook enters the Wye valley through tree-lined slopes, yet it rises from a bleak upland of limestone rocks headed by a strange geological phenomenon called Peter's Stone. This isolated dollop of limestone according to legend, was supposed to revolve each time a cock crowed in the vicinity. Given the fact that this lump of limestone has been around for an awful long time then it seems only reasonable to assume that if this was the case then it would have witnessed a lot of cocks crowing in its time, sufficient I would have thought for it to have ground itself by now into a heap of dust. Clearly this is not the case, so let us look at theory number two. This is based on a geological probability that Peter's Rock is a slippage (like Priestcliffe quarry), as it rests on a bed of clay which would aid its ability to whizz round and round, like a spinning top at every crow of a cock. The thing you have to ask yourself is why would it? And what pudding-head thought they saw this happen. You can only assume it must be something in the local water.

Another thing about this place is that at the stone in 1815, or at least somewhere near (Gibbet Field) the last man in the country (contestable), namely one Anthony Lingard was left hanging in a cage from a gibbet. His crime was strangling to death Hannah Oliver in order to steal a pair of red shoes from her to give to a local lass who had his bun in her oven as they say. He hit upon an ill-thought out plan to try and bribe the girl bearing his child with the gift of the stolen shoes to say it was someone else who had done the dastardly deed of giving her a swollen stomach. What an absolute bounder. Anyway, he had overlooked the fact that the pair of red shoes had been especially hand-made for Hannah and must have been the Jimmy Choo shoe of their time and consequently easily traced to the now dead Hannah. You can see already that Anthony was proving himself to be a sandwich short of a picnic. The thing is they became a bit of a proverbial albatross around his neck because the pregnant lass refused the shoes, being wary of how he had procured them, and quite right to. Anthony was now stuck with a pair of red shoes. They were no good to him for half-witted though he appears to be, no way was he going to be seen trotting about in a pair of bright red women's shoes, but least of all they were now no longer of any use to Hannah as she was as stiff as a board and her walking days were well over.

Sometime later the hapless Anthony must have wondered why he had bothered in the first place as he was having his neck permanently and terminally stretched at Derby gaol. His body was then transported back to Wardlow where the gibbet alone cost fifty three pounds, eighteen shillings and eight pence, without all the other expenses incurred in getting him there from Derby, thus proving that even back then funeral expenses were costly. Some things just never change. And Lingard never even had the luxury of a coffin. The up side of this tale though not from Anthony's point of view, is that the gibbeting turned out to be a real fun day for the villagers as stalls, booths and probably the equivalent of a WI cakes and crafts tent were set out around the gibbet. Even the vicar came in search of his flock because his church had suddenly become empty of worshippers and he was forced to deliver a fiery sermon alongside the gibbet in which Lingard, now looking a little worse for wear was incarcerated in a natty iron cage.

Now here was a man who did not give up easily, the vicar I mean not Lingard. The message behind sticking the corpse in an iron cage was that crime does not pay and would remain a constant reminder to people passing that way. No doubt it proved a bonus for the local crow population who must have thought Christmas had come early as they descended on the giant bird-feeder squabbling and squawking over who would get the juicy bits, the eye-balls, followed by any other part they could get a probing beak into. Yummy! This was after all, no dainty blue tit and chaffinch nut holder. This was for the big boys in black with strong sharp beaks that could take an eye out in … well, the blink of an eye! The old corpse, eventually blackened by weather, with skin dried like strips of pemmican hung around for the best part of eleven years by which time it had been reduced to a pile of bleached bones. These were only removed after the locals complained of the racket they made when the wind was blowing strongly. They were obviously oblivious to the fact that in essence what they were witnessing, albeit somewhat macabre, was the first ever wind chime thereby missing an opportunity to have it swinging outside a front door, or maybe not.

The road running along the valley floor following the Wye passes a track on the right that once served the small station of Monsal Dale, although it did have a siding or two put in for Cressbrook Mill. All that remains of this 'romantically situated station' is a length of platform and a hut, and close by in the hillside are the abandoned tunnels of a coal mine. Here an ill-considered and thoughtless piece of mining by a Mr Frogatt landed him with a fine for the sum of thirteen pounds, twelve shillings and nine pence for illegally tunnelling beneath the railway line. The consequences of this are of course obvious, the fine being a lot cheaper than the cost of a full scale railway disaster just waiting to happen. Monsal Dale station was very popular in the past with walkers, who could alight from a train and find themselves passing beneath the railway bridge, crossing the river, which prior to the bridge, was simply a ford to walk a choice of magnificent dales.

Following the road up a steep hill will bring you to the Monsal Head Hotel, which was apparently built to sate the unquenchable thirst of the railway navvies laying the track bed and constructing the viaduct. It no doubt did a roaring trade for the navvies had a fearsome reputation, particularly on payday of sinking copious volumes of ale followed by a good punch-up then back to work in the morning. If you have the good fortune to find yourself standing outside the pub on a sunny afternoon on Headstone Edge as the older locals once called it holding a pint of beer, then you will see stretched out before you one of the most wonderful and outstanding panoramas to be seen anywhere in England.

Take in the 'Arcadia of the Peak' as it has been called in the past for it is a view panegyrised (what a lovely archaic word) by virtually every writer that has cast their eyes upon it. For example, Croston wrote on first glimpsing Monsal Dale, 'we took the higher road (from Ashford) which soon brought us to the Bull's Head (the Monsal Head Hotel was rebuilt on the site of this earlier inn) and on rounding the corner of the house, the sweet vale, tranquilly reposing in the lap of loveliness, appeared unexpectedly before us, looking like a fragment rent from heaven.' Far below runs the snaking ribbon of the Wye flowing beneath the arches of a railway viaduct built around the 1860s and so utterly despised by John Ruskin. His much quoted lines from *Fors Clavigera* state that the dale was to his way of thinking once Arcadia, but, 'the valley where you might expect to catch the sight of Pan,

Apollo, and the Muses, is now desecrated in order that a Buxton fool may be able to find himself in Bakewell at the end of twelve minutes and vice versa.'

Ruskin was noted for pontificating on occasions (the dubious privilege of a critic) and in this instance he evidently preferred a horse and carriage for transport, as he was clearly not a shareholder of the Midland Railway Company. He probably pinched the term Arcadia from Ebenezer Rhodes who had journeyed through Monsal Dale in the early part of the eighteen hundreds well before the infamous railway viaduct had been constructed and called the dale the 'Arcadia of Derbyshire.' Today the viaduct is very much a part of the landscape and to have once roared out of the blackness of Headstone Tunnel in a cloud of smoke, clearing as you peer out from a carriage window to find you are flying some eighty feet above the valley floor as I have done scores of times in the past is an unforgettable experience and one which certainly lives on in my mind all these decades on. It is now part of the Monsal Trail adventure and rather ironically, Ruskin's objection is now noted on a visitor information board on the very viaduct he so detested!

When Rhodes first glimpsed Monsal Dale he stated in a somewhat exaggerated manner that it was 'Beauty resting in the lap of horror' but then again, he had scared himself witless traversing Water-cum-Jolly Dale on a fearful path. From the now famous viewpoint he refers to a small dwelling called Edge-stone House that was occupied by a young lass called Kate. Rhodes goes on to relate a peculiar story of how Kate had become brokenhearted at the loss of her lover and spent years soaked by rain, lashed by winds and half frozen by snow, a lonely tormented soul slowly losing her grip on both life and reality as she roamed the dale and rocky heights in sorrow and despair. Her malady eased with time but left behind 'traces of the mental desperation it has made.' Years later during a thunderstorm a bolt of lightning passed through the roof of Crazy Kate's (as she was now called) abode where she was seated with her parents. Apparently the lightning, 'dashed the clock to pieces, and broke some dishes; but left every other object in the house uninjured.' I find this an odd ending to the story as I feel it implies there should be some kind of connection between the events of the storm and Kate's future life, but alas there is nothing for at this point Rhodes promptly wanders off in the direction of 'Great Finn' and the Roman encampment. As story endings go, it really is a bit of a damp squib and just as I was about to reach for the tissues.

Perhaps this famous dale is best summed up by Gilchrist who gazed out upon a different landscape than that seen today for he comments on the bare rocky hillsides scattered with ruined sheds and chimneys of abandoned lead mines whose rusting machinery and rotting beams made them look from a distance like castle ruins. He finishes by charmingly describing the dale at dusk when, 'there is no sound save the comfortable lapping of the stream and at times a hollow rumble sounds in the far distance, increases and increases, and the lighted train flies across the viaduct, and, passing the little station, disappears in a further tunnel. But for this connection with modern life Monsal Dale would belong altogether to the distant past.' As a nostalgic I find this an endearing epilogue.

One of the most arresting sights from Monsal Head is the giant shoulder of Fin Cop dropping steeply some five hundred feet to the river where legend has it that near the entrance to the foreboding Demon's Dale, in the bed of the river a spirit is buried beneath a flat stone. Surely there are easier burial solutions than digging a hole in a river bed! The summit of this massive hill is marked by ancient earthworks and a tumulus where early man buried one of his own kind face-down in the ground with a slab of black marble on his skull. More recent excavations have revealed even more sinister goings on after the bones of a young female who showed signs of having died from severe wounds was found in this area. This discovery was then topped by finding eight more skeletons, all of which appeared to have been badly wounded including four babies that had unceremoniously been chucked into a ditch; and in Hobs House cave close by another skeleton was found of an adolescent who may also have been murdered. It is a sobering thought to gaze out over this beautiful pastoral prospect from Monsal Head looking towards Fin Cop knowing that beneath the earth lay the victims of violent murders that had taken place the best part of two and a half thousand years ago.

An obvious outcrop of rock on the hillside is Hob's House, or Hob's Towers where a giant was said to dwell by the name of, yes you guessed it, Hob. I wonder if he used to hob-nob with the other Hob I have already spoke of who lived in Deep Dale? Anyway, it turns out that Hob was a bit of a strange fellow for he possessed mysterious powers that were a benefit to householders. Legend relates how old Hob was a bit of a night owl as he was never seen during the day, but after dark he would sneak into folk's houses and do all the chores in a single night that would have taken a mere mortal around ten days to complete all the tasks. He sounds like a decent sort of chap who must surely have encouraged idleness among housewives. I mean, why bother to do the washing and ironing, and cleaning when all you had to do was leave the kitchen door open along with a sink filled with filthy pots and pans for old Hob to get on with. All you needed to remember was to leave out a brush and dustpan, a feather duster, the hoover, some Fairy liquid, Toilet Duck, a packet of Bold and the kid's empty lunch boxes before retiring to bed. In the morning you would awake and hey presto, old Hob had done the lot and all he requested for his labours was that you leave him a bowl of cream to quaff. Legend omits to say whether he liked single, double, whipping, sour or clotted cream, but if that was his sole diet then I guess he needed to work like a man possessed in order to stop himself becoming grossly obese and dropping dead from a heart attack. Of course being a giant does pose the question of just how would he fit into the average sized house in the first place to carry out all those chores? In spite of Ruskin's scathing comments, a crazed women and a domesticated giant, Monsal dale is a delight to walk and nature has done much to cover the scree scars where masses of debris from the excavation of Headstone Tunnel was tipped down the hillside. The dale ends where it meets the A6 coming down from the lofty heights of Taddington at a place called Lees Bottom, which does not in any shape or form resembles anyone's bottom, but it does leave you confronting the darkly wooded hillside of the unnerving Demon's Dale and the vast expanse of Great Shacklow Wood.

Continuing down this valley of riverside meadows and visible in the woods is the outlet sough, or adit to Magpie Mine. The mine itself is situated high on the tops and far from view and yet connected by this tunnel that is the best part of two kilometres in length and took eight long years to complete. Digging began in 1873 but an extremely hard rock known as toadstone was responsible for the prolonged labour, with no doubt an awful lot of cursing, an awful lot of worn out tools belonging to an awful lot of worn out miners who possibly yearned for a nice cushy office job instead. In 1962 many decades later and long after the mine had closed a roof collapse inside completely blocked the adit to such an extent that the vast amount of water now with nowhere to go created an unimaginable pressure that finally found an exit via an old air shaft in the woods where it dramatically exploded, taking with it a huge chunk of hillside sweeping away trees and a massive amount of earth. Certainly not the place to have chosen for a quiet picnic in the woods, as it really would have turned into a case of, 'If you go out in the woods today. You're sure of a big surprise.' In 1974 the blockage was cleared and an estimated three million gallons of water was released into the river. It has since calmed down to a steady flow from a grated culvert.

The main shaft of Magpie Mine is some seven hundred feet deep which a local man named Ephrain Brocklehurst can testify to, for in 1869 he apparently fell down it leaving someone with the ghastly task of having to scrape him off the floor at the bottom of the shaft. His headstone in the church graveyard in the nearby village of Sheldon reads, 'There is but one step between me and death', which is certainly to the point and had he written it himself with pencil and notebook in hand during his rapid descent, then time would not have allowed him to add more. It is said that the mine joined the workings of another called Maypits and sometime in 1833 a dispute arose between the two groups of miners as to who owned the mineral rights and who was trespassing in whose territory. The situation became heated in more ways than one, as the Magpie miners decided to settle the matter by lighting a fire of straw and sulphur in the underground workings, which resulted in a number of miners from Maypits not going home for dinner that night due to terminal suffocation. I mean, burning straw is one thing, but adding sulphur is a tad harsh by anyone's standards. Perhaps it was the ghost of one of the unfortunate miners that a party of speleologists in 1946 are supposed to have witnessed in the form of a man walking along a tunnel holding a candle before disappearing without trace. During the same trip another spectre appeared in a photograph who seemed to be miraculously standing on nine feet of water which as far as I know only one person has ever been credited with performing a comparable feat and he was taking a stroll across the Sea of Galilee.

Beyond the sough a track cuts across the meadows from the main road, crosses a stone bridge to arrive at a pair of watermills sitting on the very periphery of the great dark woods that sweep around the curve of the dale and the meanderings of the Wye. Over the years these two mills have been used to make bobbins for Coates the thread manufacturers, a sawmill for timber, as well as a place where bones from as far afield as London came to be crushed for fertiliser. I feel there is something slightly sinister about the idea of crushing bones. I think it has to do with an account I once read of a fiendish, not to mention eye-watering device employed during medieval times to make unfortunate victims confess to something they were probably not even guilty of. Anyway, putting aside this dark thought the two mills have water wheels that have not turned in decades and are rusting away at the hands of time, while the leats with moss covered walls are dry and choked by leaves and fallen branches. It is a great shame that no one is able to restore them for they are idyllic in their setting but present a sight of gloomy dereliction, with boarded over windows, a security necessity by the fishing club that now uses them. On a lighter note they featured fleetingly in the film *Women in Love* from the book of the same name by D.H. Lawrence in a scene where Alan Bates rides up to one of the mills and leans his motorbike against the wall. Admittedly this is not much in the way of a claim to fame, but that is really all there is! Close by are the remains of a water driven pump that is testimony to a time when water from the river had to be pumped five hundred feet up the hillside to the village of Sheldon so the villagers could all have a cup of tea, wash themselves and do the laundry.

More industrial remains appear on either side of the river at Arroch Quarry and Rookery Plantation. These were both sites of the once highly prized and highly collectable Ashford black marble. Geologically speaking it is not strictly a marble as we know it from say Italy, but a form of limestone containing carbonaceous (bitumen) and clayey matter. It is known to have been worked as far back as the sixteenth century and indeed even earlier, for the stone slab over the prehistoric skull found in the tumulus on Fin Cop was of this material. It only turns truly black when polished but became particularly popular during the Victorian age in the form of inlaid table tops, statuettes, urns, obelisks and all manner of decorative articles. Prime pieces were put on show at the Great exhibition of 1851 and both Queen Victoria and Prince Albert were said to be avid collectors, as well as the Duke of Devonshire at Chatsworth who purchased many pieces, in particular polished marble columns for displaying busts. As an industry it only really got underway in 1748 when Henry Watson erected a mill by the Wye to install the machines he had invented for cutting and polishing the rock, thus entering the world of mass production. It all came to a grinding halt in 1905 and only the mill foundations are visible today, along with those of another mill close by which rather oddly, made combs from tortoiseshell.

When Croston passed this way on his journey to Buxton he remarked on the marble works of Messrs Twigg & Co, who worked different types of Derbyshire marble as well as the Ashford sort which included, 'entrochal, the corroloid, the bird-eye, the rosewood and the black, the latter being procured from an excavated mine' and all were said to be, 'equal according to competent judges to anything found in foreign countries.' I can recall poking about in these mines in the early seventies and came across a muddy roof collapse that exhibited a mass of rusting metal objects along with an inordinate number of old shoes which struck me as rather unusual. Unfortunately, I was a decade and a half too early to formulate my theory that Imelda Marcos, exiled from the Philippines was hiding out in a weekend cottage somewhere above my head and had decided to throw out some of her alleged collection of over three thousand pairs of shoes, so wherever they came from remains a mystery. There must be an opening here for a joke about abandoned soles but luckily for you it eludes me right now!

Finally the river Wye reaches the idyllic village of Ashford-in-the-Water, which is situated on the ancient Portway and often referred to as The Garden of the Peak. It has been in existence for a long time and appears in the *Doomsday Book* as Aisseford meaning the 'ford of the ash.' The renowned and much photographed 17th century Sheepwash Bridge spans the river that is crystal clear and full of big 'lusty trout.' The bridge is noted for its unusual parapet that swings back on its self to form an enclosure for holding sheep when it comes to their annual bath-time. This is achieved by taking the lambs to the far side of the river where their manic bleating causes the anxious ewes to take to the water, a necessary and possibly more healthy option than today's chemical dip. Carved into the stonework of the bridge is the inscription 'M Hyde 1664' who also went for a dip here, but in his case he was thrown by his horse and found a watery grave among the 'lusty trout.'

The peaceful village with cottages of 'trim flower beds, pebbled paths in front and patches of yellow stone crop or green house leek adorning the roofs' once had a few shops and a shoe-maker. It also once had its own grammar school, but now the village has no school at all. Well, that's progress for you. One of the local pubs, the Devonshire Arms hints at the former owners of the village in the time when it belonged from the year 1550 to the Chatsworth Estate that unfortunately was forced to sell off all the properties to help pay towards some horribly expensive death duties in 1950. Imagine opening the morning mail while seated at the breakfast table in the palatial surroundings of Chatsworth house and reading a letter from the Inland Revenue demanding seven million pounds which in today's money comes in at around two hundred and three million pounds. The shock would be more than enough to make you choke on your bowl of Shredded Wheat, then either instantly try to commit hari-kari with the butter knife, or immediately pack your bags and buy a one-way ticket for the next cross-channel ferry. I am afraid that like the Grim Reaper, when the taxman cometh, there is no escape and to make matters worse, which at this point is hard to imagine, it took the Inland Revenue seventeen years of negotiations to sort the matter out with interest added on. I guess being an aristocrat is not all jolly hockey sticks, pass the port, and anyone up for bagging a grouse or two?

Ashford Holy Trinity church has bits dating back to the thirteenth century and is possibly best known for the Maidens Garlands that hang inside the church. They were funerary garlands made of paper on a hooped iron frame and decorated with flowers and rosettes. The name of the deceased would be written on a glove or handkerchief hanging from the centre and represented the death of a virgin from the village, like Ann Swindel who died in 1798. The last garland to be hung marks the death of a young girl called Blackwell who had the misfortune to drown in a whirlpool, or 'twirl-hole' in the Wye near the marble works in the year 1870. The ceremony would involve six maidens clad in white walking before the coffin and bearing between them the garland. This special tribute was reserved solely for young girls of pure repute and the tradition died out long ago. I am tempted to comment that in today's modern lifestyles there would probably be a lack of suitable contenders, but perhaps I had better button my lip. At present there are only four garlands left hanging, all looking extremely fragile, colourless and aged beneath protective coverings, yet still they exude a sense of the tragic loss of a young life.

Also to be found within the church is a memorial to Henry Watson (the black marble man) who was finally polished off from polishing his black marble. His memorial slab is of course, polished Ashford black marble ... well what else would it be? Outside behind the church can be seen a mound that is said to be the site of a fortified manor house that was granted to Edmund Plantagenet in 1319. Edmund was the brother of Edward II and therefore not to be confused with another Edmund Plantagenet who went by the hapless name of Crouchback, or indeed the better known Edmund Blackadder who is really Rowan Atkinson. All that remains of this episode of Plantagenet history at Ashford-in-the-Water is that somewhere in, or around the mound there is said to be a horde of hidden treasure that is clearly very well hidden, for as yet no one has discovered it. This is not to be taken as an invitation to storm the mound armed with a metal detector, a spade, or even a JCB digger.

There is a road out of Ashford called Longstone Lane that leads not surprisingly to the village of Great Longstone and passes Thornbridge Hall, the one-time residence of owner Mr George Jobson Marples. Now George Jobson Marples just happened to be one of the directors for the Midland

Railway Company and consequently was allowed to become one of the privileged few to have his very own private access to a railway station, in this instance, Great Longstone for Ashford via a flight of steps well away from the public end of the station platform. Here, just to be a bit showy he built a grand castellated structure complete with two towers called Woodlands that housed a set of enormous waiting rooms on the ground floor and equally spacious recreation rooms above on the first floor for his numerous staff and estate workers. However, all did not go well for much of George's wealth came from a considerable shareholding with the German munitions factory Krupp in Essen, which cost our George big time after WWI, and quite right to. By the time of WWII he was well out of it, which was in hindsight rather fortuitous for him seeing as how our bomber chaps gave the Krupp factories a jolly good pasting. Georgie boy was now sufficiently skint to the extent that he had no alternative but to turn Woodlands into flats which he rented out in order to keep his estate going. Despite the station closure in September 1962, a victim of Dr Beeching's 'hit-list' a morning and evening train continued to stop and collect a nursing sister who worked in Buxton hospital, and yet two female college students who wished to do precisely the same trip were denied the right for in the eyes of the railway board, picking three people up would be tantamount to re-opening the station. This seems rather petty and unnecessarily silly in today's climate where so many stations are to all intent and purpose closed and un-manned where passengers either pay for their ticket from a machine, or else purchase one on board the train. But then to the layman, sense and logic rarely plays a part in such corporate decisions.

Having physically worked its way past numerous mills around Ashford the river Wye gets harnessed yet again just outside Bakewell by another of Arkwright's mills (he invented the mechanisation of the process for spinning and carding), which was erected in 1779 for spinning yet more cotton. In more recent times the mill was used for the production of lead-acid batteries, including some rather big boys to provide power for submarines. From here the Wye finally gets to play the role of an unhindered river as it flows serenely through the Gothic style arches of Bakewell Bridge which was built around the 1300s and has been photographed from every angle possible and painted by many artists throughout its long life. Bakewell, or *Badde cum Well*, meaning 'the bathing well of the Saxons' or *Badequelle*, or *Baquewell* according to the Doomsday survey was at one time pretty much owned by the Duke of Rutland who smartened the place up quite a bit and even brought gas lighting to the streets. The thing about Bakewell, and this is purely personal is that I find it difficult to not use the word 'Bakewell' and the word 'pudding' in the same sentence. This could be related to the fact that whenever I am in the vicinity, or actually passing through the town I am compelled to stop and purchase at least one pudding and devour it like a man who has been starved of this cardiac inducing treat for several months, which in truth is normally the case.

The generally accepted version of the great Bakewell Pudding mystery is that it came into being as the result of a cakey cock-up by a seemingly witless cook in the employ of a Mrs Greaves the landlady of the White Horse Inn (now the Rutland Arms Hotel) that stands at the head of the town's main thoroughfare. In the year 1820, although this date is contestable, it is said that the cook was instructed by Mrs Greaves to make a strawberry tart for a client. The simpleton cook managed to get this spectacularly wrong and accidently produced what we know today as a Bakewell pudding. Despite the culinary calamity and the fact that the finished product looked like a terrible disaster that in no shape or form resembled anything remotely like a strawberry tart, it was nevertheless, served up to the customer who declared it a truly scrumptious triumph. Its future production became clothed in secrecy and upon the death of Mrs Greaves, the top secret, classified recipe was left in her will to a Mr Radford who in turn passed it on to a Mr Bloomer whose present day shop

Bloomers still produces puddings baked allegedly to the original secret recipe, as in fact do two other outlets in Bakewell making the exact same claim. But as I hinted at earlier, this legendary tale could well be bogus, for it has been said that Lady Dorothy Vernon of Haddon Hall back in the 1500s, and just down the road from Bakewell, was more than a little partial to a piece of pudding; and some say that the puddings origins lie even further back in time.

It may have been quite interesting to know what reaction it would have mustered if this culinary catastrophe had been put before the judges, had the cook been a contestant on the programme *The Great British Bake-off*, or as it would have been billed back then, *Ye Olde English Bake-off* along with Master Hollywood and Mistress Berry.

"Ye Gods! What is this foul looking object you have placed before me?" exclaimed a shocked Master Hollywood.

"Why t'is my strawberry tart Sur," proclaimed the cook somewhat sheepishly while scratching her head beneath a mop cap.

"STRAWBERRY TART!" yelled a bemused Master Hollywood unable to believe what his eyes are seeing. "This is not a strawberry tart. This is not a strawberry anything."

"Did you not read the instructions properly?" enquired Mistress Berry.

"Oh no Ma'am," replied the nonplussed cook. "I b'aint be able to read nuthin' Ma'am. Truth is, I can't write me own name."

"But this thing" ranted Master Hollywood. "This thing, this misshapen dollop of pastry with its brown, gooey filling that resembles the village cess-pool is unlike anything I have ever come across before."

"But t'is very tasty Sur," retorted the cook, fluttering her eyelids at him and heaving up her more than ample bosom.

"I have to agree," chipped in Mistress Berry with a mouthful of pudding, "despite the fact that you have a soggy bottom oozing grease, it is extremely tasty." This will no doubt create an image in your mind that would be best not to dwell on for any length of time. "And did you mix in all the ingredients properly?"

"I did that Ma'am" replied the cook. "In fact I put in a little something or other of me own."

"And what exactly was that something or other?" enquired both the judges.

"Ooooh, I can't tell 'ee that, t'is my special secret," giggled the cook.

Both judges had to agree that it was indeed a tasty pastry, but nevertheless it was still in their eyes a gastronomic accident, which of course is precisely what it was and which subsequently proved to be an unstoppable success.

The thing is for a few pounds you can now treat yourself to a tourist tea towel, Made in Great Britain (that in itself makes a change these days) one hundred per cent cotton that seems to reveal the secret recipe. But before you get too excited and rush out to buy all the ingredients and put the oven on, I am afraid that in spite of it being headed 'The Old Original Bakewell Pudding Shop' the ingredients listed are for 'The Secret Recipe' and nowhere does it have the words 'Bakewell Pudding' written on it. This is a canny bit of marketing on the part of the manufacturer to avoid being sued by thousands of customers whose attempts at making a Bakewell Pudding turned out to be not quite right, having discovered at the very last minute that the final line of the listed ingredients ends with 'and finally a pinch of …! Well, surely you did not think it was going to be that easy to get your hands on the recipe did you? After all, even the great Mrs Beeton in her 1907 updated edition of Household Management has in the index 'for Bakewell Pudding see Bakewell Tart' which is an entirely different animal altogether; and to bring the whole mystery into modern times the best that Mary Berry 'The Queen of Cakes' herself can dish up is a recipe for a Bakewell Tart. So there you have it, the secret ingredient remains as baffling as Montezuma's Lost Treasure, the Abominable Snowman and the lost Ark of the Covenant, unless of course, you really do believe that Harrison Ford, alias Indiana Jones did find it and the Ark still lies to this day in a wooden crate stored in some forgotten warehouse.

For some unknown reason writers in the past have generally overlooked the unassuming Bakewell pudding even though it's supposed place of origin, The Rutland Arms does normally get a mention. For example Rhodes on his visit to Bakewell wrote that the hotel was, 'a large and well-conducted establishment', but failed to mention puddings, though he did prefer to spend the night at the Castle, 'the first house on the right after crossing the bridge.' Bradshaw's *Railway Handbook* now made famous by Michael Portillo's television series *Great British Railway Journeys* recommends The Rutland Arms, but no mention of a pudding. Porteous speaks of the Rutland Arms Hotel but does not allude to anything to do with a pudding. Even something as relatively recent as the 1962 edition of the *AA Illustrated Road Book of England & Wales* gives a brief description of Bakewell as though it was puddingless. The first occasion this is remedied for the general tourist is in the 1939 edition of the Penguin *Guide to Derbyshire* that says of Bakewell, 'The town possess several good hotels and cafes and in most of them its speciality, the famous Bakewell pudding, may be sampled.' When reading Price's *Derbyshire Dales* published in 1953 we discover that Bakewell makes up a quartet of towns famous for their confectionary (the other three being Banbury, Eccles and Goosnargh) with Bakewell still holding on to its closely guarded secret recipe. I just feel that the world of the modest Bakewell pudding should be made broader and more expansive. After all, the iconic Australian painter Norman Lindsay for example in 1930 devoted an entire book to a pudding. Okay, I admit it was a fictitious pudding and a magic one as well, for sometimes it was, 'a rich odoriferous steak-and-kidney, sometimes boiled ham roll, and sometimes an apple dumpling', but either way you look at it, it was a deservedly fine pudding and the Bakewell pudding certainly has potential in the world of literature. Phew! I really do think it's time to move on as I am now feeling truly 'puddinged' out.

Bakewell was once home to the Union Workhouse, which was said to be, 'a large and well regulated establishment' that lay adjacent to a Dispensary and Lying-in Institution which would, 'have been of great advantage to the poor of the neighbourhood.' I wonder if a Lying-in Institution is somewhere where you could lie in bed all day, a habit still perpetuated by much of today's student population! The Rutland Arms with its noble edifice has always been the main hotel in the town and noted for its customers being regaled with, 'the choicest of viands and the best wines.' Many of its visitors came to take the waters of the tepid chalybeate spring that was accessible via 'a delightful promenade' after the bath was housed in a new building in 1697, courtesy of the Duke of Rutland. It comprised of two shower rooms and a news room where bathers could relax after a dip and read the London papers and magazines. The water running at sixty degrees Fahrenheit and containing the usual elements of iron, magnesium, with various other compounds were especially recommended as beneficial for sufferers of chronic rheumatism who would find themselves floating about in a bath measuring thirty feet by sixteen feet in water that emitted copious quantities of carbonic acid gas, the effervescent effect of which some bathers no doubt found conducive for their own effervescent gaseous contributions brought on by over-indulgence of rich foods. In J.B. Firth's book *Highways and Byways of Derbyshire* he notes that the Dukes Bath House was, 'a curious place with a narrow oak staircase, all turns and twists' and that the arched vault above the bath, 'is as bare and as cheerless as whitewash can make it.' Apparently a second chalybeate spring had been found by the Haddon Road out of Bakewell and the Urban Council immediately seized upon the idea of developing it, until that is, the Duke of Rutland got wind of their scheme and sent one of his agents along to quickly nip their aspirations in the bud. Despite its location in the Peak and the pleasantness of the town, Bakewell has never been capable of rivalling Buxton as a spa centre.

The clients of the Rutland Hotel had the privilege of being able to fish the Wye for trout and grayling and to make their lives even more comfortable the hotel laid on a private taxi service to and from the railway station that was situated on a hillside a short distance out of town. Many times in the past have I sat on a bench waiting for a train at the end of a day's walking, listening to the sounds of songbirds in Manners Wood that mantles the hillside behind the station. The buildings at Bakewell Station still remain and have been restored, but gone is the old LMS holiday 'Caravan Coach' later to be known as Camping Coaches that first came into being in 1934. Back then hiring the coach for a week's holiday (provided you arrived and departed by train) would have cost a mere three pounds and ten shillings that in 1965 had only risen to twelve pounds and ten shillings, which was still a bargain in anyone's book. Close by the station are the barely discernible bumps of an ancient earthwork called Castle Hill that is said to be the remains of a fortification thrown up by Edward the Elder in the year 924 after he had purposefully marched up from Nottingham to cause the Danes a bit of aggro by showing them just who was the boss around here.

A notable building that always gets a mention in any book about Bakewell is the church of All Saints, 'with lovely views and quaint epitaphs', perched on a hill overlooking the town. Outside the church is a Saxon cross reckoned to be from around AD750, while inside and in particular the Vernon chapel, built in the latter part of the 14th century, there is not only the tomb of Dorothy Vernon of Haddon, but also an overwhelmingly huge monument to Dorothy Vernon of Haddon. She certainly made sure she would be remembered in history, or maybe she suffered from a serious identity crisis. She would no doubt have been tickled pink had she known that a few hundred years on the film star cutie Mary Pickford would play her in the 1924 silent film *Dorothy Vernon of Haddon Hall*, a historical drama based on a novel written in 1902 entitled *Dorothy Vernon of Haddon Hall*. Clearly no problem with coming up with a title there then!

Legend has it that Dorothy eloped with Sir John Manners although it is now thought to be untrue and ranks alongside the equally questionable rumour that the same Dorothy stuffed herself on Bakewell pudding seemingly before the gastronomic mistake had happened, so it appears that someone somewhere has been spreading porkies. On both accounts, we will probably never really know for sure, but they did manage between them (that is John and Dot, not Dot and the pudding) to produce four children. Today the church is open to all visitors, whereas on the day Croston decided to call in he found the place locked. Fortunately, 'a laughing, blue-eyed girl, in a gipsy hat, who came tripping past', summoned the old sexton who eventually appeared hobbling along holding a bunch of enormous keys. The church houses many fine architectural features from differing periods as well as some interesting sculptured effigies of the departed, which will occupy you for quite some time seeking out all the treasures. Afterwards you will be in need of a good cup of tea which you will find in the many outlets the town has to offer for alas, Mrs Beswick's fine tea house opposite the church has long gone, as I suspect will be the case with Mrs Beswick herself!

Before saying farewell to the charming town of Bakewell and following the river Wye down to Haddon Hall, I feel compelled to relate the extraordinary story, part fact, part fiction, of the *Witches of Bakewell* and their subsequent hanging in the year 1608. Ebenezer Rhodes came across this tale and commented that at this period of history you only had to be 'an old, ugly, poor woman' to fulfil the recognised criteria for being labelled a witch and subjected to, if found guilty of the, 'dreadful crime, punishable with the severest of inflictions of the law', which to put not too fine a point on it meant death by drowning, hanging or being burnt at the stake. Not what you would call a great choice there then. Clearly if those qualifications were still the case in this day and age then there would be an unprecedented surge in sales of Sanatogen, Botox injections, and crowds beating a path to the door of the nearest plastic surgeon. The supposed real version of the story concerns a young Scotsman in lodgings at a house in Bakewell who was awakened one night by the voice of his landlady Mrs Stafford and her accomplice in the room beneath him apparently reciting incantations to the Devil. Suddenly the chanting ceased and the room plunged into darkness, whereupon the lodger, rather foolishly as it turns out muttered to himself the chant he had overheard and before he knew what had hit him, he found he was being prodded from a deep sleep by a watchman who had discovered him in a cellar in London wearing (the lodger that is, not the watchman) only a nightshirt. The Scotsman who understandably was more than a bit baffled to find himself so far away from his lodgings and almost indecently dressed was duly hauled before the magistrate that same morning to be charged with vagrancy. Pleading not guilty he related his story to the magistrate and offered as proof the fact that his clothes could be found back at his lodgings in Bakewell, where indeed they were found by some local officers with a search warrant. As a result of this tenuous evidence (let's face it, it was far from fool-proof) Mrs Stafford and her side-kick were unceremoniously carted off to Derby jail where they were tried, convicted and executed as witches. Oddly enough, nobody seems to have posed the question, how did the Scotsman get from Bakewell to London overnight in a few hours and wearing only his nightshirt? You can certainly rule out going by train, National Express coach or Flybe and teleportation is strictly for Dr Who. In Price's account he comments that if there is a moral to this bizarre story then Mrs Stafford should have taken the sensible step of getting rid of all the lodgers clothing, for perhaps he had been a wily young Scotsman who had not paid his rent.

While still on the subject of strange events the B6001 leads from Bakewell to Hassop, which admittedly is not on the banks of the Wye but it does have a dastardly murder pinned on its door. On the morning of Christmas Eve 1866, Edward Wager had been drinking at the local pub and staggered back home to find his wife was entertaining her neighbour Alice Hancock. Now Edward was noted for having a very short fuse and a very violent nature which his poor wife usually bore the brunt of, so when he came through the cottage door and let fly because Alice Hancock was in his house. (I might have understood it if it had been Mr Hancock his wife was entertaining.) Hannah fearing the worst ran out of the house and hot-footed across the fields with Edward in full pursuit, yelling he would kill her if he caught up with her. Tetchy or what! It transpired that later that day a miner was passing near to Deep Rake lead mine when he spotted Hannah's body floating in the dam and reported it to the local bobby. Wager was arrested in the early hours of Christmas day (which put an end to any thoughts he may have been harbouring of a hearty Christmas dinner and a game of Scrabble afterwards) and sent for trial. At the hearing two miners came forward claiming they had seen Wager kicking seven bells out of his wife near the dam where she had been found. An examination of the body was carried out by a doctor with the unfortunate surname of Wrench (just think if he had been a dentist), who declared that he had found broken bones in her mouth consistent with being kicked in the face. He also went on to say that she was very fat, with a very fat liver caused by excessive drinking, and to finish off this image of not very desirable femininity she was as bald as a coot. The wig she normally wore had presumably floated off in the water. Clearly she was no dream girl. The outcome from all this was that Wager received the death sentence that was later commuted to life imprisonment. Despite Edward Wager being a particularly nasty piece of work, I cannot help but wonder whether he was better off serving a life sentence in gaol as opposed to returning to a life-sentence with a bald-headed, booze-ridden fatty.

Not wishing to place any sort of stigma on the village of Hassop as a place to be wary of, there is another tale that results in death relating to fifteen-year-old Arthur, son of Henry VII who just happened to be strolling past the ancient cross at the village crossroads when a ghostly apparition appeared, forewarning him of an early marriage followed by an early death. Well, I bet that cheered him up no end! When he returned to Haddon Hall where he was staying and feeling a tad down in the dumps after his encounter, he was immediately sent back to London and told to make speedy preparations for his forthcoming marriage, which understandably took him by surprise. He was betrothed to Catherine of Aragon and within a mere five months of being wedded, young Arthur came over all queer, took to his bed and uttering the words, 'O the vision at the cross at Hassop', promptly passed away. This proved to be a bit of a bummer for our Catherine, but she went on to marry Henry VIII (serious mistake) who in time got rid of her (with her head by way of a change still intact) and upset the Pope along the way in favour of his new bed-mate Anne Boleyn, and the rest is as they say, history.

Leaving Bakewell the river Wye torturously twists and turns, wriggles and writhes, elbows and oxbows its way into the parkland of Haddon Hall, a stately pile that over many centuries has been occupied by the Avenells and then the Vernons and the Earls and Dukes of Rutland. At one stage of its history the house was abandoned by the Rutlands in favour of their larger residence of Belvoir Castle and consequently Haddon remained uninhabited for over two hundred years from 1700 until 1920 Then the Duke and Duchess of Rutland decided to restore both the house and its gardens to their former glory. Because it is little changed in its entirety Haddon is considered to be an outstanding example of a fortified manor house despite it never actually having been subjected to any form of attack throughout its long history. And history it certainly has for Mee notes that, 'It stands as a mirror of six hundred years in the history of the Dukes of Rutland having both Saxon and Norman stones within its walls.' In the years between 1870 and 1890 Henry James an American writer who finally settled in England after becoming a British subject wrote a variety of articles for the periodicals of the time, which were eventually published as a collection in a book called *English Hours*. He approached Haddon Hall while walking along the banks of the Wye one day and noted its grey walls as being set among some haunted old elms. At the time of his visit Haddon would have stood empty for some considerable time, which for James added an air of melancholy to the place where he suspected ghostly footfalls haunted the cold deserted rooms whose inner walls kept the past entombed and the present very much excluded. Another rather dispiriting outlook is presented in 1760 by historian, antiquarian and politician Horace Walpole who perhaps in a mildly sneering manner described Haddon as, 'an abandoned old castle of the Rutlands in a romantic situation, but which could never have composed a tolerable dwelling.' He would certainly not have lasted five minutes in a modern dwelling on a present day housing estate. Rhodes on his visit to the hall speaks of its, 'gloomy rooms, old hanging tapestries and dark carved ceilings, rich with crests and armorial bearing, all of which help feed the imagination of the visitor and take over his senses.' In his opinion, 'Haddon is a linke in the chain by which he (the visitor) is more intimately connected with a period of time and a race of beings long since passed away.' This still holds true of a visit today. Rhodes viewed Haddon as a sombre house, which he found thought provoking and not somewhere that had him splitting his sides with laughter. Perhaps at the time he was feeling a tad crabby having been harassed earlier by a phenomenal number of swallows that were nesting beneath every conceivable frieze. Shades of Daphne du Maurier *The Birds* here, though more likely to be remembered for Alfred Hitchcock's 1963 film version. Another visitor was the stoic Celia Fiennes who side-saddled on horse-back to Haddon which she says was '2 mile from Bankwell' describing the hall as, 'a good house all built of stone on a hill and behind it is a ffine grove of trees and good Gardens, but nothing very Curious as ye mode now is.' So not overly enthusiastic there then as she trotted on her way, '9 mile over the Craggy hills (no smooth surfaced

A6 in her day) Whose Bowells are full of mines.' There is something that does not quite sit well in my mind about the word 'Bowells' being used in the same sentence suggesting they are full of holes, if you see my meaning.

In contrast to the previous accounts, in the book *Evenings at Haddon Hall* written and edited by Baroness de Calabrella, she opens with the lines, 'In the most singular and romantic, and withal the most beautiful of the diversions of our all-beautiful England – the district of the Peak – is situated on the noblest of these architectural relics (Haddon) of the times of Chivalry and Romance.' Baroness de Calabrella who was born plain old Catherine Ball became a renowned English socialite, adventurer, writer and publisher who at some time during her life managed to purchase a property in Italy that came with a seigniorage which then allowed her to proclaim herself a Baroness. I must refrain from any comments about delusions of grandeur. Anyway, in her book, normally summed up as, 'a series of romantic tales of olden times', she gives a reasonably detailed account of the house's interior at the time when it would have been fully occupied and a place of great gaiety. Although the book is part fact, part fiction, the Baroness does relate a story concerning a, 'curious instrument attached to its post, resembling a handcuff', near the door of the buttery. She was informed that its purpose for any guest who at any stage of a feasting festivity refused for whatever reason to quaff a goblet of liquor being offered by the host, then this amounted to an insult and the miscreant was escorted downstairs. Here his wrist would be clamped in the handcuff which was attached well above head-height and the said goblet of liquor poured down his sleeve. As punishments go during this period of history it was pretty tame stuff, but probably somewhat uncomfortable. Rhodes also makes mention of the odd custom adding that cold water was often poured down the sleeve of an unfortunates doublet or so he was told by an old servant who was his guide that day. Today this curious relic has been moved and now hangs almost un-noticed by an entrance into the Banquetting Hall, a matter that could be easily remedied by attaching a severed arm clad in a slashed-sleeved doublet to the manacle. Now that really would be eye-catching.

Haddon Hall had quite a reputation in the past for lavish banquets and generous hospitality, yet it still boggles the mind to learn that some one hundred and forty servants would be in attendance to fulfil all of the necessary tasks. Records show that in 1789 for example, John Henry Manners the 5th Duke at the age of only nine celebrated his succession to the title with a bit of a bash that included two hundred and fifty tenants, a number that apparently swelled to near on ten thousand as the party got underway and the word obviously got around! I mean to say, this is gate-crashing big time! Refreshments came in the form of four oxen and sixteen roasted sheep, (what no jelly and blancmange!), a copious amount of ale sufficient to get anyone drunk who wished to get drunk, and other sundries like flour, groceries, wines and spirits, butter, eggs and cream, one hundred pecks of oatmeal, bread and salt. There were specialist attendants and the disco was performed by the band of the Sheffield Volunteer Corps for the sum of '£26:5s.' The total expense for this grand rave-up came to '£618:12s:6d.' Now in 1789 that was one hell of a lot of money, and that must have been one hell of a party! And while on the subject of numbers, the main Gallery in the house is well over one hundred feet in length and floored in oak said to have come from the single trunk of a mighty specimen in the park whose root alone provided sufficient twenty two inch wide boards to create the steps leading to the Gallery. That must have been some big old tree! The duke was not only famed for his boisterous shindigs where his well-heeled cronies stuffed their faces all night long before boozing themselves senseless, but also for not forgetting his tenants who occupied various parts of his estate. Both for them and the 'gentlemen of Bakewell' and surrounding areas he built in the park at Haddon a fine bowling green that on occasions proved to be extremely popular. Unfortunately it appears to have been a short-lived venture for after only a couple of years or so by the year 1816 it was reported as being neglected and considerably overgrown. One can only hazard a guess that the 'gentlemen of Bakewell' had found other pursuits and consequently lost all interest in rolling their balls across the duke's turf.

Another one-time owner of Haddon was George Vernon the uncrowned, self-appointed 'King of the Peak' who had occasion to set himself up as both judge and jury by trying a man in the Great Hall who had been arrested and suspected of murder. Now at this time in history it was commonly believed by all and sundry that if a person guilty of a murder placed his hand upon the corpse of the murdered then copious amounts of blood would gush forth from the corpse, thus proving their guilt, and as likely as not creating an unnecessary mess on the floorboards. At this particular trial old George just happened to have the murdered body to hand, so it was duly wheeled into the hall and the suspected criminal asked to perform the ceremony of the laying on of the hands. This proved to be just a tad too much for the suspect who in a flash ran out of the room and at a great rate of knots, legged it up the road where he was doing pretty well until his pursuers caught up with him at Ashford-in-the-Water. They were a very keen bunch and it is doubtful whether the criminal would have even had time to mutter to himself anything along the lines of, 'There is never a bus when you want one', before they strung him up in a nearby field appropriately called Gallows Acre, or was it so named after the hanging? Who knows? After all, just because he scarpered rather than touch the corpse does not necessarily make him guilty. I know plenty of folk who cannot stand the sight of blood, which may well have been the case here, if the suspect truly believed that by touching the body blood was going to spurt out everywhere. Anyway, guilty or not, he got his neck lengthened and that was that. The story goes that old George Vernon got a bit of a ticking off from the powers that be in London for playing both judge and jury, but he escaped a possible hanging himself by claiming he was King of the Peak and acted within his own domain or kingdom. Nice one George. Delusions of grandeur, but it paid off!

An alternative version to this tale is provided in *Pinnacles of the Peak* written by Clarence Daniel who tells of a 'Scotch pedlar' who visited Haddon a couple of times a year to sell draperies and trinkets to the servant staff and was also quite pally with Sir George. On a particular occasion he failed to turn up and enquiries were made concerning his whereabouts, which were eventually answered when the toll-keeper's daughter turned up at the hall delivering butter and eggs. She readily admitted that her father had killed the pedlar then buried his body in the garden, but for some bizarre reason had kept the head in a pan in the house. Perhaps he had notions of cooking it. Enter the old joke about always leave the eyes in when cooking a sheep's head as it will see you through the week. Well, I did say it was an old joke! Anyway, with the promise of a few bob in her pocket as a bribe from Sir George the daughter duly delivered the head to Bakewell. (Daddy is not going to be too pleased about this!) Sir George eventually took his seat on the magistrate's bench and addressed the accused as, "You rascal and villain, you have murdered my favourite Scotchman, and here is his head which your own daughter procured for me", followed by the sentence of immediate hanging. Clearly Sir George was more than a tad livid while the father of the girl was more than a bit put out at being shopped by his own daughter. A gallows was erected at Ashford Bar from which the condemned man dangled, and at the time this story was related in a barber's shop, the field was still called Galley-acre Field. In keeping with the former version Sir George was summoned to London and escaped with a salutary admonition.

Often the landed gentry would appear to be a law unto themselves and their quirkiness was quite often questionable, as is shown by the gastronomic fancies of the fourth Duke of Rutland. Not only was he given the dubious title of Viceroy of Ireland but when it came to riding, drinking and eating he tended to live life by the seat of his pants. This gung-ho trait of his does not really account for his apparent obsession of consuming eight turkey eggs for breakfast, which you cannot help but think proved contributory to the fact that he died at the mere age of thirty-four. I mean to say, who eats turkey eggs anyway, let alone eight. Personally, I think my bowl of porridge oats followed by toast and honey sounds far more appealing and I will not be changing it for turkey eggs any time soon. I bet Edwina Currie would have waggled a knowing finger at him.

I cannot leave without making mention of Haddon's greatest story which some romantics have classed as the 'greatest of English love stories' even though it has been pretty much proved that it never actually happened. I refer of course to the alleged elopement of the beautiful Dorothy Vernon and her handsome, dashing lover Sir John Manners, at least that is how the story would have you believe. Inevitably there are slight variations that have crept in over time, but generally they all revolve around a knees-up at the hall with all the guests getting rowdy and more than a bit tipsy. Now either young Dotty was sent to her room to escape unwanted attention from leering lecherous drunkards, or she just took the opportunity during all the mayhem of merrymaking to quietly bunk off into the night through the now famous and much painted (that is to say by artist and not meaning numerous coats of emulsion) doorway and down the steps into the waiting arms of her hooded lover, leaping onto a horse and galloping off into the darkness. They rode ardently down the road to Aylestone in Leicestershire where they tied the knot. The lengths some people will go to for a cheap guest-free wedding. This is the bare bones of the tale that visitors are told when standing in revered silence before the door, which is known as Dorothy Vernon's Door, which of course leads out onto (yes, you've guessed it) Dorothy Vernon's Steps. I bet someone got brain ache thinking those names up. In spite of the Vernons being Catholics and the Manners Protestants, there seems no reason to suggest that either families refused or disapproved of the liaison between Dotty and Sir Johnny or their subsequent marriage, as the two sides were not at loggerheads with each other.

This tale of romance has passed into legend, yet it still holds its own to arrest the present day visitor to Haddon and strike a starry-eyed note in the minds of those of a passionate disposition even though it had been pretty much discredited. One of the most damning pieces of evidence seems to be that both the Dorothy Vernon Door and the Dorothy Vernon Steps were according to architectural historians not built until after the pair had been married. Therefore, unless our young Dotty Vernon possessed the same magical powers that allowed Harry Potter to walk through a brick wall to catch the Hogwarts Express at King's Cross station, then I am afraid she did not pass this way. Greatly impressed by the story was one William Bennett, who fancied himself as a bit of an author and wrote in 1823 a three volume novel based around the legend called *King of the Peak, A Romance*. However, before you rush onto Amazon to try and find a copy, you may do well to listen to the words of Firth in his *Highways and Byways of Derbyshire* who says that it has such dire dialogue that he is amazed at, 'Three volumes of this trash and yet the pretty legend survived it! What a marvellous tribute to the imperishability of romance!' With or without the legend, Haddon Hall remains a truly unique piece of history and as such it has been recognised as a valuable location for films like *Pride and Prejudice, The Other Boleyn Girl, Elizabeth* and the BBC's production of *Jane Eyre*. Even Arthur Sullivan had a crack at it with a light opera called *Haddon Hall*, but it never really caught on as the public much preferred operas by both Sullivan and his partner Gilbert.

Finally on a more sombre note, many tourist to Derbyshire will have experienced the frustration of not being able to get even a glimpse of Haddon's splendours through the barrier of beech trees and others beyond in the park that obscure all but the very tops of the chimneys This tantalising peek is still very much the same today and there is only one way to overcome the matter, which is to put your hand in your pocket and pay out the two shillings entrance fee it would have cost you in 1949. Alas it is not 1949 and it will now cost you ten pounds. Neither could the house be viewed in the days when it was possible to pass by on a train. Prior to this the 6th Duke of Devonshire at the time would only allow the railway to go through his property provided it could not be seen from his very grand Chatsworth house and vice-versa. The constant wrangling and changing of plans took so long that the duke passed on and his successor refused to have the railway anywhere near his property. This left the only other possible route through Haddon's grounds and the Duke of Rutland jumped on the previous band-wagon by also dictating that the line could only pass through his estate provided he could not see it when he was having a morning stretch in his jim-jams by the bedroom window. In order to comply with his wishes the railway went to ground, so all you would see as you chuffed along would be a glimpse of the sooty walls of the one thousand and fifty yards long Haddon Tunnel that eventually took the railway forward after fourteen years of wrangling and arguing. Unfortunately, the topography of the land meant that the tunnel could only exist by constructing a 'cut and cover' section which in essence was an artificially built tunnel and only then would the railway be out of sight from the Dukes windows. I wonder if he slept well on the night of 2 July 1861, or even had it on his conscience, for earlier that day his demands had caused the death of four navvies when part of the artificially constructed roof collapsed killing them in an instance. The railway has long gone and the tunnel now sealed off although it continues to collapse in places which is not surprising as it was a very difficult task to undertake and despite all the many times I passed through it on a train, I had no idea that some of the covering in places consisted of only eight feet of earth! The other anomaly connected with this section of the railway is that the esteemed Joseph Paxton who had been instrumental in originally trying to persuade the Duke of Devonshire to allow the line

to pass through Chatsworth estate promptly built a fine Italianate station at
Rowsley which then became redundant because it was in the wrong place
when the line was re-routed towards Haddon. I bet he was truly gutted.
The station building does still exist as part of the commercial outlet of
Peak Village, sitting among a miscellany of retail outlets like an island of
railway architecture, solid and well-proportioned as is to be expected of
a Paxton design. At the time of writing it was occupied by a shop selling
old varieties of sweets along with jams, cheese, oatcakes, odds and ends
of bric-a-brac and some galvanised buckets. I am sure Paxton would turn
in his grave. All is not totally lost from this era for a short distance down
the road heading south on the A6 will bring you to Peak Rail, a heritage
line running steam trains to Matlock; and here you can purchase a ticket
and trundle down the line following the river Derwent viewed through the
window of a swaying carriage. Here you can see the sights, sniff the smells
and soak up the sounds of nostalgia, as I have done along this line that I
travelled so often and so many years ago. It is pure escapism and absolute
therapy, because as A.G. Bradley so rightly says in his *Rivers and Streams
of England,* 'It would be preposterous to deny that there is both poetry and
sentiment in the corner seat of a railway carriage – everyone with a spark
of sensibility must have felt it.'

Finally we are on the last lap of the river Wye as it continues to all but
tie itself in a convolution of watery knots on its way to the final destination
of Rowsley. Its wriggling ways inspired poet John Gisborne to put pen to
paper and write;

The tortuous Wye
Appears. Mark how reluctant he withdraws!
How he turns back on many a lingering curve,
As if enamoured of the groves and towers
He lately passed. (Haddon Hall)

The poor old river seems to wallow in confusion to the extent that it no longer appears certain of just which direction it should be heading, so to solve the problem it splits in two to create an island before joining again in time to merge quietly into the waters of the river Derwent. Rowsley is mentioned in the Doomsday survey for there has long been a settlement here and in the period 1870 – 1872, John Marius Wilson compiled his Imperial Gazeteer of England and Wales in which he describes Rowsley as, 'a village and a township of Bakewell parish', where it, 'stands on the river Derwent at the influx of the Wye, and on the Derby Buxton railway.' He quotes the following statistics of, 'a railway station with telegraph, a post-office under Bakewell and a hotel.' The population was a mere two hundred and ninety-five persons and fifty-three houses. Bradshaw in his railway compendium tells us that there are omnibuses available to meet all trains that will take you to either Bakewell or Chatsworth for the grand price of sixpence. There were also Post Horses in readiness.

Most references to Rowsley mention the Peacock hotel. It is Rowsley's equivalent of Bakewell's Rutland Arms hotel. The Peacock was originally built in 1652 by John Stevenson who was an agent for Lady Grace Manners of Haddon Hall, and with its stable block to the rear it is almost a stately home in its own right. If I may digress here for one moment there is an odd reference to Lady Grace Manners by Gilchrist when he visited Haddon. He remarks that the 'dominating spirit' as he entered the Long Gallery was of her, 'death mask that hangs in a glass case under the great east window. It is the face of a sad and worn-out lady with the bitterness of death upon her lips.' The thing about this is that a mask taken from the dead face of Lady Grace is never going to portray her looking her best, now is it? I mean to say, what was Gilchrist expecting a cheery grin and a wink! Lady Manners is still on show today looking tight-lipped and grey-faced and not at all well. In days past when I stayed at Sandon Hall as guest of the Earl of Harrowby, outside my bedroom door was a death mask of Napoleon gazing at me every time

I left the room, and apart from his skin having turned very black, he did not look too well either! The connection of the hotel with the exotic bird the peacock is that it appears on the Manners family crest. Before it became a coaching inn, it was for a time the dowager house to Haddon. There is an extraordinary tale that relates to a porcelain Minton peacock that once stood in the reception area of the hotel. Apparently the Minton factory may only have made five of these birds and the one in reception was salvaged from the wreck of the Loch Ard, which had sunk of the coast of Victoria in Australia and by fair means or foul had found its way back home. Many noted people have stayed at the Peacock including the poet Longfellow, and the painter Landseer, famed for his painting the Monarch of the Glen and not so famous for occasionally having it away with the Duchess of Bedford. Well, a chap needs some relaxation from painting. Croston who by now had virtually explored the entire length of the Wye also stayed a night at the hotel and entered through the ivy-clad porch that was festooned with, 'piscatorial implements suspended in the porch', or fishing rods and creels to you and me; and here, 'within the snug and comfortable old parlour, we spent a pleasant evening in the society of cheerful friends.' How enviably civilised that sounds. Henricus also remarked that the Peacock inn was, 'one of the most comfortable (and at the same time reasonable in charge) in Derbyshire.'

Close by stands another fine old building the Grouse and Claret which was formerly the Railway Hotel having been constructed after the arrival of the railway to Rowsley in 1847. The railway itself has been responsible for Rowsley having in the past its fair share of dignitaries, although in truth they were on their way to Chatsworth and rarely glimpsed beyond the station platform. Many left via the subway that protected them from the gaze of the public as they were escorted to a waiting carriage, which would whisk them up the road to the Duke of Devonshire palatial home. Among the rich and the celebrated came King Edward VII, and King George V accompanied by Queen Mary. In its heyday the railway at Rowsley had been a massively important freight terminal, containing a myriad of sidings at least one of which belonged to the Express Dairy who set up shop in 1933 on railway land. Express Dairies built a creamery which became a huge collecting point for all the dairy farms in the area and I can recall seeing milk tanker wagons containing thousands of gallons of milk waiting to be hauled down the line by steam train to Cricklewood. I bet the factory workers were never short of a spot of milk at tea breaks.

Meanwhile, back at the river, the island caused by the Wye developing a last minute split personality was land that became the site of many mills over the centuries all draining the final dregs of power from this very overworked river. One mill still remains as a reminder of a past industrialised age in the shape of Cauldwells, and this particular mill became distinguished by being uniquely driven by a water turbine machine. Formerly it had two water wheels to do the work of turning eight pairs of millstones for grinding flour and another three pairs for animal feed. Although today it is no longer able to produce flour, it is nevertheless an attraction in its own right with a shop where numerous different types of floury products can be bought which must surely set it aside as a baker's Elysium. It exists as a tourist venue for the curious, housing a forge and old stone workshops alongside worn cobbled walkways and the background rumble of turning mill machinery.

From here the Wye flows a short distance before it loses its identity and merges effortlessly with the waters of the Derwent to continue its diluted journey south. Rhodes like Croston had pretty much travelled the course of the Wye and bade it an emotional farewell with the words, 'Adieu, thou lovely river! I have traversed thy lovely banks from thy source in the vicinity of Buxton, to where thy clear and silvery stream mingles with the yellow waters of the Derwent.' A fitting finale to one of the county's most captivating and picturesque of rivers. For me a fitting finish would be to cross the old packhorse bridge (it has been widened twice to meet modern demands) that spans the Derwent and sit down with a cup of tea and a bun in the tea house which used to stand opposite the bridge. Sadly it is no longer there and neither is my tea and bun. A pint of ale in the Peacock? Why not.

4.

Telling Tales of
Two Rivers.

Compared to the Wye the river Lathkill is comparatively short being only around five miles in length on a good day. I say on a good day because you cannot always guarantee it will be there as it often chooses not to put in an appearance from the dark confined recesses of Lathkill Head cave, its usual source, but chooses to gurgle up out of the ground some distance on near Cales Dale. Even after that it can occasionally get temperamental and decide that enough is enough and promptly disappear back underground and emerge further on. This as you can imagine causes the fish a bit of a headache as they often become stranded in pools and fissures in the river bed not quite knowing what to do next apart from curse evolution for not giving them even a couple of legs to enable them to climb out of the water and leg it down to the next pool.

Charles Cotton, Izaak Walton's sidekick and a keen angler himself declared the Lathkill to be, 'the cleanest stream in England', for it teemed with the, 'reddest and best trout in England.' The Lathkill has not been a heavily worked river for it only passes one place of habitation, the small village of Alport, but nevertheless, it has had to work a few mills en-route connected with both corn and mining. The top end of the dale beyond the resurgence cave of Lathkill Head is a dry dale known as Ricklow Dale noted mainly for the mass of tumbled rocky waste from the past industry of quarrying marble; and a little way on beyond the end of this dale lies the village of Monyash, which is a good place to begin.

Monyash is another early Peakland settlement, being recorded in the Doomsday book as 'Maneis' which is assumed to mean 'many ash trees' of which centuries ago there were, but few now remain. Whereas nearby One Ash Grange that presumably only had just the one ash tree now has many. As far back as Saxon times de-forestation of the area was well underway clearing for farmland and for use in the lead mining industry, all of which took its toll on the local tree population. The village of Monyash sits in a basin of limestone beneath which lies a squidgy layer of clay, and being impermeable it traps water that rises to the surface in the form of ponds or meres and once formed the village's water supply. Now only Fere Mere remains and like almost everyone else in the country the dwellings are now on mains water supply for which they get billed. No more free water for them. In its industrial hey-day when Monyash was referred to as the 'Lead mining Capital of the Peak' the village was a hive of activity with blacksmiths, shoe-makers, dress-makers, joiners and wheelwrights all plying their trades. The Barmote or Great Court that decided miner's claims and settled their disputes met here and the High Peak Miners Standard Dish, a measuring device that held sixteen pints (the Low Peak Miners Dish holding only fourteen Winchester pints was held in Wirksworth) was for ore valuation and not for filling with beer, which would make the traditional drink of a 'yard of ale' look pretty tame stuff. Predictably, the lead mining industry declined and even the marble quarries ground to a halt after two hundred years of operation in the early 1900s, and the last lead mine Eagle mine closed in 1925. Consequently the village of Monyash declined along with its population who went in search of work elsewhere. The village was once on the mail coach route for passengers travelling from Leek to Bakewell via Longnor, Crowdy Cote and Ashford. Monyash is now back on the map as a popular centre for tourists, which it certainly was not shortly after the war as is apparent in Nellie Kirkham's description of the place in 1947. She says the village, 'lies still and peaceful about its pond, but the verges of all the roads leading to it still tell loudly of the war, for they are piled high with bombs.' Off-putting and unnerving to say the least!

The name Lathkill probably derives from the Norse 'Hlatha gyll' meaning 'ravine with a barn.' Now Lathkill Dale is not short on ravines, but the barn, well that is another matter altogether. It is not unreasonable to assume that the headwaters of the river Lathkill begin to gather on the clay layer of the Monyash squidge basin and by various underground passages and abandoned mines makes its way to Lathkill Head Cave where it gushes forth in wet weather, well sometimes. Gilchrist in the *Beautiful England* series wrote, 'Beyond the dreary upland the Lathkill gathers itself in mysterious underground passages, and appears suddenly as a fair sized stream' and he goes on to praise it for in his opinion, 'Of all Peakland rivers the Lathkill is the purest; its waters have the clearness and lustre of rock crystal.' The head of the dale is a bleak ravine of limestone outcrops and sparse vegetation made even more inhospitable by the jumbled heaps of limestone spoil that serve as a reminder of the marble quarries that once operated here from around the 1700s for two hundred years or more. They were mining a type of grey crinoidal limestone that was popular with the Victorians as ornaments, table tops and fire places, but sadly the quarrymen did not make any effort to clear up the mess after they had finished and as a result they have left us with some very big rockeries. Rhodes describes it as a place where, 'the rocks had been blasted and rent to pieces with gunpowder, and their natural features defaced.' He seemed not to be over-enamoured of the place. Then again it was clearly not a favourite spot with Croston either, for he declares, 'the scenery here is of an extremely gloomy and savage character', with, 'great grim lifeless walls of naked rocks.'

I think it is safe to assume that in their eyes at any rate, Ricklow Dale scores 'nil points' but it would take more than that to dissuade woolly-hatted, woolly-headed Arnold from turning up with his hapless walking group. In all likelihood he would have positioned himself on a suitably commanding block of stone to launch into an address akin to William Wallace giving a rousing speech to his warrior highlanders prior to the battle of Stirling Bridge. It is a foregone conclusion that Arnold had done his homework, which would enable him to deliver a spellbinding talk (or so he misguidedly thinks) beginning with, were any of the group at all aware that they were standing in a gully that was begun in the late Pliocene times. Errr, No. During the stunned silence that followed Arnold retrieved from his rucksack a claw hammer he had got from his shed that morning and proceeded to bash a piece of rock which shattered in all directions thus proving that without his large round spectacles, Arnold would have most certainly taken out one of his own eyes. Holding aloft his geological trophy and undaunted by his near miss, Arnold gabbled on to the fidgeting group how this rock containing fossils some three hundred and sixty million years old is a combination of bioclast wackestone and gigantroproductid packstone. Now despite wackestone and packstone sounding like a firm of solicitors Arnold failed to hold the attention of the group until he let slip that he had been lead to believe that a good specimen of this type of limestone could be found in the entrance to the Bull's Head in Monyash. At the mention of the Bull's Head the assembled group of walkers by now completely bored out of their skulls scarpered quicker than a pack of crazed lemmings in the direction of the pub, not so much to see the legendary entrance slab, but to buy themselves a desperately needed pint. Bemused Arnold was left behind alone on his rock with only the faithful, lovelorn Enid Barroclough who seized the opportunity to coyly sidle up to her hero and ask if she could have his rock specimen to place on her bedroom window sill. No man could ask for more.

Today Ricklow quarry has an eerie desolation about it with its shattered fallen rock faces and unstable looking holes and cavities that lead off into a dark world. As Rhodes commented a couple of hundred years ago, 'We supposed we should find some little spot yet unprofaned by

avarice, where rock and foliage intermixed compose a beauteous picture:-
we were mistaken;- neither tree nor shrub find a home in Ricklow Dale.'
Clearly not a place he will be re-visiting! Nature is slowly meeting the
challenge to re-vegetate the spoil but it will never be able to fully disguise
the destructive hand of man which even now is evident on a very minor
scale as fossil hunters continue to bash away at lumps of rock to release
the shell of a few million years old gigantropod. It is worth including here
Croston's description of his descent with a companion into Ricklow Dale
and its quarry if only for its dramatization. He recounts the event as, 'an
undertaking difficult and dangerous withal, every few yards bringing us
to the verge of some crag or precipice, beyond which a step would with
certainty have precipitated us into the depths below. Nothing daunted
we began the task, creeping slowly round a ledge of rock, then struggling
down the hillside through crag and brake and over slippery heaps of
shingle and loose stones. Manifold difficulties beset our path; sometimes
we had to crawl between the roots of bushes, then to wade through heath
and fern, and among copse wood and briar which thickened in places
until they became barriers to further progress.' Before actually reaching
the bottom of the dale there were, 'crumbling boulders that afforded but a
treacherous footing, now and then plunging ankle deep in hollows, thick
with decayed brown leaves, and concealed from view by the overhanging
vegetation.' After which there was, 'more scrambling, battering, and
scratches, another slope or two, and then the bottom of the dale was
reached, when we had time to breathe and look around us.' What bravura!
What drama! It sounds more like they were descending into the Grand
Canyon than Ricklow Dale.

Having touched on the subject of unrequited love with mention of Enid
Barroclough, no self-respecting dale could call itself such without having
a Lover's Leap, and Lathkill Dale is no exception, for there is a rocky bluff
known as Jane Hambleton's Rock where, and this will come as no surprise

to you, local lass Jane Hambleton flung herself into space in the name of love. However, there is more to this story as rather stupidly she did not stop at just the one go. Oh no, our Jane was keen as mustard to prove her undying love in front of her spectator boyfriend who egged her on for reasons which on the face of it seem to be more than questionable. His idea was that if she wanted him to take her up the aisle to wedded bliss then she had to jump off the precipice, which she did, landing safely in front of him. This is where his intentions become debatable for he asked her to perform her flying act again. Brimming with passion, or consumed with sheer lunacy, Jane throws herself off yet again and lands unscathed apart from a broken finger. I venture to suggest that as far as her boyfriend was concerned things were not quite going according to plan, and so as a show of her true love for him he asked her to fling herself off a third time. At this point you have to ask yourself, was Jane so utterly smitten as in 'love is blind', or 'love knows no bounds' or is she really a sandwich short of a picnic? The answer will never be known for jumping Jane (no relation to *Jumpin' Jack Flash*, the Rolling Stones 1968 ... Ye Gods, I can't be that old surely!) launched herself one more time into space but despite having now practised two reasonable landings she hit the deck so badly that she never got up ever again. No surprise there then, after all, she had pushed her luck somewhat.

One writer relating this tale comments that poor Jane did indeed fulfil her wish of being taken up the aisle but sadly in a coffin, which is not at all what she originally had in mind. I guess it saved her from the expense of a wedding dress and a reception. As for her supposed lover, well he may very well have been smiling to himself in a pew on the back row during her funeral, but I would have thought that the stigma of his former girlfriend's demise resting fairly and squarely upon his shoulders would surely have cast considerable doubt on the future likelihood of a horde of local lasses beating a path to his front door for a date.

Another anecdote concerning Lathkill Dale, and we may as well get all of the deaths out of the way early on, relates to another outcrop of rock called Parson's Tor, and no prizes for guessing who took off from the top of that precipice. The victim was one Rev Robert Lomas, incumbent of Monyash and of dubious character. The simple version of his fall is that Rev Rob trotted over to Bakewell one day to have a chat with the vicar there who it turns out was away giving the last rites to a dying man. The Rev hung around until the vicar returned who asked him to dine with him, which he did as by now he was feeling a tad peckish and had not brought any sandwiches with him. By the time dinner was over it was dark outside and Rev Rob rode away into a dismal night of drizzle that later turned to sleet. Unable to see exactly where he was heading he dismounted and unwittingly tried to pull his horse onwards over what turned out to be a precipitous drop. The horse having more sense than Rev Rob was having none of it and during the ensuing tussle the reins snapped and Rev Rob was pitched into eternity where he was found the following morning as a cold corpse lying at the base of the tor on blood stained rocks. Not quite the sort of sight you want to come across if you have just had breakfast. Rev Robert Lomas was buried in the churchyard at Monyash. This version of the tale, take note, was written at a later date by a curate who seems to have glossed over several issues, if the following account is to be believed.

This rather more illuminating version concerns a bit of a melee that took place between Methodist preacher John Benet (no relation to Gordon) and a drunken clergyman the Rev Robert Lomas. Lomas is said to have barged into the chapel with a rowdy mob of boozed-up miners just as Benet was getting the congregation tuned up for a bit of hymn singing, as you do. Lomas, who was clearly off his trolley pulled Benet off a chair, tore his clothes and gave him a good shaking. You can see they were not the best of friends and a clash of religious fervour took centre stage, with the pair of them trying to out-preach each other. One member of the congregation was so appalled by this unprecedented turn of events that he rose to his feet no doubt pointing a finger of disapproval at the drunken clergyman and prophesised that Lomas would die a deservedly violent death. In 1776 Rev Robert Lomas was discovered with his neck snapped at the bottom of Parson's Tor. I know which makes the better story, but I wonder which one is nearer the truth? As with so many Derbyshire legends and stories of half fact and half fiction, the not really knowing is the key that holds our continued curiosity.

Meanwhile back in the living world the next notable feature is Lathkill Head Cave from which the river Lathkill appears, at least in wet weather, for it issues from a 'cavern in a mass of broken rock' which Rhodes calls 'pleasingly romantic.' Firth describes it as where the river, 'springs from a cavernous opening in the rock in a long, rugged defile.' When I passed it in March 2014 it was most definitely 'springing' with gusto and running crystal clear. By August of the same year it was as dry as a bone. More often than not it refuses to surface until somewhere around the junction of Cales Dale where it gurgles up among the rocks and decides to make an effort at becoming a river. This was not the case after the wettest of winters in 2013–14 when Lathkill Head Cave was most certainly doing its job as the source of the river. Cales Dale is a short, steep ravine that leads at its head to One Ash Grange which is now a farm. The Grange was once part of the Haddon estates held by the Avenells and one William Avenell being in a generous mood or perhaps he was just fed up with doing the weeding gave the land to Roche Abbey in Yorkshire which is how it came to be associated with erring monks. It was operated as an outpost, a kind of monastic penal colony where hooded monkish miscreants (Were they the equivalent of present day Hoodies?), were sent to farm the land, although history does not record just what constitutes being a naughty and unruly monk. Please, no jokes about unclean or disgusting habits. By the side of the path leading to the Grange is a ruin thought to be a cold store or cold pantry for the monastery. It has a well-built arched stone entrance which leads to a chamber hewn out of the rock where a pair of storage shelves can be seen consisting of stone slabs on stone plinths. This would certainly be a necessity in the days before chest freezers, particularly if the monks consumed anywhere near the amount of food for example, that the religious order of the Winchester Brethren ate during certain recognised festivities like Christmas, Twelfth Day and Candlemas Day. Records show that on one occasion a forty-six and a half pound chunk of roasted sirloin of beef, three large mince pies and copious amounts of ale were consumed at dinner and for supper they ate plum broth with three joints of mutton with more beer. On Palm Sunday they were given green fish (sounds like they would be reaching for the Rennies after that one), milk pottage with three pounds of boiled rice in it, three pies containing twenty-four baked herrings and of course, more beer. Admittedly this menu would not warrant a Michelin Star, but certainly a good reason for the need of a sizeable larder. Unfortunately at the time of my most recent visit the larder at One Ash Grange was inhabited by a trio of alarmingly large plastic figures who seemed to be under the impression they were in Bethlehem despite Christmas having passed the best part of eight months ago. I have to say an out of season nativity is not a good sight especially as Joseph was on his back and completely out of it. Clearly he had had more than enough of Christmas and I felt it best to leave him like that. Compensation for this incongruous spectacle can be remedied by purchasing an ice cream for two pounds in a nearby barn where the money is put in an honesty box, unless you are in a Duke of Edinburgh outdoors pursuits group, in which case you are banned because one of you was not very honest!

A few yards further brings you to what are assumed to be the original medieval piggeries and an ingenious construction of a sloping slab of rock in the outer wall allowed swill to be poured down into a trough, the whole thing being protected from the elements by an overhanging slab roof, thus the monks were spared the risky business of running the gauntlet of hungry pigs which as we all know will eat anything including a monk. At a later date One Ash Grange was held by the Bowman family who were Quakers and had possession of the farm for over two hundred years. More recently during World War I a certain Henry Bowman of Monyash drove over to France in his car where he offered both himself and his car as an ambulance service for transporting wounded soldiers from the frontline. During this heroic gesture 'Jerry' on two different occasions successfully chucked a shell or two at Henry's car, but heroic Henry was having none of it and undaunted he carried on with his mission that eventually resulted in the Quakers setting up a proper troop ambulance service.

Cales Dale quite naturally contains a number of caves including One Ash Cave, which is reckoned to have been used by Paleaolithic reindeer hunters as some ancient bones and abandoned tools were excavated here. Obviously times have changed for they would certainly be in for a long wait nowadays in anticipation of a reindeer waltzing down the dale. (Well, maybe not on Christmas Eve.) The other thing they would find somewhat off-putting is that Cales Dale as Nellie Kirkham quite rightly observes is, 'neck-deep in nettles in the summer', for which it has gained quite a reputation and is no place to be found without your trousers on never mind rushing about chasing wild animals clad in little else than a reindeer loin cloth! Ouch! And ouch again! On the hilltops beyond the head of Cales Dale lie a scattering of tumuli almost within bone throwing distance of the recumbent stones of Arbor Low. This impressive stone circle is the principle prehistoric monument in Derbyshire and is often referred to as the Stonehenge of the Midlands. The site sits on a bleak mound over a thousand feet above sea level and was once connected by an earthen rampart to the great tumulus of nearby Gib Hill. The henge and the nearby tumuli have over a period of time yielded a collection of both human and animal bones, flint and antler tools, and burial urns containing human ashes. Predictably, no one really knows what the purpose of the circle was for, and equally predictable has been its connection with druids and also the troublesome malevolent boggarts, those pesky mischievous spirits that haunt such places being hell-bent on giving anyone who crosses them a hard time. What a pity they did not set about the clown who decided that a spray paint design on the centre stone would be appropriate. The whole area is very atmospheric and none more so than when standing in the circle of stones in the failing light of a wintery day, amidst the desolate windswept uplands that seem to exude prehistory from every shape and shadow to the extent that in the wind you could be forgiven for mistakenly hearing the murmur of strange tongues, or even the distant rhythmic tramping of feet from a passing ghost legion along the old Roman road a little to the west. There is a legend that treasure can be found buried under one of the stones, but with over fifty to choose from searching for this is going to be a tall order, and there is little doubt that both English Heritage or the farmer who owns the land are going to take a pretty dim view of you turning up with a spade over one shoulder and pushing a wheelbarrow. Access to this mystical site can be gained by a gold coin you are requested to put in the honesty box for permission to cross the private farmland on which the circle lies. To my way of thinking in this day and age this is value for money even though back in 1949 for example, the fee was only three pence or a penny/halfpenny if you were in a group of twenty or more people. My first visit to Arbor Low was as a young lad out for the day with my family and we walked from the euphoniously sounding Parsley Hay train station which *The Homeland Guide* advices, 'the train service is infrequent and it is best to ascertain times prior to leaving.' Wise words indeed, although now days you can arrive at Parsley Hay station anytime you like, because for train read bicycle.

Meanwhile back in Lathkill Dale at the junction with Cales Dale, if by sheer coincidence you happened to be standing in the dark and sleet on the night of 11 October 1776 at this particular spot armed with a pair of night-vision goggles and this is you understand pure supposition, then in all probability you would have witnessed the one and only solo flight of Rev Robert Lomas and the terrible mess he made of landing, for more or less opposite you is Parson's Tor. As I said, it was mere supposition. The footbridge crossing the river here was once a simple stone affair and it is said that the original stone uprights were held in place by the canon wheels from the time Cromwell's armies passed this way. The idea of hauling a canon along the pathway through Lathkill Dale even today is enough to make you question your sanity, but back then in untamed terrain you would have to be completely insane and I can only assume that severe wear and tear was sufficient to make the wheels fall off, which is how they came to be supporting the bridge, if the tale is to be believed.

Continuing downstream the river Lathkill meets its first form of employment in the shape of, although barely visible, a sheep dipping station, and adjacent to a small abandoned tufa quarry that in the past had supplied material for the once fashionable Victorian taste for garden rockeries. Close by is a green and mossy cascade comprised of tufa, which Croston described as 'glistening sheets, boiling and eddying and swirling and splashing.' I detect here shades of Robert Southhey's *The Falls of Lador,* 'And dashing and flashing and splashing and clashing...' The river now begins to take shape becoming wider and deeper as it approaches a weir and the site of Carter's Mill. This was once a corn mill but all that remains is the weir, a few stones and two original grindstones that have been left to gather a covering of moss as they prop each other up alongside a wall. The weir also created the headwater for a leat that ran down the valley to power a waterwheel for Mandale Mine.

On the opposite bank is the vegetated defile of Calling Low Dale that harbours among the trees a rock shelter where Neolithic man not only left an arrowhead or two lying about, but also his own old bones. Skeletons were discovered here of children along with the bones of a woman who had a particularly nasty looking hole in the front of her skull which must have given her the mother of all headaches and probably a lot worse. Anyway, this is where they all ended their days and perhaps it was purely a case of needs must and a hole in a rock face is as good a place as any to lay down your weary bones; and of course a lot less trouble than hauling unwieldy slabs of limestone across the hilltop and then having to dig out tons of earth with only a deer antler to chuck over the top of them to make a tumulus, a word they had never even heard of! You cannot help but sympathise with them for settling for the cheaper, no nonsense, less effort family funeral plan.

The river continues for a fairly straight stretch through a densely wooded valley which in summer almost hides the sites of the Lathkill and Mandale mines. The former was owned by the Quaker run London Lead Mining Company, who embarked upon a costly undertaking of driving a drainage sough through the hillside. This venture took a mind-boggling thirty years to complete costing the company ten thousand pounds that resulted in only seven and a half thousand pounds worth of ore being extracted causing the mine to close somewhat out of pocket. Someone seriously got their sums wrong here. Then in 1825 along came mine agent Bateman brimming with determined enthusiasm and cutting edge technology in the shape of a revolutionary pumping engine to alleviate the flooding of underground tunnels and chambers. He also sunk another shaft beneath the floor of what is known today as Bateman's House, which in most people's minds would be a pretty strange thing to do, but I suppose it did away with the need to have a waste bin in the kitchen. The original use of the building is deemed to be industrial with the shaft being sunk in secrecy from the prying eyes of other mine speculators. Quite how you can dig a massive great hole without people knowing is questionable.

They definitely did not employ *The Great Escape* disposal of waste technique by surreptitiously dropping soil from the bottom of their trouser legs on their way home each day to avoid any suspicion! Little remains of the house now apart from a corner section, a mullioned window and a door-less doorway above some semi-circular steps. When Firth came across it he took it to be a, 'homestead, which the last occupant must have quitted with regret, if he had eyes for beauty or ears for the music of the rippling of the stream.' In its heyday it would have been a place awash with the noise and mayhem associated with mining activities and far from the bucolic scene it presents today. The shaft within the ruined walls of Bateman's House can now be descended by means of a metal ladder for visitors to get a glimpse of the world of mining aided by a device on the wall which by winding the handle will illuminate the drop where water rushes noisily into the unknown. I can only hazard a guess at what the light reveals for when I was last there the handle was missing, and naturally I did not happen to have a spare handle with me. Well that would be the last thing you would think of bringing on a day out! Anyway, like a man possessed Bateman decided to site a massive water wheel for the mine that apparently pumped out over eighteen thousand litres of water per minute, and yet in spite of all this expense and effort Lathkill Mine ground to a halt finally closing in 1842.

After the closure of Lathkill Mine interest shifted to next door Mandale Mine that had been in existence at least as far back as the 13th century until its demise in 1851. Its extensive system of tunnels and soughs has been blamed for lowering the water table and contributing to the river Lathkill doing its famous disappearing act as it frequently does in the summer months. For twenty or so years Mandale Mine was in the hands of Messrs Alsop, Taylor and Co. and was the, 'scene of active industry and profitable labour.' The drift entrance is situated a little way up the hill above the ruined engine house and is now gated. I suspect this was possibly the entrance I once explored in my youth where wading through knee-deep water I spotted just in time a flooded shaft in the floor which saved me from a cold immersion. The engine house once held a Cornish beam engine, which had been brought in 1847 to replace the old original fifty-two feet diameter waterwheel as the engine was more efficient and reliable at draining the mine. Part of the engine house remains to this day set back from the path among the encroaching trees. Also in this area was situated a hut or shealing where lead was stored before removal to a furnace after first being washed, pulverised and separated from the quartz spar and, 'other adventitious substances which adhere to it in its natural state.' The waterwheel has long gone, but part of the original stone piers in varying stages of decay remain that supported the launder transporting water across the river via a leat from Carter's Mill to power the huge overshot wheel. Firth was particularly damning of their appearance saying rather scathingly that they were a shame on their builders and, 'no relics of clever brain and honest work, but mere rubbish.' They certainly ruffled his feathers. In a similar scenario to Lathkill Mine, miners were also engaged in digging a drainage tunnel through the north side of the hill, which ended at nearly two kilometres in length and took twenty-three years to complete. Again the vast expenditure coupled with the costly installation of new machinery lead to the eventual closure of the mine in 1852 with the phenomenal loss of thirty-six thousand pounds! All the equipment was sold off and the story goes that it took forty horses to haul the massively weighty beam of the Cornish engine back up the steep hill to Over Haddon. Now that would have been a sight well worth witnessing never mind all that garden fertiliser left behind from forty straining horses.

The thing is, mining was a costly and risky business and raising a profit was no easy matter, so its hats off to the person who in 1854 started the rumour that a little further down the dale there was 'gold in them thar' hills' and so the Lathkill Klondyke gold rush got underway. Now it did not quite take off to the extent that Lathkill Dale was inundated with shanty towns, over-run with hordes of drunken brawling miners, brothels, gambling dens and honky-tonk saloons swarming with billowing bosomed good-time gals, due to the simple fact that it was not too long before the penny dropped that it was pyrites or 'fool's gold' that had been found. However, the initial interest pretty much turned the mine shares overnight from a pound a time to thirty pounds, so some entrepreneur or con-man very quickly made a lot of money, whereas the miners all found themselves looking at lumps of pyrites and empty pockets. They were not happy bunnies.

Beyond the mines a lane comes snaking down the hillside from the village of Over Haddon to Lathkill Lodge a former fishing place and an adjacent mill originally for grinding grist (grain) and both owned at one time by the Duke of Rutland. He was also responsible for the construction of weirs to form trout pools and a hatchery. The old duke clearly liked to see a fine big trout on his plate. Crossing the river here used to be by means of a ford until a simple stone clapper bridge was built so the monks living at Meadow Place Grange – another monastic outpost up the hill on the other side of the river – could cross without having to hoist up their habits and sling their sandals over one shoulder before wading through the water. Meadow Place Grange once had its own chapel, but it is no longer there and the grange is now a farm.

Like One Ash Grange it too fell victim of Henry VIII's avarice and was dissolved. All this was of course due to King Henry falling out with the Pope because he would not let King Henry divorce his present wife Catherine of Aragon so that he could wed his new bed mate that saucy little minx Ann Boleyn. Old Henry who always got his own way promptly denounced the Catholic faith and finding his latest bank statement in the red speedily set about relieving all monasteries of their land and wealth, which made him pretty well-off at the expense of a lot of hapless, homeless monks. Close by are the remains of a pump that once supplied water up to Over Haddon perched high on the hill. Attached to a tree near the now deserted looking mill is a notice informing you that there is 'No Public Road' at this point through the dale, but it is, 'Open to Visitors except Thursday in Easter Week', where a 'Toll of One Penny' must be paid. So if the Thursday in Easter week is the day you are planning to explore the beauties of Lathkill Dale north of Lathkill Lodge then you had better start saving your pennies now.

Over Haddon sits eight hundred feet above sea level overlooking the river Lathkill and according to Mee it is, 'a hardy little village in upland country with endless stone-walled fields, glorying in its place above the dale.' In the 1950s intrepid ramblers who slogged it up the short but steep hill out of the dale would be rewarded by a stop at Yew Tree Cottage where, 'in addition to more solid refreshment, beautiful big brown cups of tea may be obtained.' Halcyon days for the rambler of the past for those big brown cups of tea have alas, passed into history. This small village can however lay claim to two people of renown. The first is a man of more recent times who lies in the churchyard beneath a headstone bearing the name Maurice Oldfield, who was born and bred here and became a former head of MI6. It is said that he was the inspiration for Flemming's character 'M' in the James Bond films. I wonder how he would have viewed the role being played by a woman we all know as Judy Dench.

A rather more incredulous tale comes from the distant past and concerns a young girl called Martha Taylor who in her short life became a bit of a celebrity albeit for particularly strange and slightly unbelievable circumstances. She was born around 1650 and became known as 'the fasting girl,' or 'the Derbyshire Non-such.' Martha was born in Over Haddon and is said to have come from 'mean parentage.' When still a small child she was thumped on the back by the local miller, presumably from Sough Mill at the foot of the road in the dale, though whether in jest or anger is not known. Ultimately it did not much matter as the damage had been done and from that day forth she suffered lameness and developed spinal complications, both of which had a debilitating effect on her general well-being. You can already see that this is not looking too good for poor Martha and she was probably wishing she could tell the miller just where to shove a bag of his own flour. Feeling more than a bit poorly she took to her bed in 1662 by the fireside in a lower room of her home where she remained in a sickly state, until five years later on 22 December she decided to abstain from any form of solid food sustenance.

I would have thought she might have taken this decision the other side of Christmas dinner when many people try to make an effort to cut down after the seasonal blowout. But not our Martha, she had made up her mind and that was that, and she certainly took her dieting to the extreme for she soon began to waste away. Now records show that from this point on she would only take an occasional, 'few drops of the syrup of stewed prunes, of water and sugar, or the juice of one roasted raisin.' I find it quite inconceivable that anyone would wish to bung syrup of prunes into a virtually empty system. This must surely have rendered her internal pipework cleaner than a whistle! And the other thing I find quite amazing and questionable is just how much juice can you get out of only one raisin and a roasted one at that! A collation of several accounts pretty much agrees on this diet, so it must be true. Now and then her lips were moistened with a feather dipped in sugar and water. Whether this was a treat or out of necessity can only be wondered at, but it sounds to me like the forerunner of lip salve. Anyway, young Martha kept this up for well over a year and in spite of her claiming that at one time she stayed wide awake for five weeks, 'her countenance remained fresh and lively, and her voice clear and audible.' Because it was the 1600s and nobody had invented the radio, or television, or the computer to play games on Martha occupied her time learning to read and seemingly, 'attained some knowledge in sacred mysteries', which was rather apt seeing as how she had become one big mystery herself. By now she was becoming well known and her condition, a cause for curiosity, came to the notice of the Earl of Devonshire who took an interest and sent along 'physicians, surgeons and other persons' to spend a two week period recording and authenticating her state. The last recorded date of Martha's self-imposed fasting was 30 March 1669 until her death on the 12th June some fifteen years later in 1684. The unanswered question is did she make an unlikely recovery from what can only have been a terribly wasted and emaciated condition, or did she actually carry on in this state for all those years, which on the face of it would be quite extraordinary! Two accounts of the malaise of Martha Taylor are said to be stored in the archives of the British Museum and consist of one written in the year of her death in the form of a 'quasi-scientific document' by Joseph Reynolds, and another by someone who simply calls himself H A who presents the story 'for religious edification.' Now what I see here is a clear-cut case of someone being born at the wrong time, because had this been a present day phenomenon then our skinny weight-losing Martha could very well have made herself a small fortune by selling her slimming technique and diet to a readily available and ever-increasing market of obese individuals who yearn to be waif-like; and with this comes the added bonus of an amazingly low weekly food bill. Young Martha would have been on a winner.

Stepping swiftly out of the distant past and back into the verdant valley of the Lathkill, the river continues over numerous weirs before reaching the massively walled and very low arched medieval Conksbury Bridge, and it was on this spot that a young Norman Price gazed over the parapet into the clear water of the pool below. While watching the myriad of plump trout swimming lazily in the river he addressed an elderly chap standing close by saying with childish innocence, "You'd only have to put your hand in to have trout for supper."

"Nay, lad," replied the man, "them sort are none catched that-a-way. It looks easy, but it b'aint."

No prizes for guessing who did not get trout for supper that evening. Near the bridge lie the barely perceptible traces of the medieval village of Conksbury that was abandoned long ago. The bridge was the original route from Ashbourne to Bakewell and has been structurally improved during late Victorian times. On a warm summer's day (Remember those? No I didn't think so!), it is a place overrun with day trippers both on the banks of the river as well as in it and the wise trout swim elsewhere.

A short distance downstream along a riverside path which one guide book noted, 'is private, and fishermen take a dim view of trespassers' (probably a bit tetchy because they had failed to catch anything), a delightful and graceful one arched packhorse bridge spans the Lathkill where the water gleams as it tumbles over a horseshoe weir. It is known by the somewhat uninspiring name of Coalpit Bridge as it was originally crossed by teams of packhorses carrying cargoes of coal from the mines by Chesterfield. Firth came across this bridge on his walk and says, 'We reached a little arched bridge with the daintiest of pretty weirs by its side, and a stone's-throw away under the trees may be seen the Fishing House of the Marquis of Granby.' These aristocrats certainly enjoyed their fishing. Today the fishing house painted a faded egg-shell blue with white trimmings resembles nothing more than a summer house you could purchase at any reputable garden centre and certainly not a patch on Walton and Cotton's fishing house in Dove Dale. The heavily laden packhorses would have descended the dale and crossed the bridge for the uphill trudge past Raper Lodge, an old keeper's house. This house perched above the river on the hillside was used as a setting for part of the 1970 film *The Virgin and the Gypsy* that was based on a D.H. Lawrence book of the same name, which he penned in 1926. The film is typically Lawrence being a tale with undertones of brooding sexual tensions and had among its stars a young Honor Blackman playing the part of adulterous Mrs Fawcett. Honor Blackman was of course already extremely well-known by this time for her role as Cathy Gale in the television series *The Avengers* that was screened in the early sixties; and what red-blooded male could have failed to control a pulsing heart beat as he watched her throw herself about in her black figure-hugging cat-suit! Phew! Easy now! The track on the other side of the bridge zigzags steeply up a wooded hillside towards the site of the one-time Raper fluorspar mine, which later became opencast in the form of a quarry. It was in the hands of the Bacon family, so in essence this makes it a Bacon mining operation, which of course sounds highly misleading and highly implausible!

In no time at all the river Lathkill enters the village of Alport and gets nudged from the right by the equally crystal clear water of the Bradford in the valley of the Dakin after passing beneath an ancient stone bridge built in 1718 for the passage of packhorses trains on their lengthy journey to London. The Bradford like the Lathkill also has the habit of occasionally going to ground, and on one notable instance in 1881 the river completely disappeared by running underground for the best part of six miles possibly through old mine workings before re-appearing at Darley Dale where it joined the river Derwent! However, it eventually found its way back home to flow through the short, but picturesque Bradford Dale below the village of Youlgreave.

Alport is a quiet place devoid of shops, cafes, pubs or a post office and Rhodes said it, 'is a pleasant place, and the greater part of its inhabitants appear to be in reputable circumstances', although he does note that there are, 'of course some inferior dwellings', but not to any great extent for a village of this size. This was not always the case for in the past Alport was a bustling place with an inn which was originally known somewhat uninspiringly as The Boarding House Hotel. Later this took on the more acceptable sounding name of Three Rivers Inn that pulled its last pint in 1924 before being demolished years later to make way for a new road scheme. A refreshment stop according to an old *Penguin Guide* on Derbyshire called The Lathkill View Café once stood by the road to Elton and had been around since the 1930s where footsore ramblers could refuel with tea and buns. Now days you will only your hunger sated provided you have remembered to bring your own sandwiches and a thermos of tea.

Alport has an industrial past with connections to paper production and woollen manufacture and still boasts an ancient mill once used for corn which was possibly the same mill as mentioned in the Doomsday book. Unfortunately there were also mining products brought to the vicinity of the village and the biggest headache (quite literally) was a lead smelter and lime kilns whose acrid toxic fumes made for a particularly unhealthy environment and many of the inhabitants also bore the scars of 'red plague postules', or smallpox as it is now more commonly called. The flues for the smelting mills ran hundreds of feet up the hillside and were built of stone, with some high enough to be able to stand upright inside and looked similar in appearance to mine soughs. With industry came a mixed population of locals which included miners, Irishmen and redundant soldiers who had finished shooting at Frenchmen in the Napoleonic Wars and now needed a job. This influx of dubious characters no doubt lead to the notice (a replica) sited on the gable end of the Coach House which once served as a no-nonsense reminder to any vagrants. It states, 'NOTICE TO ALL VAGABONDS FOUND LODGING, LOITERING OR BEGGING WITHIN THIS HAMLET WILL BE TAKEN UP AND DEALT WITH AS THE LAW DIRECTS', thus enlightening them, should they be in any doubt of the 1824 Vagrancy Act. Luckily you can now loiter in the streets of Alport and admire the fine houses without fear of having your collar felt and being carted off to the nearest village lock-up to spend an uncomfortable night prior to a spell in gaol wearing a natty two piece suit sporting arrow heads and a not very bijou manacle and ankle chain.

Although this may not necessarily be a big crowd puller Alport does have the best exposure of tufa rock in the county in the form of 'a large mass of rock, from forty to sixty feet high.' In the past it was named by a true visionary, Tufa Rock, but is now more commonly referred to as Bradford Tor. Geologically speaking, or as bobble-hatted, bobble-brained Arnold would tell you, tufa is a calcium carbonate deposit formed by chemical precipitation from springs and the like that are rich in dissolved calcium. Therefore the heavy concentrate of calcium means that whatever the water runs or drips over becomes naturally coated in calcium carbonate giving it a stone-like appearance. (Thank you Arnold, you can go home now.) The petrification of objects was particularly popular during Victorian times and the well at Matlock Bath was a source of fascination as indeed was the better known Mother Shipton's petrifying cave and well at Knaresborough in Yorkshire. Despite the name petrifying this is not some hole in the ground that is so horrific that you become petrified with fear to the extent that you are scared witless, have nightmares and require psychiatric treatment for the rest of your life. Petrifying in this instance refers to water droplets losing their carbonic gas, which 'precipitates earthy particles upon the substance on which it falls, thus forming a stony incrustation.'

I have seen a variety of objects from a bowler hat, an umbrella through to a birds nest complete with eggs seemingly turned to stone, while in the Victorian era wigs and sheep's heads were popular items for petrification. I suppose in theory if you were daft enough to stand beneath such a flow for long enough you could become your own garden statue. The Alport tufa is comprised mainly of vegetable matter and Rhodes notes that, 'in the tufa rocks they (animal and vegetable remains) are often embedded in their native state: branches of trees are frequently found within them; and in some places they appear an accumulation of sticks, straws, and weeds, closely enveloped in calcareous incrustations; amongst these the natural snail-shell, not in the least altered in appearance.' There is a tale that long ago the entire head of a stag with antlers attached was taken out of the tufa here and is 'now in the possession of a gentleman at Bakewell.' Curiously, there was no body attached to the head, but then it is possible that the locals saw this as a tasty opportunity not to be missed and for one brief moment in the distant past the village of Alport hung heavy with the aroma of venison casserole cooking in numerous homesteads.

It would be unforgivable to not create a very pleasing diversion up Bradford Dale which is a rather charming, albeit short dale as it is only about two miles from end to end. Like the river Lathkill, the river Bradford is a river of weirs and pools for trapping fish and near its top end is an ingenious construction of stone-walled enclosures for trapping and washing sheep. There are overgrown leats and cobbled mill races for umpteen mills that now no longer exist. Halfway along the dale a bridge crosses the river carrying a path up the steep hillside to the village of Youlgreave, or is it Youlgrave, or as the locals call it Pommy or Pommie? Who knows? Maybe it will always be disputable. It is mentioned in the *Doomsday Book* of 1086 as being in the hands of that owner of villages, Henry de Ferrers and valued at sixteen shillings which seems very reasonable for an entire village, so put me down for half a dozen. I know a bargain when I see one! The village is perched on the lip of Bradford Dale and dominated by the hundred feet high tower of the 15th century All Saints Church that boasts an aged stone font some eight hundred years old, plus a painted glass east window executed by the well-known Pre-Raphaelite, Sir Edward Coley Burne-Jones who was matey with the equally famous William Morris who allowed his workshop to be used for the windows creation and assembly. Another window within the church has a rather poignant association, for it has been presented as a memorial made from individual pieces of glass collected from numerous bombed-out churches in Flanders by the brother of Rennie Crompton Waterhouse who died in 1915 at Gallipoli. It is a sobering shrine of heartfelt remembrance from one brother to another.

On a recent visit to All Saints church one warm early spring afternoon I came across a very elderly lady on her hands and knees pulling out weeds with her bare hands from between the stone slabs by the entrance gate. With some effort she stood up to talk to me complaining that she was really too old for this sort of work and I was inclined to agree. She said there had been a funeral the previous day and thought the entrance was looking a tad unkempt, so she took it upon herself to do the weeding. She told me that the mound to the left of the gateway was the burial mound of past village children who had died of scarlet fever and diphtheria, but their families had been too poor to provide their children with even the most simple of grave markers and so they were all put into the one mass grave.

Also within the confines of the churchyard is the grave of Jane Shimwell, who later became Lady Jane after her husband Alexander McDougal had been officially recognised as the inventor of Self-Raising flour and where would we be today without that on our kitchen shelves! It would be a world of flat scones and sunken cakes. Margaret, which may or may not be the real name of my churchyard guide – for she showed a degree of reluctance to be named when I asked her – then pointed out a carved arrowhead in the church wall which she believed was a bench mark to prove we were standing, or to be more precise, the church is standing at six hundred feet above sea-level.

I then drew her attention to a delightfully decorated stone shop front across from the church that had a carving above its window ending in a bunch of grapes at one end and what appeared to be oranges at the other end. It must surely have been a grocers shop. Wrong, said Margaret, it was called Hunters, a general store that sold everything under the sun including bags of sugar, for she told me that when the property was re-roofed a while back hundreds of the old blue sugar bags were discovered in the roof space. I shook her soil-stained hand and left her to her weeding.

Further down the street a rotund stone structure rises out of the road sitting on a solid plinth of granite blocks, surrounded by railings with a stepped shallow trough at the front. It bears the date 1829 and is the Conduit Head that was once capable of holding five thousand gallons of water and was for many years the villages water supply, having been piped all the way from Mawstone Spring. Again according to Margaret much of Youlgreave is still on spring water supplied by the Youlgreave Water Company, but it no longer comes from this structure which Firth called 'a barbarously ugly conduit in the market place.' However, whatever your own views are of the conduit, facing it on the opposite side of the road is the splendid imposing building of the former Co-op that opened in 1887 and operated right up until 1968. It still retains the original gold lettering on the arched ground floor windows advertising Groceries, Provisions and Clothing but is now under the ownership of the YHA, and although the diversity of buildings used by the YHA is well known, few, if any can boast as this one does that you can spend a night in Haberdashery or – and take this whichever way you like – in Ladies Underwear!

Tucked away around the corner from the Conduit, or the Fountain as it is often called in an attempt to prettify the debateable visual and architectural merits of the water tank is a delightful 'one-up, one-down' cottage known somewhat ostentatiously as Thimble Hall which contrary to its name is said to be the smallest detached house not just in Derbyshire but in the entire world! This illustrious title has been officially imposed upon Thimble Hall or Cottage by none other than the *Guinness Book of Records*. The two rooms were connected by ladder and the only thing it had in the way of home comforts was a 'Cinderella' fireplace. It measures a mere eleven feet ten inches by ten feet three inches and reaches the dizzy height of twelve feet two inches.

Given the thickness of the stone walls this reduces the interior room measurements to less than eight feet square and at one time in its history it housed a family of eight, which even for a tribe of pygmies would be a bit of a squash. In the past the house has also been used as a retail outlet by both a butcher and a cobbler. I would have thought that another very close contender for being the smallest house would be the much photographed, much painted and better known 17th century House on the Bridge at Ambleside in the Lake District. This equally small house oddly enough, also once had a family of eight living within its walls, and coincidently had also been a cobblers shop. Clearly a house of this size has its limitations commercially speaking and it is never going to be a supermarket or sell grand pianos now is it?

And now here is the weather forecast for Youlgreave and much of the Peak District for 16 January 1615 according to parish records that hold 'a *memorial* of the great snow.' A detailed account states that snow fell with a vengeance until it was nearly four feet deep with, 'drifts of snow, they were very deep so that passengers, both horse and foot, passed over gates and hedges and walles.' It tells of how the snow fell on ten separate occasions smothering all the countryside and increasing in volume until 12 March 12 when it ceased and a thaw set in until, 'or the heapes or drifts of snow were consumed', which took until the 28 May with only snow remaining on Kinderscout for a longer period. As a result of these adverse weather conditions, 'it hindered the seedtyme, consumed much fodder and many wanted fewell, otherwise few were smothered in the fall, or drowned in the passage.'

Certainly a winter to remember and not unlike our present winters, which for one reason or another are becoming memorable. The Derbyshire weather then changed to the extreme as the snow was followed by a drought that lasted until well into August, 'so the greater part of the land was entirely burnt up.' Of course we still moan about the weather today and used to blame it on the Russians, but now hold global warming as accountable, a hypothesis that had never even been heard of back in the 1600s; and would Michael Fish (he who predicted the 'nothing much to worry about' Great Storm of October 1987 that killed eighteen people and pancaked fifteen million trees! Oops!!) Have been able to forewarn them had he been on the weather scene in those days, armed only with a bit of bladder-wrack dangling on a piece of string from his bedroom window and a knowing nod from a sky wary shepherd?

Like so many Derbyshire villages Youlgreave had connections with the lead mining industry which died out long ago, although mining for fluorspar and calcite is still carried out in a low-key manner in the neighbourhood. About half a mile from Bradford Dale is the site of Mawstone Mine where in 1932 five miners died after what was presumed to be a gas explosion underground, which filled a chamber with deadly carbon monoxide. A sixth miner luckily escaped death and surfaced to alert the mine manager of the disaster. It seems that the mine manager and two other miners were totally unaware of the terminal effects of odourless carbon monoxide because they descended the mine intent on a rescue mission and predictably missed their dinner that night and every other night after becoming the victims of poisonous fumes. The mine closed shortly after this disaster.

Miners of old tended to be a superstitious bunch and prone to hearing 'knockers' and seeing spirits and ghosts often generically referred to as 'T 'Owd Man' particularly if the spectre is associated with dead miners. The following legend has been recorded in other parts of the country with minor variations, as is the case with so much of folklore and Youlgreave has its own particular version. The tale relates to a poor miner living in the village who was hovering on the brink of total destitution and all this hapless individual had to call upon was his three sons. The eldest who was ambitious and tired of being penniless decided to leave home and seek his fortune wherever he could. Sometime later he sat down in a wood to eat his meagre fare of bread and cheese when suddenly he was confronted by a small red hairy man. He asked the young lad for some of his snack, as he was more than a tad peckish, but the lad who was clearly in a bad mood gave the hairy man a good kicking instead. Exit one limping red hairy and very vindictive man. After that episode the lad found he was continually out of luck and was forced to return home as poor as a church mouse.

Undeterred by his brother's failure, son number two set off with the same goal in mind. Down in the same wood he got out his lunchbox and predictably out popped the still very hungry red hairy man. Son number two begrudgingly gave the hairy man what few crumbs remained after he had finished eating and as a reward the hairy man showed him a mine in the woods. The lad took one look at the state of the shaft and decided it would be a waste of time as regards making him rich, so he turned tail and went back home without so much as a brass farthing in his pocket.

At this point the third son who was called Jack (you can tell he is going to be the lucky one with a name like Jack, plus the fact that he is the only son that is named) also set off in search of wealth and a better life and yes, once again out came the lunchbox and yes, once again out popped the hairy man. Do you get the feeling that this tale is beginning to sound a bit like the *Three Billy Goats Gruff* with the Troll beneath the bridge, or even the opening lines of a gag about, 'there was an Englishman, an Irishman and a Scotsman.' Anyway, on this occasion our Jack showed compassion and shared his lunch with the hairy man who by now was almost out of his mind with hunger and was rewarded by not only being shown the old mine shaft, but was also lowered down to the bottom where he found himself in a wonderful land. Here at the bottom of the mine shaft the hairy man mysteriously appeared on the scene and without further ado rolled a copper ball down a tunnel asking Jack to follow it where he would come across a copper castle where he had to fight a giant and rescue an imprisoned maiden.

I bet Jack the lad had not bargained for all this when he woke up that morning. So Jack carried out the deed, slayed the giant, rescued the princess who thanked him and cleared off home (ungrateful little b …). Next up the hairy man rolled a silver ball down the tunnel and gave Jack the same instructions as the previous venture, along the lines of find a silver castle, kill the giant and rescue the princess, who also went home without so much as a kiss my arse or a thank you. (I hope you believe all this and not think it's just a made-up story.) Round three involved a golden ball and … well, you know the rest, except by now Jack was getting a tad hacked off, never mind getting out of breath chasing balls down tunnels like a demented dog, beating up giants and then not getting so much as a smacker on the lips from a bunch of ungracious princesses. He was feeling more than a little jaded with all this physical exertion and was half wishing he had not been so generous with the contents of his lunch box. But the tide was starting to turn for Jack as the last princess got the 'hots' for our lad and quicker than you can say 'well I'll go to the foot of our stairs', they were happily married and Jack was given all the gold he wanted.

Well that put a smile on his face I can tell you, so he built a home for himself and his new bride and also a house for his poor aging father, rather than put him in an old folks home. No prizes for guessing who was son number one, and well done him. Now if you are thinking of having a break and putting the kettle on then forget it, for this is not the end of the tale. When Jack's two other brothers got wind of his success they both raced each other to the mine and had a bit of a scrap about who was going to descend the shaft first. In haste and overcome by avarice they both leapt into the bucket and descended the shaft much faster than either of them had anticipated, due to the fact the rope broke and the pair of them crashed to the bottom in a heap.

Now whether or not they survived the fall history does not relate, but in truth it would be of no consequence for if they were feeling a little dazed from their fall and scratching their heads in wonderment it would have been a very short-lived moment, because seconds later the sides of the shaft collapsed and buried them both forever. They really did have a very bad day and should have stayed at home. The moral of this tale is self-explanatory, so if you ever find yourself in a wood eating your lunch and a red hairy man pops out from the trees, then you would be wise to share your sandwich with him and a couple of fingers of Kit-Kat, or alternatively call the police!

From Youlgreave the river Bradford climbs past many weirs with hooped iron sluice mechanisms dated 1890 and 1891 and the sites of long gone mills. A side valley reached by crossing a bridge with the words, 'STILL GLIDES THE STREAM AND SHALL FOREVER GLIDE THE FORM REMAINS THE FUNCTION NEVER DIES' (make of that what you will) carved along the parapet leads up to Lomberdale Hall built in the 1850s by Thomas Bateman, having inherited the estates of his grandfather. Grandfather Bateman was a bit of an archaeologist and a philanthropist having rebuilt the village of Middleton in the 1820s that overlooks the head of the Bradford. Thomas Bateman was also a keen archaeologist and over a period of time erected an extension to Lomberdale Hall to house his ever growing collection of finds, for it is reckoned that during his lifetime he excavated and opened over five hundred barrows or tumuli. His long suffering wife Sarah no doubt held her breath every time he came through the front door dreading another invasion of more old bones and pottery shards to dust.

"Oh my God! What have you brought home this time?" enquired Sarah with hands firmly placed on her hips.

"It's an almost complete skeleton of a Neolithic man," replied Bateman excitedly. "Isn't it simply marvellous?"

"No! It is not simply marvellous," snapped Sarah. "It's just a heap of mucky old bones, and get them of my kitchen table I'm just about to make some pastry.

"But my dearest they … "

"No buts and no bones. Remove them and yourself from my kitchen NOW!!"

Bateman's tomb, for he died at the early age of forty-one displays a large replica of a bronze-age cinerary urn and lies in solitude on a hillside behind an old chapel, surrounded by railings and almost roofed over by the dark green hanging branches of a yew tree. Carved into the stonework at the front is an interesting spelling of the word entrance which has been spelt 'ENTERANCE'.

Back in the steeply sided and well wooded dale and further along is another bridge carrying a track up to Middleton itself and here in the past the river has been harnessed not only in a leat to serve a now ruined mill, but also diverted into a complexity of stone-walled holdings where sheep were once driven into for a mass washing session. I wonder if the water back down the dale that was pumped up to the conduit in Youlgreave ever had a mildly discernible hint of fleece grease and sheep droppings about it. By the track, which ascends a rocky ravine is a huge detached section of the rock face known as Fulwood's Rock and is big enough to hide a man, which is precisely what it did back in the 1600s, and the man was none other than Sir Christopher Fullwood himself. Prior to the Bateman takeover of the area the Middleton estates were in the hands of the Fullwoods who built a fortified house known as Fullwood Castle and it was here that the Cavalier son of Sir George Fullwood, Sir Christopher Fullwood got himself into a spot of bother with Cromwell's marauding Parliamentarians.

They had got wind that Sir Chris had managed to rally a thousand obstreperous miners hell-bent on marching to Derby in support of King Charles and decided that they had to be stopped in their tracks. Consequently a troop of Cromwell's chaps headed for Middleton and set about raiding Fullwood Castle. During the ensuing melee it became blindingly obvious to Sir Chris that things were not really going his way, so working along the lines of, 'he who fights and runs away, lives to fight another day' (he was in for a nasty surprise), he nipped smartly out of the back kitchen door, clambered down the side of Bradford Dale and hid himself in a cleft behind the big slab of rock. Unfortunately for him this turned out to be not a very smart move, because shortly after he was discovered and so with his back against the wall, or in his case against the rock and with nowhere to go he was an easy target for the musket ball that headed his way. Badly wounded Sir Chris was carted off in the direction of Litchfield, but never reached his destination as he died from the shot wound during transit. For him it had been a memorably bad day and all there is to show in his memory is Fullwood's Rock, which he unwittingly proved is not a good hiding place should you ever find yourself being sought out by a bunch of murderous Parliamentarians. After his death Fullwood Castle fell to ruin, which the locals took full advantage of by helping themselves to masses of free building material, some of which was used in the construction of the present day Castle Farm that stands adjacent to the field whose tell-tale mounds are all that remains of the old castles foundations.

Middleton to be topographically accurate is called Middleton by Yougreave to distinguish it from Derbyshire's other Middleton, which is called Middleton by Wirksworth in order to differentiate itself from Middleton by Youlgreave. Well, that's sorted that little matter out. Middleton by Yougreave is not unlike Alport at the other end of the dale insomuch as it does not have a shop, a café or a pub and comes over as little more than a hamlet going very quietly about its business and not too bothered about being in the present. Even the post box is a left over from the reign of King George and beside it is a Victorian stone water font inscribed with the words 'THE LORD'S GIFT', which clearly the Lord had reclaimed as the font was as dry as a bone.

A short way down the road from here is a slightly unusual memorial inscribed on a bronze plaque that reads, 'In Memory of the Crew of Wellington Bomber RAF No.BJ652 which crashed at Smerrill on January 21st 1944'. The aircrew of six ranged from the eldest at twenty-seven years of age to the youngest a mere nineteen. The epigraph RIP had not been included, which I felt was apt considering the memorial had been placed at the edge of a children's playground where peace of any kind would not be forthcoming when the place was in full swing. I left the village to slumber on in the sunshine and made my way back into Bradford Dale and down river almost to Alport where a kindly couple invited me into their garden for a chat and a much needed mug of tea.

Beyond Alport the river Bradford joins forces with the Lathkill and together they follow the curving line of a wooded hillside known as Priest's Hill on which is visible the ancient stone gables of Harthill Hall, parts of which are said to date back to the time of the Crusades, when the Christians were knocking seven bells out of the Muslims in an attempt to reclaim Jerusalem. Some of the halls complex is now available as holiday accommodation, which seems quite apt, as no less a person than Henry VIII apparently stayed for 'Bed and Breakfast' a long time ago. Maybe he was taking a bit of a holiday from the hustle and bustle of court life in London to come and close down a few Granges and fill his coffers with their wealth.

In complete contrast and almost spilling out of the trees on the opposite side of the road to the tranquil Harthill Hall is the rather less attractive spectacle of Shiningbank Quarry. Being part of Haddon it provides labour for the estate workers producing limestone for road building. At literally a hop and a skip down the road the diluted waters of the river Lathkill and the Bradford finish their journeys by joining the Wye at Fillyford Bridge and another fascinating saga of legends, tales and unexpected facts comes to an end. However, there is still one more river to follow that will yield more mysteries and more stories and in spite of its questionable beginnings it metamorphoses into arguably the counties most beloved and most scenic of dales.

5.

Dilly-Dallying
along the Dove.

It seems altogether unmerited that what many consider to be the most picturesque dale in the county and one that rates as one of the finest dales in this country, with a world-wide reputation (I remember in the 1970s spotting a 'Dove Dale' tea towel hanging behind a bar in a remote mountain village in Spain's Picos de Europa Sierra) should have such a drab beginning. Like the river Wye the Dove starts its lengthy forty-five mile journey on the slopes of Axe Edge, across the road from the aptly named Dove Head Farm in what can be a gloomy and austere landscape, especially on days when blankets of grey mist unfurl down the barren hillside smothering everything in its path. Naturally, when the sun shines there is a marked improvement if only for the view that can be seen from the A53 road.

The true source of the river Dove has often been questioned, but it is generally accepted that the stone-slab structure sitting in a slight depression among a scant copse of trees and partly engulfed by overgrown vegetation is, on rare occasions, sufficiently wet to be called the birth place of the river. On a recent visit I noticed that above the spring head and on the other side of the road vast quantities of water was seeping down the hillside creating a huge sodden, muddy, water-logged morass, that appeared to be coming from a barely perceptible dip, which had been tented over by the cut-off, upturned, back-end of a low-loader lorry that was an utter visual abomination, but nevertheless was more in keeping with what one would expect to see as the source of a river.

When Firth visited the site, he describes how he went through a wall-gate and down a flagstone way to the spring where earth had been banked up and covered with a flat stone. He saw a stone cracked by frost during the severe winter of 1903 that had the intertwined initials of those legendary anglers Walton and Cotton carved into it, although the alleged visit of these two celebrities to this remote spot is usually accepted as a mere flight of fancy on someone's part. Less than half a mile down the road in Staffordshire, for the source of the Dove lies practically on the county border, is the remote Traveller's Rest pub. In a field below among rough pasture, and it accounts for little more than a large armpit sweat stain on the ground is the source of the river Manifold. Now I only mention this fact rather scathingly because it gets announced in blue letters on the Ordnance Survey Map, whereas the better known (internationally speaking) Dove gets no recognition at all! The one advantage the source of the Manifold has is that you can dilute your disappointment by downing a pint or two in the nearby pub.

You could of course argue that the 'blink and you'll miss it' hamlet of Dove Head which is marked on the map ought perhaps to be recognised as the source, but it seems it has been falsely named, otherwise I feel certain that some whizz-kid would have jumped on the commercial bandwagon and made a killing by selling, 'We have been to the Source of the Dove' T-shirts, tea-towels and car stickers. I wonder if Dove Head Farm has considered this to supplement their income. Anyway, the river in one way or another and from somewhere on the hillside finally gets underway from its humble beginnings to very quickly cut down into a clough consisting of a combination of shales and grits. The area here is rough upland pasture dotted with isolated farmsteads and criss-crossed by low stone walls, wire sheep fencing and narrow roads that wind up and down crossing the infant Dove on tiny stone bridges.

In general the landscape is fairly uninspiring until the river drops into a steep sided valley to emerge at its first place of habitation, the small community of Hollinsclough. There are no shops here or a pub, only a smattering of houses and the church of St Agnes that was built in 1840 originally as a Chapel of Ease, which in times past was also a rather rustic euphemism for the old earth-bucket outside lavatory. I mention this lavatorial fact just in case such aspects of social history interest you. St Agnes on the other hand according to various sources and many variations was a good looking lass about twelve or thirteen years of age, who refused to renounce her faith after being falsely accused of becoming a Christian by a chap, or maybe more than one chap who all wanted their evil way with her.

This however was never going to happen as she had given herself to her faith and none of them stood a cat in hells chance of getting inside her robes! (Nobody wore pants in those far off times.) She was subsequently hauled up before the powers that be and threatened with all manner of nasty things that would be done to her, but our Aggie did not really give a hoot, so in recognition of her stubbornness she was decapitated, or stabbed to death, or burnt at the stake, depending on which story appeals to you most. For her pains she was given the role of patron saint of gardeners, chastity, girls, engaged couples, rape victims and virgins, so no eternal rest for her for with all that lot to look out for she certainly had her work cut out. Back in the 1700s Hollinsclough once had its own silk weaving industry, but now the quiet little hamlet is noted as a gathering place for walkers attracted to the nearby group of spectacular hills.

These sharply ridged and very distinctive shaped hills called Hollins, Chrome, Parkhouse and Hitter are in fact extremely ancient reef knolls that once formed a shallow lagoon comprising of an un-estimable number of sea polyps and coral. All this took place some three hundred and forty million years ago, give or take a week or so, and clearly there are no more lazing on the beach days to be had here, as the tide went out an awful long time ago. Somewhat incongruously in this amazing landscape someone chose to turn the most northern bump of High Edge hill into an underground storage dump during World War II for bombs. Now had there been an unfortunate accident involving a tremendous explosion then the former High Edge hill might very well have had to be renamed Low Edge hill or even No Edge hill.

Chrome hill was also burrowed into in the 1800s by miners in search of the mineral calamine that was used mainly for medicinal purposes. At this same hill apparently you can witness the odd phenomena of a double sunset, so if you feel inclined to finish your day twice with two lots of Pimms at sundown, then this is the place to be. Between Chrome and Parkhouse hills is waterless Dowel Dale a onetime tributary to the river Dove and where a cave was discovered to have once been inhabited by six adults and four children who left their bones in sealed off sections along with what was presumably their pet dog, who was buried here minus its head. A headless dog would really not have been a lot of use to anyone, although it would never get on your nerves barking and neither would it ever need feeding. You should always look for the upside in circumstances such as these.

While on the subject of headless things, close by is the village of Earl Sterndale, probably best known for the pub that bears the strange name of The Quiet Woman, which has a sign depicting a headless woman, and you cannot get any quieter than that! The signboard showing, 'a woman in a black dress, arms pugnaciously akimbo', is accompanied by the questionable epitaph, 'soft words turneth away wrath', which you can interpret as you wish. The story behind this is that a former landlord's wife, who it seems never knew when to shut up and was nicknamed 'Chattering Charteris' proved to be a bit too much to handle and was quite obviously getting on the poor man's nerves. According to his account of the facts, 'Chattering Charteris' even ranted and raved in her sleep which finally pushed the landlord over the edge. In what was without doubt a successful effort to silence her for good he lopped off her head, which on the face of it seems a tad drastic, then again, drastic situations call for drastic measures. She was clearly a bane in the lives of the locals as well for it is said that on hearing the good news and in full support of the landlord's actions the villagers had a bit of a whip-round in order to help out with the funeral costs.

Now is that not an outstanding example of village community spirit at its best. Earl Sterndale has another dubious claim to fame with its church, which is the result of a rebuild in 1952. This was necessary after the church of St Michael (a saint who at one time was associated in the minds of most people as the patron saint of Marks and Spencers vests and underpants for men) was singled out by an over eager pilot in the Luftwaffe who scored a direct hit on the building in 1941, an achievement that must surely have aided Hitler's war effort no end! Anyway its claim to fame is that this is the only church in Derbyshire to be hit by a German bomb.

St Michael, just to put the record straight is noted for not being at all matey with Old Nick, but he does come to visit you on your death bed to ask if you have any regrets about all those naughty things you have done during your life, like that brick you threw at next doors cat, along with the time you were accused of frottage with a woman in front of you in a bus queue. If some people do confess to the saint you have to ask yourself just how much time does he have! St Michael was made the patron of grocers, mariners, sickness, and somewhat bizarrely of the police and paratroopers. Were police and paratroopers around in his day? And now that I have touched on the subject of war, there is by the edge of the village a home called Woodbine Cottage that was the former residence of one Billy Budd a veteran soldier who fought in the Afghan War of 1880 and of whom it is said once walked from Kabul to Kandahar, a distance of around three hundred and fifty miles with his feet wrapped only in ragged cloths. History does not seem to relate just how he came to be without his shoes and socks in the first place.

One road leaves Earl Sterndale to cross the river Dove at Glutton Bridge where a corn mill once operated that went off the map in the 1940s. It then carries on to Longnor which as I am striving to stay on the Derbyshire side of the Dove as much as it is possible to do so, then I am going to by-pass this village. No offence intended Longnor. Another road runs in the general direction of the Dove passing the hill of High Wheeldon on the left, which has been given to the nation as a memorial to the soldiers of the Staffordshire and Derbyshire regiments who never came home from World War II. On the hillside is the well-known cave of Foxhole that over the years has yielded a stone axe, bowls, blades and the bones of deer and wild boar, along with those of several individuals who may very well have rested in peace had it not been for the antics of a deranged dog hunting for rabbits.

The over enthusiastic dog managed to get itself stuck and consequently had to be dug out, whereupon the cave was uncovered. Surely it should have been named Rabbit Hole, or even Dopey Dog Hole. Beyond the site of the cave a lane (Green Lane) branches off from the road to where a wooden footbridge takes you across the Dove to Longnor. This is Beggar's Bridge which was once a particularly busy packhorse route, although this is hard to imagine in its present pastoral setting, but in times past perhaps the passing trade was sufficiently brisk that beggars found it a profitable place to seek alms, or put in modern parlance to sponge, scrounge and bum.

The river Dove then wriggles its way past the small hamlet of Crowdecote, or Crowdicote, or Crowdy Cote, whichever name takes your fancy and a name thought to derive from the Saxon 'cruda' who was possibly a farmer who first settled here. Predictably it was once the scene of a busy packhorse route from Hassop to Newcastle-under-Lyne, as well as being on the Leek to Bakewell mail coach run. The old bridge carries the narrow road uphill past the appropriately named Packhorse Inn and on up to a sharp bend, which if you are driving then forget about stopping there as it is an accident waiting to happen, but does give fantastic views down a wide, flat-bottomed valley with the Dove meandering along down to Pilsbury.

Pilsbury sits on a dog-leg bend on a single track road beyond which can be found the remaining lumps and bumps of the 'motte and bailey' castle that once stood there in the time of the Normans. It was undoubtedly De Ferrers who as we have already seen was a mega-landowner (courtesy of King William) that originally knocked up the wooden fortification around the latter half of the eleventh century to occupy the prominent limestone outcrop. De Ferrers owned Pilsbury itself, which was valued at ten shillings or fifty pence in today's money. He was certainly one for snapping up a bargain was that De Ferrers fellow. There are few houses in the hamlet and the scene is very much dominated by the noble looking Pilsbury Grange, which is where John Farey writing a report on the industry and agriculture of the area in 1815 recorded the first known recipe for the humble oatcake that in ages past has sustained many a weary traveller at a wayside inn. Now you need only pop along to Morrisons in Buxton and buy a wodge to take home and chuck into a frying pan. This narrow track that continues to skirt the valley side heading for Hartington is gated every so often and can provide an active drive if you have no passenger in your car, but the views over to the Staffordshire side make it worthwhile as you drive past remote farmsteads and the adit of a long abandoned lead mine. The track finally drops down to a quintessential English village with its church, inns, quaint shops, pump, greens and duck pond. You have arrived at Hartington, which for many is where the real beauties of Dove Dale begin.

Hartington is often referred to as 'The Gateway to Dove Dale' and topographically speaking it does pretty much herald the start of the river Dove's most impressive and arresting scenery as it cuts through limestone country. Firth called Hartington, 'a clean, breezy, upland village' while Croston referred to it as, 'an old-fashioned and somewhat important country town.' In his book *A Summer Saunter Among the Hills and Dales of Derbyshire*, Croston in typical fashion arrived at Hartington late at night having followed the Dove from Ilam and writes how very pleased he was to see, 'the lights gleaming from the windows of the Sleigh Arms', which he entered just as the, 'inmates were preparing for bed.' He goes on to say that the Sleigh Arms (named after the family who owned it and nothing to do with tobogganing or Santa) was, 'a quiet, old-fashioned country inn, where good entertainment and a cheerful but unaffected welcome are sure to await you.' Clearly the landlord was not as hacked-off as I would have imagined he might have been with Croston arriving on his doorstep at bedtime.

At this time in history the Sleigh Arms – now the Charles Cotton Hotel – shared the square with a wheelwright, a blacksmith, more public houses and a few shops including a baker, butcher, tailor, undertaker and the ubiquitous oatcake maker, all of whom have faded into the past. And with them went the Red Lion where in 1727 two irreverent chaps were reported for playing bowls on the Sabbath and were duly whisked away and charged at Derby Assizes. The lesson to be learned here is never get your bowls out on a Sunday. The same square today hosts two pubs, a post-office and tearoom, a clothiers, an antique shop and a cholesterol inducing chocolate shop. The village's old solid town hall is now a general purpose store and of course there is the cheese shop, the only remaining reminder of Hartington's famous cheesy past. Once upon a time it was world renowned for its production of Stilton and Buxton Blue cheeses, which ended rather sadly in 2008 when the creamery closed causing a substantial loss of jobs in the immediate locality. Luckily King George V had passed on some time before all this took place, for it is said that he would only have Hartington Stilton on his royal table, and quite right to!

Another member of royalty did leave his mark here in the village, in the unlikely guise of one Prince Oberlensky, who once resided at Dove Cottage after fleeing from Russia during the revolution of 1917. Prince Alexander Sergorvitch Obelensky to give him his full title is mainly remembered for his prowess as a rugby player and his short life that ended abruptly at the age of twenty-four after he crashed a Hawker Hurricane in Suffolk while training as a fighter pilot. Tragic though this is, I think it would be fair to say that although his life was a short one, it was nevertheless, more fulfilling here in England than the one that would have awaited him back in Russia at the hands of the Bolsheviks, where in all probability Prince Alex would have found himself doing a bit of long term mining alongside a lot of other Russian aristocrats in deepest Siberia. He would not have been having a fun time.

Overlooking the daily comings and goings of village life in Hartington is the church of St Giles, and of course in keeping with previous references to saintly beings in this book I feel that you as reader will be in need of a summation of the life of St Giles. The thing is, you are going to get it anyway unless you wish to skip this paragraph and then kick yourself later on when a question about St Giles pops up in your local pub quiz. To cut a long story short – for most of these saintly tales-cum-legends are lengthy – St Giles was living the life of a hermit in a cave (where else) in a forest somewhere near Nimes in France and had bestowed upon himself a pet hind deer that apparently provided him with a daily pinta, which you have to admit was very obliging of it. One day a group of the king's huntsmen appeared in the forest, saw the deer doing whatever deer do in forests and gave chase. The deer fled back to St Giles and an overexcited bowman let loose an arrow that missed the deer and a rather surprised St Giles was suddenly aware that he had copped for it in his leg.

Understandably poor St Giles was more than a tad miffed about this sudden turn of events, but seemingly took it on the chin (or leg) so to speak. When word got back to the king relating the old hermit's stoicism and the permanent hole he now had in his leg through which the wind whistled tunefully, the king duly honoured him by building St Giles a monastery all of his own where he could one day lay down his bones when he eventually decided to call it a day. So, didn't he do well! And because old St Giles was left with a limp for the remainder of his life he was made the patron of cripples … and blacksmiths, and breast cancer, and breast-feeding, and horses, and rams, and insanity (which he must have been teetering on the edge of himself when he heard about all this lot) and a whole load of other things that would be more than enough to put you off ever wanting to become a saint in the first place. I mean to say, it's an unpaid job and you are never going to get a minutes peace to yourself!

This very same church, or to be more precise, the churchyard was once the scene of a fracas during the Civil War when a bunch of fleeing Royalist were pursued by a band of belligerent Roundheads who always being on the look-out for a bit of a scrap set about the Royalists among the headstones of St Giles's churchyard. Being Cromwellians they had no respect for their surroundings and continued to slash, stab and maim among the graves of the local dearly departed, until a final few Royalists managed to escape into the church where they barricaded themselves inside and escaped being slaughtered.

But to finish on a lighter note it would seem that St Giles church lay at the heart of one parishioner in particular called Mary Flint, who many decades ago left an endowment of four pounds a year to enable fuel to be purchased for the church stove, after spending a life time attending the house of God freezing her backside off in winter. It was without question a gesture well-meant but in today's stringent economic climate four pounds is not even going to buy one bag of coal, so without some form of more modern heating the good people of Hartington would still be blowing into cupped hands during a service.

On the subject of winter there is an account of an exceptionally harsh one where it is said the snowfall was so tremendous that drifts piled up to the eaves of the houses and anyone who wished to leave their home had to tunnel out through the snow like a mole. The tale also related that every path that was dug that day lead not to the post-office, or the shops, but to the nearest ale house. Well that sounds perfectly logical to me, and certainly no surprise. Normally the weather around this part of the Peak District does not inhibit visitors and Hartington can be a busy place all year round, as walkers in particular flock to spend a day in the dales of the Dove. For many it is merely a day trip but others take advantage of the accommodation available, one such place being the stone mullion-windowed Hartington Hall that was built in the 17th century and is now in the ownership of the Youth Hostels Association. It is alleged that in 1745 Bonnie Prince Charlie stayed here long before it belonged to the YHA of course, after all he would not be bunking-up in a bed in a communal dormitory with a bunch of hairy-legged ramblers now would he!

Another interesting building was once connected to the silk industry that operated here in the 1700s and was later turned into a workhouse for the locality. Now it is somewhere you can stay for a holiday and boasts conditions considerably better than those experienced by its former inmates, namely the poor and the destitute. For starters you can have a decent breakfast (not bread and gruel) and the rest of the day you are free to go out and enjoy yourself rather than being forced to spend your day breaking stones, sweating it out in a steamy laundry room or tediously pulling oakum apart for use as ships caulking. In fact you've just never had it so good.

In 1899 Hartington was able to pride itself on having its very own railway station. It was announced in a November edition of *The London Gazette in 1889* that a railway to be called the Ashbourne and Buxton railway would commence being laid from, 'the township of Clifton, in the parish of Ashbourne and terminating in the township of Hartington Middle Quarter' where it would shortly join the Cromford and High Peak Railway some four hundred yards south of the sidings at Parsley Hay. During the construction of the Hand Dale viaduct, which crosses the road travelling east out of Hartington, it is said that when the digging commenced for the foundations of its piers the navvies broke into some old mine workings where a number of lead miners had perished at some time in the past. Whether or not they dug up the actual bodies I was unable to ascertain. In keeping with the other stations on this line Hartington was what could be called a low budget wooden affair. In the 1950s for example, two trains a day ran from both Ashbourne and Buxton and one each way on a Saturday. Sunday service did not exist. There was also a bus running from Buxton (40 minutes to Hartington) and from Ashbourne (50 minutes) that dropped you off outside the Devonshire Arms which was quite advantageous seeing as how the railway station was quite a hike away. Unfortunately the buses did not operate on a Sunday either, so clearly you could not get within cheese sniffing distance of Hartington on the Sabbath unless you had your own form of transport.

Today of course, it is an entirely different story for on most Sundays during the year the world and his wife seem to turn up in the centre of the village. However, the railway was responsible for bringing hordes of booted ramblers to the village and the area in general, but after 1963 even they were out of luck for the station was closed and with it went the excursion services and the line was eventually taken up and the station buildings pulled down with the exception of the Hartington signal box. This still remains in situ sitting beside the Tissington Trail a popular route for both walkers and cyclists. If you care to stand on the steps of the signal box on a quiet evening, then with a little imagination you might just be able to conjure up in your mind's eye the sounds and sight of the Manchester to London Express thundering and clattering at great speed across the bleak landscape of limestone walls and dark, silhouetted clumps of trees.

Hartington station like so many country stations of the past was erected to serve the community, but in essence it was too far away and was quickly superseded by a local and far more convenient bus service. This saved you the best part of a two mile trek from the train if all you had was 'Shanks's Pony' and you just happened to be laden down with a number of suitcases and trailing small children continually grizzling and carping on about having to carry their own bucket, spade and shrimping net after a seaside holiday at Colwyn Bay or Southport.

To discover the river Dove we leave Hartington by a footpath, which was, 'just around the corner and at the side of Ellis's Garage', but not anymore. Today the starting point for the path is marked by a decorative, green cast-iron sign dated 1907, which proudly announces, 'Dove Dale via Beresford & Wolfscote Dale, altitude 753 feet' and directs you up some steps where your nostrils are unexpectedly assailed by a heady pong of lavatory disinfectant as you quickly pass the doorway of the public conveniences. A somewhat unbecoming beginning I feel to the arresting sights that follow for the dale walker. The dales of Beresford, Wolfscote, Mill and Dove have truly stunning scenery which has inspired many painters, writers and poets to attempt in paint or words whatever romantic scene has captured their imaginations and pleased their souls most.

Up to this point on the journey of the Dove the countryside already covered has been considered to be, 'pleasurably diversified, though it does not exhibit those bold and striking features which give so much interest to the lower divisions' and because of this fact the outstanding scenery in the lower section of the river has created a whole plethora of names to accompany its many and varied visual attributes. For example there is Pike Pool, the Celestial Twins, Drabber Tor (Drabber than what?) Peaseland Rocks, Gypsy Bank, Iron Tor, Lion's Head Rock, Reynard's Arch, Reynard's Kitchen, Reynard's Hall, Tissington Spires, Jacob's Ladder, Lovers Leap (there just had to be a Lovers Leap) the Watch Box, Shepherd's Abbey, the Straits, the Twelve Apostles, Dovedale Church and the ever popular Stepping Stones; so clearly no shortage of things to look out for, particularly if you want to indulge in a spot of I-Spy as you walk the dales.

Having successfully negotiated the toilet block (with or without a bladder stop) the path traverses green sloping fields before dropping into the wooded top end of Beresford Dale. This dale is particularly well known because here on the Staffordshire side of the river is sited Izaac Walton's and Charles Cotton's world famous Fishing Temple, 'a quaint, quiet-looking little building of square form, with a lofty roof surmounted by a hip knob.' Almost every avid angler that ever cast a line comes to pay homage by gazing dewy-eyed across the river, a creel slung nonchalantly over one shoulder and a Timber Wolf or Dry Grizzly Hackle pinned jauntily on his hat, and that folks is as close as you are going to get to this hallowed shrine. This is because the building erected in 1674 now lies on private land and is completely inaccessible to the casual visitor. Only a modest glimpse can be had from the Derbyshire side unless you are prepared to clamber over a wire fence and had the forethought to come armed with a machete to tackle the otherwise impenetrable undergrowth. The only two remaining options open to you would be the over the top expensive hire of a helicopter, or the far cheaper solution of floating down river lying on your back with a periscope held aloft on something light and portable such as an inflatable air bed which to be perfectly honest is a bit daft. Eccentrically English, but daft all the same.

The square building has a pyramidal roof of stone tiles and over the doorway is a slab bearing the inscription PISCATORIBUS SACRUM 1674 and within its walls the two great anglers according to a passage in the 17th century best-seller *The Compleat Angler* starring Charles Cotton as Piscator, and Izaac Walton as Viator, 'smoked pipes which was their breakfast.' Hardly as nutritious as a bowl of porridge, but that was their preference, a bowl of shag to start the day. The Fishing House has been immaculately restored over recent years for it had previously fallen into neglect at the hands of vandalising visitors and it was reported in 1814 as being, 'much dilapidated with broken windows, wainscoting torn from the walls and furniture smashed', yet still the uncaring visitors continued to scrawl, scratch and carve their names and initials upon any available surface. Consequently this world-renowned Fishing House is no longer very visible, which for all who come to view it presents a bit of a conundrum, but its inaccessibility does at least ensure its future safety.

Since writing this chapter the Fishing Lodge has now come on the open market and can be yours along with a substantial amount of river and woodland for a mere £450,000 pounds. I cannot help thinking that this is a tad steep for what in essence is just a stately summer house with historic connection. It is not as though you could really take up residence in the place, for it has no services and apart from the grand fireplace that you could sit beside on a cold rainy afternoon toasting Derbyshire pyclets for tea, there is not a lot else going for it.

By now your mind will probably be awash with piscatorial pre-amblings and fishy thoughts so you could be forgiven for thinking that the next object of wonderment the Pike Pool is in fact a pool teeming with pike. WRONG! This placid green-grey stretch of the river with a towering limestone pinnacle rising some thirty feet out of the water, which one might assume has been fancifully likened to a rocky version of a pike is perhaps the reason for the Pike Pool being so called. WRONG again! Of course if this had been the case and worse, if it had been a real pike standing on end, then given the aggressive nature of a pike it would not be at all wise to hang about looking gormless exclaiming 'Wow! That's a monster pike. I wonder if it's very dangero'… SNAP! … CRUNCH!!' The truth of the matter is rather more mundane and comes from *The Compleat Angler* after Viator exclaims, 'What have we got here? A rock springing up in the middle of the river!' to which Piscator remarks that it is called Pike Pool due to the sharp pinnacle of limestone resembling a spike or point. Yes, it is a bit disappointing. Well I think that is more than enough of things pike-like and time to move on. The path now continues on the Staffordshire bank of the river flowing beneath a high crag surmounted by a stone tower believed to have been constructed from stones taken from the nearby demolished Beresford Hall.

Beresford Hall was the one-time home of Charles Cotton who was born there in 1630. Cotton eventually inherited the place after the death of his father who was also called Charles Cotton. They were clearly not at all imaginative in the Christian name department. Charles Cotton the younger married his cousin Isabella Hutchinson in 1656 and, so it has been suggested, above his station. His poems and writings failed to bring in sufficient funds and he has also been accused of spending too much time fishing the Dove with Isaac Walton whom he had befriended early on. Accounts differ but it has been recorded that Cotton fathered three sons and five daughters that would strongly suggest he had been busy fishing with his tackle in more than just the river Dove! If not engaged in fishing or procreation, Cotton would find it very necessary every so often to seek refuge in some cave close by where he could hide from the many money debtors that came knocking on the door of Beresford Hall.

Things went from bad to worse and Cotton was finally forced to sell the hall in 1831 when his bank account showed he was grossly in the red and he died a few years later stony broke, leaving his estates to his growing list of creditors. He had never been good with money. The only remaining tangible and visual evidence of the Cotton family now lies in St Peter's church in Alstonfield a short distance away from where the hall once stood. St Peter's is perhaps an apt location seeing as how he too was a fisherman, although with regard to his request to be crucified upside down, then the shibboleth, 'a glutton for punishment' springs to mind. Anyway it is here inside the church that the rather cumbersome box pew that once held the Cotton family is housed. It has been moved from its original position and is an old carved oak affair, of which the best that can be said of it is that it resembles an early roofless compartment of a railway carriage, where only the very top of the occupant's heads or possibly only their hats would be visible to the rest of the congregation. Highly anti-sociable! Sadly at some time in the past 'some barbaric vicar' allowed the pew to be painted a peculiar shade of duck-egg green (not so much Farrow & Ball, but more your Homebase Value emulsion), which seems an incongruous choice of colour. However, on a happier note and despite the slightly late hour of my visit to St Peter's church it is the only church I have ever come across where you can avail yourself of an electric kettle to brew a cup of tea or coffee, which can be drunk from the church's personalised cups. Biscuits were also on offer. Of course they were custard creams. I mean to say, just how thoughtful and unexpectedly civilised is that!

Not quite so idyllic – at least in times past – is the mound of Steep Low, lying northwest of the village, which was the site of one of the last gibbets in the country. They certainly liked to *Hang 'Em High* (Clint Eastwood film 1968) in Derbyshire. A jolly good hanging has always been a popular form of entertainment for the locals in days past and was usually treated as a bit of a day out for the wife and kids, and although I am all for resurrecting old traditions and customs I suppose one has to draw the line somewhere. I personally have nothing against the ancient tradition of Morris dancing for example, but it does lack the cut and thrust of a good hanging.

Beresford Dale is a particularly calming dale where the river seems unhurried as it meanders among trees before emerging into a more meadowy landscape. In times past it might not always have seemed so serene, if you happened to be foolishly splashing about in the river and fell foul of the formidable water bailiff Dora Olive, who once frequented this stretch of the river and who was not a woman to get on the wrong side of. You could find yourself, as indeed many did fleeing down the riverbank in sopping wet trunks like Billy Bunter being pursued by the 'beastly' Mr Quelch!

Further along where the river flows out of Beresford Dale and into Wolfscote Dale there is a ford of sorts known as Bear Ford where, as legend would have you believe is the place where the last bear in England growled its last growl. Of course there are many other areas in England that claim to be the site of the final demise of the last bear, to the extent that there were probably more last bears killed than there were actually last bears, if you see what I mean. That last sentence needs thinking about. Wolfscote Dale on the other hand does have connections with wolves, which no doubt will come as no surprise to you as the clue is in the name. Here in this dale it is said that the last wolf in the area was killed which is far less contestable as the word area is not specific and could extend for miles. Hypothetically it could extend as far as the once wolverine locality of Wormhill that sits high above Miller's Dale where in the 15th century the countryside was heavily forested and positively swarming with wolves giving rise to the following jolly jingle:

'Cruel as death, and hungry as the grave –
Burning for blood – bony, and gaunt, and grim –
Assembling wolves in raging troops descend.'

Obviously there were more wolves here than you could shake a stick at, which actually would not be a smart thing to do. Wolf hunters were also thick on the ground and decapitated wolfs heads almost became a form of local currency, for it is said that many paid their rent in wolves heads. As a substitute for real money it would, naturally have its limitations like nipping into your local 15th century ale house for example.

"E'ven' Gyles, What be 'avin'?"
"Th'usual jug Ranlyn, an' one f'sel'."
"There ya'r. That'll be two an'alf wolf 'eads."
"I got three'uns" grunted Gyles. "Now don'tee be givin' me no change. They 'alf-eads just tear big'oles int' smock, an' missus allus goin' on 'bout sewin' up they'oles." (I make no apology for the mixed dialect)

You can see why the good old English groat caught on as a more practical coinage. Tradition states that Wormhill was previously known as Wolfhill, so do we assume from this that after all the wolves had been bumped off the place became infested with some kind of ferocious scavenging worm instead. You can see where I am coming from on this. Shades of the comic horror film *Tremors* perhaps.

Anyway, back beside the Dove a bridge crosses the river and here are two curiously shaped upright stones which presumably at some time served the function of being a knee-trapping, ankle-bashing stile. In Wolfscote Dale two separate limestone buttresses loom out of the hillside called the Celestial Twins, although it is difficult to relate them to anything either heavenly or divine. The left twin houses a couple of caves with one of particular archaeological significance that lies out of sight around the side of the cliff. This has the dialectic name of Frank I' th' Rocks like the old coaching inn, the Bull I' th' Thorn on the A515 south of Buxton. The cave was excavated in the 1920s and the skeletal remains of Neolithic Mam, Dad and their eight kids were unearthed. Quite how they all fitted inside the wet muddy ascending passageway beggars belief, for that is one big family. Folklore has it that at a much later date the cave was inhabited by Frank himself – who was a cobbler – although business must have been a tad slow in such an isolated spot, despite being close to Beresford Lane an old packhorse route.

Now if Frank had been plying his trade during Roman times then he might have fared much better for a legion of Roman soldiers tramping about the area, as indeed they had, must surely have provided Frank with umpteen pairs of sweaty, grimy clapped out sandals to cobble. Some past writers have simply referred to the cave as Frank's Hole, which suggests something rather salacious and clouds the mind with a degree of uneasiness and hesitation when considering scrambling about inside Frank's Hole. Okay, I hold my hands up and readily admit that is the way my mind tends to veer. And yes, I probably should seek psychiatric advice!

The rather more obvious cave entrance in the front of the cliff is Wolfscote Grange Cave. Wolfscote Grange itself has been knocking about since Doomsday and is a mere stone's throw away down the dale. For my money the cave has more going for it as a place to live than Frank's pad around the corner. Crichton Porteous passed this way around 1950, but omitted to see its potential as a residence, as he had done concerning Dale Abbey Hermitage cave much earlier on in this book.

Admittedly it is a fifty-foot uphill climb from the water supply, but nevertheless it is a delightfully situated rock shelter facing south west and consisting of a cosy chamber with two dinky side windows, a tall internal chimney and an easy-clean stone floor. It also has the unusual feature of a back entrance along a 'slim people only' passageway and a fine rock sun terrace ideal for summer barbeques from which there are far reaching views over the dale, allowing you plenty of time to panic should you spot an ill-tempered hungry bear heading up the hillside in your direction. Now be honest, who could resist such a place and yet it remains empty. I can only presume that the rather high slippery doorstep that has been polished to a glassy finish by centuries of inquisitive visitors has rendered it a dangerous liability. However, it is a first class cave to sit in and dangle your legs over the lip while indulging in a lunch-break, as I did myself and as many have done before me including the person who probably staggered off into a blurred dale as I found their abandoned spectacles on the floor of the cave.

Continuing for a moment along the thoughts of things highly polished reminds me that the popularity of walking alongside the Dove can be measured by the smooth sheen on the wooden post tops at some stiles and also the stone ones where the limestone has been polished to an almost obsidian-like finish by millions of grasping hands, where people have in some cases had to squeeze themselves through. I mention this last fact with regard to the circumstances that more than a few walkers find themselves in, which has given rise to complaints that some of the uprights seem to be unnecessarily close together. I witnessed such an event at a stile where Biggin Dale joins the Dove, for here an elderly gentleman was experiencing considerable difficulty in extricating both legs from between the two uprights.

While trying to make light of his dilemma he was beginning to get flustered and aware of the growing queue of walkers waiting behind him. In truth he was really far more concerned by the unnerving possibility that he was in serious danger of leaving something behind at the stile and he did make reference to this. Not only would this have been an eye-watering experience, but also embarrassingly messy as the disconnected part of his anatomy would not be something anyone would rush to pick up in a hurry, unless they happened to be fortuitously in possession of a 'doggy-do-dah' bag.

The length of Wolfscote Dale is lined by ragged, rocky limestone crags and steep slopes of scree. Along here another small rock chamber lies up a short footpath opposite Peaseland Rocks, one of the many hanging outcrops of bare rock perched high on the Staffordshire side of the Dove. Just before this feature the steep mass of Drabber Tor rises up from the valley floor hiding from view the oddly named habitat of Dunge Bottom. It would not be out of character for me to say that Dunge Bottom does tend to sound like an uncomfortable medical condition, whose symptoms are perhaps best left to the reader's imagination, or not if you so prefer. Oops! I seemed to have succumbed to yet another rectal reference.

Despite its unfortunate sounding name Dunge Bottom does in fact have commanding views over the surrounding countryside and really deserves a more euphonious epithet. The long bleak and dry Biggin Dale sweeps in from the left to join the Dove and is a dale which was given to the National Trust by Sir Robert McDougal a Derbyshire landowner and of course the man who got flour to raise itself, instead of just lying about doing nothing in a big white heap. Biggin Dale is a pleasant walk through shady coppices of Ash, Hawthorn and Hazel before emerging onto a more open landscape of walled pastureland. MacDougal also bequeathed the Staffordshire side of Dove Dale from Biggin Dale down to somewhere around the Twelve Apostles, which was indeed a very generous gesture on his part.

There was actually a report of this fact in 1938 in the July edition of *The Children's Newspaper* along with the announcement that another nine hundred acres was up for grabs in the Manifold valley for a mere thirteen thousand five hundred pounds. Interestingly, the article attempted to encourage all child readers to put their hands in their pockets and dish out their pocket money to help raise the required sum! I wonder how many children now days would be sufficiently countryside conscious and willing to part with their funds instead of spending it on a new computer game or the latest mobile phone. I strongly suspect it would fall on deaf ears. Across a footbridge is a cardiac-arresting climb straight up the front of Gypsy Bank, which presumably had Romany connections sometime in the past although it would be the last place anyone in their right mind would park a vardo.

The path finishes at Alstonfield and ultimately at the door of The George with its patriotic signboard, where many a life-saving pint has been guzzled in record time after that climb up from the river Dove. Back on the Derbyshire riverside are the remains of Iron Tors pump house that was once a water action device for pumping a supply of water up the severe hillside to a farm way up on the top.

The next section sees the Dove wriggling through some seriously steep rocky sides, which Croston in his usual dramatic fashion described as, 'sombre and savage' as he crept, 'round a ledge of rock so narrow that no beast of burden could follow.' I suppose in all fairness the scenery did probably take on a more hair-raising aspect for him being heightened by the fact that he was doing the walk by moonlight with still quite a way to go before reaching the Sleigh Inn at Hartington. When Firth passed this way in the early 1900s and more sensibly in daylight he found the scenery far more appealing as well as witnessing a tried and tested method of sheep dipping in the river. A long pole with a loop of chain at one end was slipped over the head of the sheep that was then dragged up and down the river a number of times by the 'brawny arms of a shepherd' until it had been sufficiently dunked. This sounds like exhausting and strenuous work. Firth compares this technique to a more 'Homeric spectacle' that he had witnessed earlier on lower down the Dove where the sheep one at a time were simply chucked into the river and caught by a shepherd who took the protesting sheep in his arms and dunked it under the water. This sounds like seriously exhausting and seriously strenuous work! Imagine standing in the freezing cold river for hours at a time wrestling with frantic sheep. You would have to be near Herculean as well as perhaps considering a career change.

Further downstream is Lode Mill where a simple one arched bridge spans the Dove and replaces the original river crossing, which was merely a ford when in 1658 a woman met an untimely end by drowning trying to cross the river. The old corn mill still stands by the bridge and is now being converted into a dwelling. The road crossing the bridge drops down the vertiginous hillside from Alstonfield and climbs one equally as steep up to the A515 where the nearby French sounding village of Alsop-en-le-Dale can be reached. This small and somewhat isolated village lies around a mile from the Dove valley and has a Norman church of early 12th century origin, St Michael and All Saints, and a fine stone-mullion windowed Elizabethan Hall which was built in the late 16th century. It was the seat of the Alsop family for seventeen generations until 1688.

The village took its name obviously, from the family as was the norm in such far off times and in plain language means Alsop in the Dale, which is where Alsop chose to live. Setting aside the fact that it would be nothing short of stupidity to build a house in such a place, it is nevertheless fortunate for namesake that Alsop chose not to build his house in a bog! In spite of its somewhat remote location Alsop-en-le-Dale was once served by the single track Ashbourne to Buxton railway and had its own station a sensible half mile away. For a while the station bore the name of Alsop-en-le-Dale for Alstonfield, which could be a bit misleading given the fact that not only was Alstonfield nearly two miles distant it also required a steep descent down into the Dove valley and an equally steep ascent up the other side, which could be reason enough for catching a bus instead. It might very well prove to be an energetic trek on foot, especially if you were burdened with a week's shopping after a now regrettable spending spree in Ashbourne.

At this point on the map the railway line had already begun descending an incline after first having passed through the spectacular sixty feet deep Cold Eaton cutting just to the north, where apparently some three hundred thousand tons of limestone was excavated during this undertaking, which by any stretch of the imagination would make one hell of a gigantic rockery! Passenger services ended here in 1954, but excursions continued until 1963 and my parents being ardent ramblers certainly took advantage of this short lived pleasure. After complete closure of the station its buildings were for a time used as a sort of barracks for schoolboys on field trips from Nottingham High School, a school which has been around since at least 1513 but which now, shock horror is considering taking its first contingency of girls. Another nail in the coffin of it ever becoming a man's world once more!

Be that as it may, back down in the valley of the Dove at Lode Mill, with or without handfuls of shopping bags the road known as Lode Lane has a side road that branches off to the left and hugs the bank of the river the short distance to Milldale, a tiny serene hamlet much frequented by visitors and famed for its wonderful packhorse bridge. Known as Viator, or Wheelbarrow bridge on account of Viator (from *The Compleat Angler*) pronouncing that in his opinion it was only suitable for wheelbarrows due to its extreme narrowness which he goes on to say is barely 'two fingers broad' and hardly wide enough for a mouse to pass over. The words gross exaggeration immediately spring to mind here followed by the theory that too much booze had been consumed for breakfast at the Fishing Temple or else a trip to the opticians might be beneficial. In its original state the bridge would probably have been built without any sides which would have made it appear perilously narrow, but two fingers wide?

According to Firth this bridge, along with Alstonfield church, has been constructed from stone mysteriously quarried from nowhere in the neighbourhood. Shades here I fancy of the equally mysterious Stonehenge bluestone, but perhaps not on such a grand scale. Milldale is a popular turning point for walkers coming up the dale from the Thorpe end and their efforts were once rewarded by Mrs Bailey of Dove Mount who for the best part of forty-eight years served among other things, 'a rambler's-sized cup of tea.' Over those forty-eight years that would prove to be an inestimable gallonage of tea being poured down the parched, gasping gullets of Dove Dale walkers. Today the needs of walkers are met in the shape of Polly's Cottage where refreshments are served from a half-doorway, and it was here on a sunny but chill day in early March that I was glad of a cup of steaming tea and a particularly scrummy, home-made Nelson Square liberally dosed with almond essence. Extremely scrummy and highly recommended!

While still on the subject of feeding faces there was in the past a well-known character Nancy Bennington, who used to walk the three mile round trip from Milldale to Reynard's Cave downstream carrying a basket brimming with bottles of water, fizzy 'pop' along with sweets, postcards and even films for cameras. She was a true entrepreneur and plied her trade cum rain or shine during the summer months for nearly forty years. She constructed a rough and probably uncomfortable (for uncomfortable read haemorrhoid inducing) chair from rocks beside the entrance to Reynard's Cave and here she spent the day sitting beside a fire, brewing tea. Porteous recalls seeing her on several occasions during his walking trips and makes the comment that she must have known the dale in all its moods better than anyone, and what a great shame she never wrote down all she knew and had seen. He freely admits that anything he might have to say about Dove Dale alongside what Nancy Bennington could tell would be 'simply claptrap.' As unstoppable old age crept on she found herself unable to make the daily walk down the dale so settled for selling her wares by Viator Bridge.

Such delights were not on hand for Croston when he reached Milldale for it was already twilight and he remembers seeing the villagers lounging about their doorways, or grouped on a grassy bank by the riverside chatting among themselves and enjoying the coolness of the evening. He caught their attention when he crossed the bridge whereupon they, 'gazed at us with an air of inquiry, and wondered at our temerity (for temerity read what daft buggers) in coming through the dale so late without a guide.' Croston was advised to take the road to Hartington and warned against continuing along the riverside, as the path was difficult and lonesome. Croston paid no heed to their advice and took to the dale in the ensuing blackness, where he hoped he would be blessed by moonlight for most of the route and consequently finish his days rambling without any mishap. He describes the scenery as 'dark, wild and forbidding' with 'strange, uncouth, shadowy forms' of 'blackened rock' and 'foliage, grim and spectral looking.' The thing is what else could he be expect to see wandering about this rugged landscape at night. A landscape I might add that would have been far more appealing had he witnessed it during the day. He really should have set out earlier and not spent so much time faffing about along the way.

The river Dove now continues through the section for which it is world famous, where geological wonders and accompanying names fly thick and fast, plus a few tales thrown in for good measure. This is the part of the

Dove of which Lord Byron wrote to his poet friend Tom Moore saying, "I assure you that there are things in Derbyshire as noble as in Greece or Switzerland" and how right he was. Of course we do not have a Parthenon or a history of smart-arse philosophers, or a questionable obsession for Cuckoo Clocks and jammy sponge rolls (Okay, so Swiss rolls don't come from Switzerland), but Dove Dale is supremely rich in fabulous scenery and certainly takes some beating.

A side dale enters on the left winding down along the bottom of The Nabs a limestone outcrop from which after an exhausting and sweaty climb to the top you will be rewarded with what is claimed by many to be the finest view in the entire country, provided of course it is not lashing down with rain and blanketed in grey mist. Beyond The Nabs the countryside is said to be haunted. Nearby is Hanson Grange, the name Hanson being a corruption of a corruption, which basically means Hill of High Sin where, as Firth implies 'dark deeds' may have been committed between antagonistic Danes and unneighbourly Saxons. However, the really sinister bit can actually be linked to the almost adjacent Bostern Grange for here a dark deed was indeed committed and the ghost that roams the hillside can no doubt testify to this, if you happen to come across it one dark night and can summon the courage to ask either before or while you are soiling your underwear in fright.

The alleged spectre is that of John Mycock (unfortunate surname if ever there was one) who in the year 1467, which makes him a very old ghost indeed, was viciously set upon by some particularly unpleasant chaps. For reasons not at all clear poor Mycock appears to have got on the wrong side of John de la Pole from Hartington to such an extent that John of the Pole felt it necessary to bash Mycock severely about the head (presumably with a pole) in anger. Unfortunately for Mycock Johnny the Pole had brought along some accomplices who were pretty keen to get a piece of the action, so Henry Vigurs of Monyash who had clearly taken the trouble to travel some distance to attend the party and therefore wished to make it worth his while, stabbed Mycock in the chest. As if this was not enough, and clearly it was not, John Harrison of heaven knows where shot the dazed and bleeding Mycock in the back with an arrow. By now poor old Mycock would have realised that things were not going his way and he would not be going home, so it would be no use his wife putting his dinner in the oven for later. Not wishing to disappoint him and possibly just for good measure Mathew Bland also from Hartington cracked Mycock's skull with a hefty club-staff. Well I guess they certainly did a jolly good job of making absolutely sure he was never going to get up and walk away. By now Mycock was looking more than a little worse for wear as he lay expiring on the ground in a pool of his own blood, whereupon everyone more than satisfied with their efforts went home apart from Mycock, who was definitely not going anywhere! The story goes that at a later date somebody blabbed about the heinous crime as some two years on in 1469 the four murderers were ordered to be tried before no less a person than King Edward IV himself. However, it turned out the king was in for a bit of a disappointment due to the fact that on the appointed day none of the accused showed up which King Ed probably thought was a bit of a bummer having got all dressed up for nothing. It is assumed that Pole, Vigus, Harrison and Bland had powerful friends in high places who wangled it so none of them was ever brought to justice. Little wonder then that the ghost of John Mycock wanders the hillside still seeking retribution for his grisly end. I bet he's right livid!

On a lighter note this area of Dove Dale was once frequented by the philosopher and naturalist Jean Jaques Rouseau who arrived here at nearby Wootton Hall after taking refuge from France in 1765, where he was convinced (imagined) that he was being persecuted by his enemies back home. His real problem was himself, for he assumed (imagined) everyone and everything was against him and consequently some scheming dastardly plot was always being hatched by someone somewhere that would result in him being murdered in his bed or else some similar fate would befall him. At this juncture the words paranoia, neurotic and psychotic spring to mind and Rhodes described him as being a, 'quarrelsome, unamiable, petulant and angry man' and proud to his own detriment. 'It was' continued Rhodes, 'indeed impossible for anybody to be on terms of friendship long with the eccentric and ill-humoured Jean Jaques Rousseau.' Quite obviously J.J. Rousseau would not be someone you would want to find yourself stuck sitting next to during a long-haul flight. Surprisingly in spite of him seeming to be a tad nutty, and bad tempered, and generally disagreeable he did manage to bring with him to England his mistress Therese le Vasseur who I can only presume to be either a tad barking herself, long-suffering, or else had a face like the back-end of a tram smash and nobody else would look at her. During Rousseau's calmer moments which seemed to be few and far between he is said to have, 'sewn rare and curious seeds in this sequestered spot' and collected plants for his own studies. So, not all bad then!

The first highlight to arrest the attention of the walker south of Milldale is Dove Holes, which is not to be confused with Dove Holes. Yes I know they both sound the same and are even spelt the same, but the former in this instance refers to two very large holes, whereas the latter refers to a village lying north of Buxton which sits next to a very large hole, namely Dove Holes quarry. While the Dove Dale Dove Holes is very much an attraction that has engaged the curiosity of centuries of passing visitors, the village of Dove Holes can boast no such claim and was once deemed – somewhat harshly I feel – to be the ugliest village in the entire United Kingdom. In all fairness to the place it can claim to have one antiquity, namely the Bull Ring, which was the site of an ancient stone circle said to be on a par with the one at Arbor Low, but unfortunately at some time in the distant past the locals borrowed (nicked) all the stones to do a spot of building, leaving behind a grassy mound with a ditch. This is not a great crowd-puller.

However, the two Dove Holes caves set above the footpath, although only shallow inside, have impressive entrances that to my mind resemble a pair of empty eye sockets in a skull half buried in the ground and are said to be yet another hidey-hole of Charles Cotton, when his creditors came looking for him. These huge cavities were formed by tributary streams dissolving the rock as underground waterways, which were eventually left high and dry as the river continued to cut downwards, taking the water table with it, or at least that is the generally accepted theory, and who am I to argue. Normally as in keeping with this book such a geological discourse would be proffered by our old friend Arnold, the well-known rambling 'know-all' accompanied by the near swooning Enid Barroclough hanging on his every word. Luckily he has not been seen in the vicinity which is fortuitous as he will not be reappearing any time soon as it is far too close to the end of the book.

Moving swiftly on just in case I am forced to eat my words, the path passes beneath the grand spectacle of Pickering Tors at the end of which sits a rather precariously balanced mass of rock called The Watchbox, an, 'enormous cubic rock weighting anything up to fifty tons or even more' and, 'looks ready for a 400 odd feet drop at any moment.' This I would have thought would be more than sufficient to discourage anyone from gazing up at it for too long in case it chooses that moment to detach itself and render some hapless victim a terminal nanosecond headache. On the opposite side of the river is a hundred feet plus limestone pinnacle sometimes called Pickering Tor but more usually Ilam Rock. This, 'mighty pillar of insulated rock whose conical summit penetrates the clouds' (somebody getting a little bit carried away here) is in spite of its severity climbable, although it remained relatively untouched for some time after an ascent by Siegfried Herford, whose harrowing account of climbing Ilam Rock scared the pants (or climbing breeches) off others who were suddenly not so keen to follow in his footsteps.

I climbed a route up its side in the mid-sixties and I have to say that after all that effort it is sadly short of space on top to have any sort of a picnic. Access over the river to this popular site used quite literally to be by a tree-trunk bridge, but no doubt health and safety in some form or other stepped in and condemned the Amazon-style river crossing and replaced it by a proper affair with handrails on either side. The river here would have been crossed by many, as at one time there used to be a tea hut situated close by that was nothing more than a wooden hut with a grand sign announcing that this was the Ilam Rock Refreshment Room and as far back as the late 1800s decently dressed chaps and gals in outdoor casuals, which still look very formal by todays (generally sloppy) standards would partake of tea and tit-bits at a table-clothed trestle table. It must have been a considerable feat to get the hut down into the dale in the first place, but then few things daunted the innovative Victorians.

A short distance on where the Dove is hemmed in by rock walls a place described by the over enthusiastic Croston as, 'so narrow as would hardly afford footing for a goat', the walker is forced to pass beneath the jaws of a great beast, namely the Lion's Head Rock, a natural feature with a truly remarkable likeness to the head of a lion. It is a fine piece of limestone sculpture aptly summed up by Price when he writes the tools used were, 'needles of rain; an emery-wheel of winter winds; the sharp chisel thrusts of frost and the mallet blows of spring thawing', have created something so unmistakably leonine that is most obvious when viewed coming down dale. The thing you have to bear in mind when wandering along the often dicey pathway is that all the time you are craning your neck trying to spot and name the many different formations of towers, pinnacles and outcrops you could be teetering on the hazardous brink of a narrow path, not looking where you are placing your feet. This in turn could lead to you to unexpectedly finding yourself in for a bit of hospitalisation, or worse, a cooling off period in a mortuary which is definitely going to put the dampers on your day out in Dove Dale.

With this scenario firmly fixed in your mind it might be more prudent to stick to the features that are blindingly obvious unless you have already had an accident and are being carried out unconscious on a stretcher, in which case you will miss the massively impressive natural arch of Reynard's Cave. According to some folk it got its name from the old term for fox which is Reynard, or as others say in homage to a hermit who once lived here called, would you believe, Reynard. Through the arch is an open area due to the roof collapsing in the distant past and within can be found a few small caves that have been inhabited at least as far back as the Bronze Age.

I bet Bronze Age man wished he had been around at the time when Nancy Bennington was running her refreshment pitch and brewing tea by the arch for she could certainly have provided them with a welcome dietary change. The pathway if you can call it such up to the arch and beyond is little more than a slope of slippery scree being a, 'steep and rugged path strewn with loose stones, where you tread with caution for fear of being precipitated over the slippery crags into the stream below.' It can be a bit of a scramble especially in wet weather but to quote Disraeli at this point as Firth did, 'If you like that sort of foolishness, that's the sort of foolishness you like.' Profound stuff, yet somehow stating the obvious!

And speaking of foolishness here is a first-class example of somebody being an utter twerp. Rhodes, among others relates the true story of the unfortunate Rev Langton the Dean of Clogher who through his own folly prematurely earned himself a tombstone in Ashbourne churchyard. It transpired that a group of ladies and gentlemen decided to spend the day in Dove Dale along with the Rev Langton who for reasons best known to himself was accompanying them on horseback. With some difficulty he managed to get as far as Reynard's Arch along with the rest of the party. It was here in what may have been a flash of macho inspiration (for macho inspiration read utter lunacy), that Rev Langton took it upon himself to endeavour to ride his horse up the rock strewn hillside on a route that was never meant for a horse. A rabbit possibly, but a horse definitely not! Probably to his surprise he was asked by a Miss La Roche in the party if she could join him in the saddle for what was without doubt a hair-brained idea. One can only assume that Miss La Roche was either overcome with an irrepressible sense of adventure or else she was plain stupid.

Rhodes is rather more refined in his choice of words and says that Miss La Roche had more 'courage than prudence' and so with feisty Miss La Roche clamped firmly to the back of a no doubt enraptured Rev Langton the pair of them set off. They were watched by their, 'companions below (who) were shuddering at their danger, and gazing upon them with an anxiety intense even to pain', or put another way they were all getting a tad unnerved and stressed out by the whole thing and just waiting for an accident to happen, and they were not to be disappointed. Predictably, and I do feel it was predictable, the poor overburdened horse struggled up the slippery slope until it ran out of hoof-holds, and being unable to turn around or complete anything resembling a perfect backward somersault rolled heavily down the hillside in an alarming manner. Also rolling down the hillside in an even more alarming manner was Rev Langton and Miss La Roche who were not doing so well as the horse as they only had four legs between them. Rev Langton successfully finished the course by crashing all the way to the bottom of the dale and much to everyone's surprise was found to be still alive, a state which as it turned out was a short-lived affair for he died soon afterwards. Miss La Roche on the other hand who was obviously a latter-day Lara Croft tumbled down the hill in a particularly unladylike manner, for which her attire was not suitable and escaped with a few minor injuries despite being, 'rendered insensible with the fall.' Another account states that she was saved from disaster by getting her long hair tangled up in a bush. Now that sounds painful. There is a half-happy ending to this story because the horse survived and fully recovered from the accident and no doubt dined out (or ate hay) on the saga whenever it found itself in the company of other horses.

Langton's horse, "Hi there, how are you?"

Second horse. "I'm fine. Hey, aren't you the horse that fell down the side of Dove Dale?"

Langton's horse, "You're dead right and let me tell you all about how I escaped that death-defying fall. You see what happened was I ..."

Second horse, "Sorry mate. Can't stop. Got to rush, I've just been bitten by a bot fly."

And so like an equine equivalent of Coleridge's *Ancient Mariner* Langton's horse felt compelled to spend the remainder of its days wandering fields and relating his tale of daring-do and death to any horse he could get to listen to him. Miss La Roche also survived to tell the tale and lived the rest of her life very much regretting her foolishness, and as for Rev Langton, well one can only say that as a man of God he certainly got to meet Him a lot sooner than he had ever expected!

I have said this before and I will say it again. No self-respecting dale can call itself such without a lovers leap and happily Dove Dale has such a leap. Lover's Leap stands as a hundred and twenty feet high promontory of outcropping limestone, a little way down from the scene of the dean's demise, towering above the river Dove. The steps leading to the top of this outcrop were built by captured Italian prisoners of war during World War II, which must surely have been a welcome relief from running about dodging bullets because a deluded Benito Mussollni had sold out to the Germans. Anyway, legend has it that a distraught young girl being convinced that her beloved had been killed while fighting in the Napoleonic Wars decided life was no longer worth living. Standing on the brink of the drop she launched herself into space, or would have done had it not been for the fact that she never made it to the bottom as her skirt became tangled in a bush that left her dangling ignominiously, her mission unaccomplished. At this point and feeling a tad hacked off she freed herself and stomped off home where she discovered to her surprise that word had just been received from her loved one that he was indeed alive and kicking. So who felt a bit silly now?

Another tale tells how a young woman fell over the edge unintentionally and her fall was arrested by her hair getting caught up in possibly the same bush. This does sound similar to the Miss La Roche incident and I wonder if it became a fairly common sight to see women leaving Dove Dale with blood dribbling from their heads in a partly scalped condition. There is yet another tale telling of how a young girl jilted in love leapt over the edge into space until she too was stopped by that confounded bush again. She also called it a day and went home. Apparently she remained single for the rest of her life after this debacle, or was it perhaps because she failed to attract any further suitors because she really never looked too good after crashing headlong into a bush.

The thing that strikes me about lovers leaping when I look back on legends like Hannah Baddeley for example, is I cannot help but think that perhaps their hearts were not really in it and they could have planned things better. With a bit more effort they could easily have got themselves over to Matlock Bath, had a nice day out before climbing to the top of High Tor and yelling 'Geronimo' as they plummeted through space at a great rate of knots. This naked limestone massif stands around four hundred feet high and is pretty much devoid of bushes. Consequently you would be shifting at a fair pace by the time you hit the bottom thus guaranteeing the desired effect. In fact far too fast to be stopped by your skirt snagging on a tree branch or even by your hair getting tangled in one. In the latter scenario, surely your hair would be ripped completely off your head leaving you to be found in a crumpled heap at the base of the cliff giving the appearance that some passing (albeit unlikely) Commanche Indian had scalped you for a trophy to hang from his belt. I put forward the suggestion that High Tor is the ultimate Lover's Leap and could well become Derbyshire's equivalent of Beachy Head.

The end or start of Dove Dale depending on which direction you are coming from is marked by the Stepping Stones which were laid in the river during Victorian times so the fairer sex could cross the water in a lady-like manner and not be forced to throw decorum to the wind by hitching up their many layers of skirts and in so doing create an almost un-suppressible lust and slobbering from their male companions, as they glimpsed a hitherto forbidden shapely ankle. Prior to this event (the laying of the stones that is, not the glimpsing of an ankle) crossing the river would have been a wet-feet experience although not particularly deep. Rhodes explains in his guide section in *Peak Scenery* that, 'Travellers in carriages may go to Ilam first, return over the fields to Bunster Dale, and ford the river (Dove), which may be done conveniently at the foot of Thorp Cloud where Dove Dale commences.' Since these times millions upon millions of people have crossed the stones from Staffordshire to Derbyshire, or vice-versa having passed between the two sentinels that guard the entrance to Dove Dale. On the former side looms Bunster Hill at one thousand and seventy-nine feet, while on the latter side the volcano-shaped hill of Thorpe Cloud rears up at a mere nine hundred and forty-two feet, a whisker off making it a true mountain.

Certainly in the fifties during the summer period the Stepping Stones was yet another outlet for teas, ice cream, minerals, postcards and all the other paraphernalia associated with British beauty spots. It goes without saying that this was particularly popular with the visitors, but it did probably create a down-side unless visitors were better behaved than many of their predecessors which is debatable. Croston notes for example that Reynard's Hall was a favourite place for picnic parties who left behind, 'broken glass, orange peel and other fragmentary remains' and Firth writes blaming the half-day trippers, courtesy of the new railway for littering the dale to the extent that it is 'often choked' by these trippers 'who fail to respect their surroundings.'

The availability of public transport was without a doubt massively contributory in getting the masses to Dove Dale. Again in the fifties when owning a car at least for the average working man was still a novelty the following choice was on hand for the ardent walker and picnicker on their return from a day in the dale. On Monday, Tuesday, Thursday and Friday a local Hulley's bus left Thorpe at 5.30pm for Ashbourne, and on Wednesday and Sunday from June until the last Sunday in September a good old bright red Trent bus would transport you from the Dog and Partridge pub and the Peveril of the Peak Hotel to Ashbourne and on to Derby. The beauty of this service was that the instant the bus was full it would leave and further buses continued to do so until quite a late hour. How wonderful was that! Can you envisage that happening now days? No chance! Another coach company North Western also ran a summer service leaving at 5:45pm to Matlock, and with the railway station a mere half a mile away you could hop on a train at 6:44pm to get to Ashbourne and Derby, or catch the 4:25pm to Buxton. For some reason the train service did not operate at weekends, which would have been its busiest time and this only occurred when excursions were put on towards the decline of the line.

Almost without warning the river Dove flows away from all the spectacular scenery and is diluted by the river Manifold coming in from the Staffordshire side where the two of them amble away through a landscape of fields and cultivated meadows. It leaves behind the power and momentum that forced it through all those wild rugged limestone valleys and gorges and takes on a much calmer mood as though it has finished showing off and appears to completely lose interest in Derbyshire altogether as it runs away into Staffordshire. This is a point near where Celia Fiennes wrote round 1695 after having had an outing to 'Tetbury' (Tutbury) Castle, 'I pass ye river Dove on a stone Bridge Called Dovebridge wch Enters me into Darbyshire.' The river Dove from its humble beginnings on the bleak slopes of Axe Edge leaves behind a legacy of unparalleled beauty as it deserts us for another county and we never see it again in the Peak.

Within a stone's throw from the entrance to Dove Dale lies the tiny village of Thorpe and a Norman church believed to have been built around 1100AD, so we are talking mega-ancient here. It is the church of St Leonard and it would be remiss of me not to give St Leonard an airing as has been the case with other saintly saints and their churches. For starters he is patron of political prisoners, imprisoned people in general including prisoners of war and then we change to something completely different for Saint Leonard then takes on women in labour, (the man must be out of his mind!) horses and cattle diseases. So a bit of a mixed bag there then!

Legend has it that all a prisoner was required to do to gain freedom was to invoke the name of Saint Len in their cells and hey presto, their chains and leg-irons would simply snap open before their very eyes. Pretty neat trick, thus giving every prisoner the potential to become a bit of a Harry Houdini! Clearly most prisoners were rather chuffed about this and would seek out Saint Len bearing all their iron restraints as proof and in homage to him. At this time our goodly saint happened to be living a peaceful and tranquil existence as a hermit in a forest outside Limousin when he slowly found himself being surrounded by an ever increasing mob of ex-prisoners and an ever increasing pile of scrap iron in the form of rusting chains and leg-irons, which he had to admit to himself was something he had not banked on when pursuing the quiet life among the trees. Enough was enough, so he got up one morning, upped sticks and went off to found an abbey where almost in the blink of an eye a village grew up around it. Poor old Saint Len, he could not get away from his followers, but they did name the village St Leonard-de-Noblat. Of course there is no proof to imply that St Leonard ever visited Thorpe to bless the church with his name, any more than there is to say that he spent a sunny afternoon in a deckchair on the beach at St Leonards-on-Sea thinking to himself, 'Do you know what, I'm going to name this place after myself. I quite like it here.' I mean to say, it seems highly unlikely all things considered!

Anyway, getting back to his church the south porch apparently bears the marks where allegedly hundreds of arrowheads were sharpened by local archers during the reign of Edward III. This came about according to local lore, because just as the Great War of 1914–18 wiped out so many of the male population, similarly, though not as discriminating for it killed off women as well, the Black Death wiped out much of the male population to the extent that king Ed found his protective band of archers was a bit thin on the ground. Consequently in order to rectify the matter King Ed issued a decree that all men should not use their free time playing football, drinking and generally arsing about, but take up the practice of archery, or ELSE! The theory being, although slightly tenuous that because most people at this time lived in wooden huts there was nowhere else the men could sharpen their arrow tips apart from on the stonework of the church. Hmmmm.

As I have already mentioned it was the coming of public transport that opened up Dove Dale along with other dales to the common man and as a result the village of Thorpe became known as yet another Gateway to Dove Dale, and in 1899 a wooden station went up on the nearby railway line with a station board announcing Thorpe Cloud for Dove Dale. Over the following decades thousands upon thousands of visitors poured out of carriages onto the platform laden with picnic baskets and blankets, or shod in hob-nailed boots, clad in windcheaters and slacks, prepared for a day of rambling along the Dove, unless it was the month of May and the train was the Well Dressing Special excursion, in which instance many would stay on board to travel a little further up the line and visit Tissington and its amazing floral tributes. Today the droves appear by car or by coach, the latter for a glimpse of Dove Dale before travelling on to Ilam for a glimpse of the Manifold Valley. Despite being sorely tempted to include this beautiful dale in the book I decided against it purely on the grounds that it runs entirely in Staffordshire, and although it is still a part of the Peak District I would have to change the title of this book. Okay, so that's a pathetic excuse, but I am sticking to it just the same, and before you say anything I am not being disrespectful to the Derwent Valley either but I do have to adhere to some sort of criteria in limiting the length of this book.

Not far from the village of Thorpe is an inn with a somewhat mixed reputation called the Dog and Partridge, which in times past was very much an isolated rustic public house, and one where many travellers stayed overnight before continuing on their journeys. Rhodes found himself in the vicinity of this inn just after dark one night and wrote, 'we literally groped our way to the Dog and Partridge.' However, on entering he was immediately overcome by an unwelcome feeling of foreboding after spotting a sinister group of men sitting by, 'a solitary farthing candle, around a few almost extinct embers in the grate, which cast a feeble light upon their pallid faces.' Not quite the sight he was expecting to lift his already jaded spirits. Feeling more than a tad unnerved by what might have been, or was possibly still going on he turned tail and fled being faced with no alternative but to slog it the four miles to Ashbourne in the hopes of finding some accommodation for the night. He arrived at midnight and found the town, 'nearly deserted; not an inn door was invitingly open to receive us, and no lights were to be seen, except here and there a solitary bed-candle twinkling through the windows.' What else did he expect at this time of night, and yet surprisingly he not only managed to find, 'a tolerably good inn' but also indulged in a 'hearty supper' before retiring to bed. Can you imagine the kind of reception you would get these days if you banged on the door of a pub after midnight asking for supper and a bed for the night! I am pretty confident that you would be showered with a torrent of verbal abuse accompanied by some form of erect digital gesture.

The following morning after a whistle-stop tour of Ashbourne, Rhodes finally headed off towards Dove Dale passing the Dog and Partridge where he plucked up sufficient courage to seek some refreshment before continuing his journey. He noticed on passing through the doorway blood stains on the floor and when he was shown to a seat there was more blood as well as some heavily bloodied clothing hanging over a chair. After the previous night's brief encounter with the disquieting group of men huddled around a candle, Rhodes felt he was sitting where a horrendous murder had taken place and was feeling more than a little uneasy. After a pint and a pie, or a packet of dry-roasted nuts, or whatever it was he had Rhodes learnt much to his relief that the landlord the night before had gone out to cut hay from a stack close by and had accidently fallen upon his cutting blade and, 'been wounded in a dreadful manner. Profuse bleeding ensued', hence the spilt blood on the floor and the blood-drenched clothing draped over the chair. I guess back then customers sensibilities were not much of a priority as clearly no one had bothered to wash the floor or remove the stained clothing, so obviously the Dog and Partridge was not at all interested in chasing the Pub of the Year Award.

At the time of writing I notice the pub is for sale presumably because of a lack of customers. You know, some one really should give that floor a damned good mopping. From here Rhodes enters Dove Dale, waxes lyrically about its wonders as far as Mill Dale, then climbs up out of the valley to the A515 as it now is and on to Tissington, Hopton, finally polling in to Wirksworth at God alone knows what time of night as that is a fair old distance, where he no doubt annoys some unsuspecting inn-keeper yet again who has just gone to bed and is already snoring for England.

And now like Rhodes, Croston, Firth and all those other writers and wanderers of Derbyshire's Peak District, it is time to bid it a very fond farewell. Throughout the pages of this book I have attempted to lift the lid on the lore and legends, and the fact and fiction of a part of Derbyshire's rich treasure trove and provide an entertaining, informative and modern slant on the interpretation of these aspects. I have, metaphorically speaking lifted and looked beneath boulders and fumbled among the tangled undergrowth of the past by peeking, peeping and peering, as well as poking, prodding and prying, which has led me to revel in an unnecessary amount of alliteration. However, there are still vast areas of the Peak District I have not covered and they all have their tales, and legends, and facts waiting to be discovered.

I sincerely hope that I have provided not only humour, but enlightenment and information and I would wish for no more than Croston does as he ends his book, which I have personalised by saying, 'if I should by means of inducing any studious book-worm, any bilious clerk, or toiling artisan, to leave his library, his desk, or his workshop, and follow in my footsteps, my object will have been accomplished.' It only remains for me to finish my rambles through the dales by ideally heading for Thorpe station to catch a train, but I fear I will be standing there a very long time and slowly growing old waiting for a train that is never going to arrive. I am, alas, fifty years too late. Luckily I came under my own steam so I will be heading for the car-park instead. Now where on earth did I put those damned car keys…